JOE T.
ROBINSON

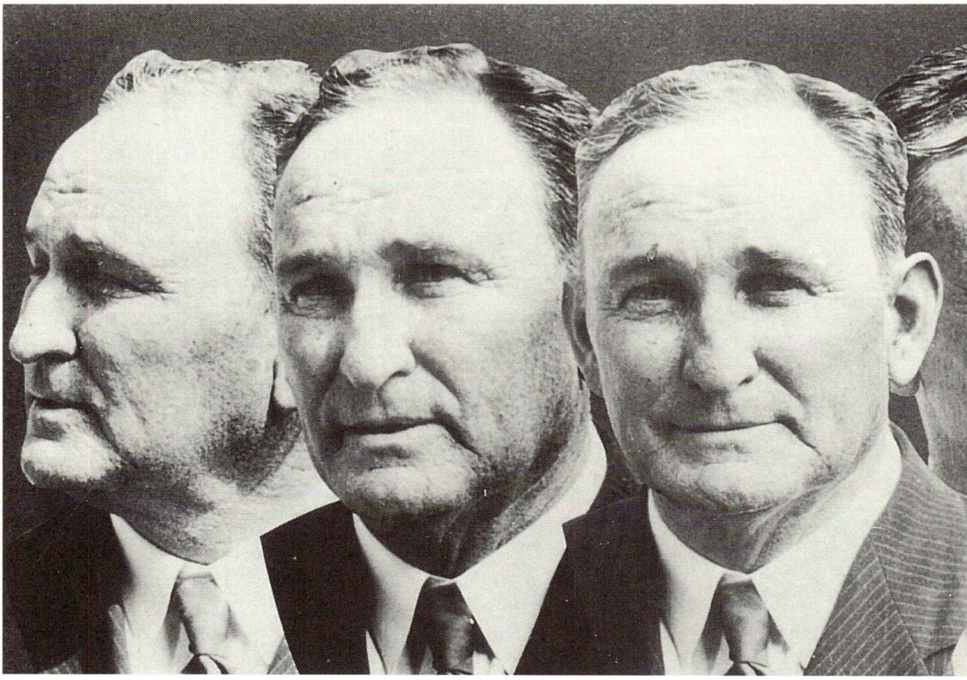

JOE T. ROBINSON

Always a Loyal Democrat

Cecil Edward Weller Jr.

The University of Arkansas Press
Fayetteville 1998

Manufactured in the United States of America

02 01 00 99 98 5 4 3 2 1

First paperback printing 1998

Designed by Liz Lester

⊗ The paper used in this publication meets the minimum requirements of the American National Standard for Permanence of Paper for Printed Library Materials Z39.48-1984.

LIBRARY OF CONGRESS CATALOGING-IN-PUBLICATION DATA

Weller, Cecil Edward, 1961–
Joe T. Robinson : always a loyal Democrat / Cecil Edward Weller, Jr.
p. cm.
Includes bibliographical references and index.
ISBN 1-55728-513-6 (cloth : alk. paper)
ISBN 1-55728-544-6 (paper : alk. paper)
1. Robinson, Joseph Taylor, 1872–1937. 2. Legislators—United States—Biography. 3. United States. Congress. Senate—Biography. 4. Legislators—Arkansas—Biography. 5. Arkansas—Politics and government—To 1950. 6. Democratic Party (U.S.)—History—20th century. I. Title.
E748.R66W45 1998
328.73'092—dc21 97-43301
CIP

Photographs are from Special Collections, University of Arkansas Libraries, Fayetteville. The George W. Donaghey photograph is from the George Washington Donaghey Papers. Reprinted by permission, Special Collections, University of Arkansas Libraries, Fayetteville.

Dedicated to my wife,
Lanetta Lyn Hollis Weller,
the best part of my life

ACKNOWLEDGMENTS

No one can finish a project such as this book without owing a debt of gratitude to the many people who assisted at some time in the project; I am no different. This manuscript started out as my doctoral dissertation at Texas Christian University. I must, therefore, first and foremost thank my graduate advisor, Dr. Ben Procter, who has read and reread every incarnation of this work. Without his meticulous training, his hearty laughter, his forgiving nature, his warm friendship, and his oft-used lash, I would have never finished this biography. No matter how long I live, nor how hard I work, I will never be able to repay him for his care and kindness—care and kindness he has freely given to graduate students over his forty-year career at T.C.U. In addition, I owe thanks to other faculty members who offered suggestions at different times, including Professors Grady McWhiney, Spencer Tucker, Ken Stevens, Frank Reuter, D. Clayton Brown, and Richard Waits. A number of friends and colleagues, to whom I am indebted, have read portions of the text and, thankfully, made suggestions, including Richard Bailey, John Belohlovak, Walter Brown, Walter Ehrlich, Darleen Garrett, Ron Law, Vista McCroskey, Janet Schmelzer, and J. Howell Smith.

I owe special thanks to the staffs of several libraries and research facilities who have been invaluable, including the David Mullins Library at the University of Arkansas (especially Michael Dabrishus, Betty Austin, Andrea Cantrell, and Sandy McCraw), the T.C.U. Library, the Library of Congress (in particular, David Wigdor, Manuscript Division), the Franklin D. Roosevelt Library, the Herbert Hoover Library (especially Dwight Miller), the Arkansas Historical Commission, the Martin Luther King Jr. Library (Washington, D.C.), and the San Jacinto College South Library (especially Richard McKay and Richard Harper). Many individuals, in numerous ways, aided this project, and I owe them tremendous thanks: Mr. and Mrs. Richard Newberry, my older sister and her husband, for opening their home to me many times while I did research at the University of Arkansas and for always finding a way to make those weary research trips fun and enjoyable (and my nephews Allen and Tim); Mrs. Phoebe Procter, for always knowing the right thing to say at the right time; Mr. and Mrs. Grady Miller Jr., who opened their home, their family records, and, most kindly, their hearts to a young graduate student researching their uncle; Mr. Joe T. Robinson Jr., Mr. W. T. Robinson, and Mrs. Lloyd Willmon, for sharing their insights and family records with me; Mr. Matt Fels, for proofreading countless drafts, offering insightful editing, and always believing that the book would someday be finished; Mr. Roy Plattel, for his computer expertise and friendship over the years; Mrs. Lynn Freeman Scott, for aiding me in research at the Columbia University Oral History Project; Mr. Norton Robbins, for his support and understanding while I was in graduate school; Mr. Richard Millard, for saving me countless hours of retyping because of his computer knowledge; Mr. C. Ray Baker, for his enthusiastic love of history; Mrs. Lorine Lay, Mr. Tom Oliver, Ms. Dorothy Hosford, and Mrs. Billye Bumpas, for their love of the English language and their desire to teach others how to write; Mr. and Mrs. Robert Bass, for employing me while in graduate school and then allowing me to leave, seemingly at will, for research trips, while, along with Mr. and Mrs. Thaxton, always encouraging me to continue.

On a more personal note, I am especially grateful to the encouragement and love given me by my late father, Cecil E. Weller, and by my mother, Sarah Weller; anything good I do in life is because of them. Most importantly, I could never have finished this project without the love and support (and proofreading) of the most wonderful person I have ever had the pleasure of meeting—my wife, Lanetta.

CONTENTS

PREFACE

When working on a book like this, a historian must choose whether to do a biography, which keeps the manuscript focused on one person, or a "life and times," which casts the person as one of many in a certain era. From its inception, this book has been a biography. Even though Joseph Taylor Robinson participated in politics, especially the Senate from 1913 to 1937, this book does not claim to tell the story of America, nor even American government, from the 1870s through the 1930s. Robinson *is* the subject, and anything which takes him off the page for too long is distracting and off the topic. Without apologies, therefore, I have prepared a biography of one of the most powerful senators of the twentieth century and, until the election of Bill Clinton as president, the most powerful Arkansan in history.

I have worked to tell the story of Robinson as he was; if he remained silent on a subject, in most cases so does the book. After spending more than a decade "getting to know" Robinson, I am still uncomfortable trying to guess what he was thinking, if he did not give an indication in his papers or to his family. Nor do I try to hide his weaknesses. Surely some may say he is less noble than the book at times portrays him, while others will certainly complain that he is at times treated too harshly. My hope is that the balance in the book represents the makeup of the actual man.

After the years of research a picture developed of an honorable man with many fine qualities. Perhaps foremost in his character was loyalty. From his earliest days, he learned to be faithful to his friends, family, colleagues, and the Democratic Party. Nothing angered him more than perfidy. He could never understand anyone who turned on a close comrade. And to him the Democratic Party was almost part of his family. He could never understand, nor truly forgive, any party member who bolted in 1928 over Al Smith's nomination or who attacked the New Deal; surely that person must have a flawed nature.

Robinson was also a man of integrity and honesty—even in politics. At his death, his property holdings, while small, could be traced to his law practice before he entered politics or during the congressional recesses. And all told they were worth far less than just one year of the $100,000 salary a New York law firm offered him in the mid-1920s. When he made a deal, he stuck by it, even when it caused him personal hardship. If he agreed to a measure, he would support it to the end, no matter the calumny heaped upon him.

Throughout his lifetime he was a Progressive. From his first stint in the state legislature, through his terms in the House of Representatives and the Senate, to his days as majority leader he continually supported the working man. In a speech in 1912 he forecast the need for a system similar to social security. He fought for industrial reform with his proposal for a railroad rate commission for Arkansas in the 1890s, with his sponsorship in the Senate of legislation to end child labor in the 1910s, and with his arduous efforts in passing New Deal legislation in the 1930s.

Personally, his religious tolerance, acceptance, even defense became famous. Robinson was friends with people from all faiths. Then because of his loyalty, he often defended them and their faith. In 1928 his extemporaneous attack on Sen. Tom Heflin (D-Alabama), who was verbally assaulting the Catholic church, was not surprising, even in a day when the Ku Klux Klan still wielded great power. In the 1930s his defense of Jews against attacks in Germany even brought about an "official rumor" that Hitler had heard that the senator's name was originally "Robinsonowski," which explained his views.

Robinson also loved and cared more for his family than for the spotlight his position gave him. He spent most evenings at home with his wife, Billie, shunning the parties to which he was often invited. Although the Robinsons loved children, they were unable to have any, so at times their many nieces and nephews filled in, staying for extended periods with the Robinsons in Washington. And whenever one of them needed money for school or needed a job, "Uncle Joe" could be counted on. In fact, numerous relatives served on his staff throughout his career. And he depended on his family, particularly brother-in-law Grady Miller, to keep him apprised of events and politics in Arkansas.

Yet everyone, no matter how good, has a bad side. Perhaps most famous for Robinson was his temper. As a young man he almost broke into fights on both the House and Senate floors. As he grew older, more than once he hit someone, usually younger and larger than he was, when his temper exploded. For instance at the 1920 Democratic National Convention he knocked a man out, while a few years later he was kicked out of the Chevy Chase, Maryland, Country Club for fighting on the golf course.

More disturbing, however, were his actions and inactions when the Arkansas delta erupted in violence in the mid-1930s. He did nothing to help the poor tenant farmers nor their organization, the Southern Tenant Farmers' Union, as their rights were trampled and members were battered, beaten, and flogged. At first he saw it as "foreign" interference and tried, incorrectly, to blame New York reformers for causing trouble in the South. Obviously he would have liked the situation to have just gone away, but it did not. Eventually he did acquiesce, even supporting the Bankhead-Jones Farm Tenancy Act in 1937.

In some areas Robinson appeared hypocritical. In Arkansas he campaigned as a prohibitionist—although no reference of him having "signed the pledge" exists. And whenever he was in Arkansas, he refrained from drinking. Yet while in Washington he often imbibed, even during prohibition. An inconsistency also exists on the importance of religion in his life. As a lifelong member of the Concord Methodist Church, he contributed regularly to its finances. When in Little Rock, his home after 1912, he attended the First Methodist Church. Yet he rarely attended church when he was outside of Arkansas, unless for a formal function. Both of these stances seem to have been done in order not to antagonize the more religiously conservative voters in Arkansas.

On the issue of race relations, Robinson was clearly a man of his times. He was opposed to integration and apparently looked down upon African Americans as needing paternalistic protection and help. Early in his career he spoke in favor of the literacy test and of the poll tax, though in his later years he rarely even discussed the subjects. And he did nothing to help African Americans gain their civil rights.

Yet he was not a race baiter or demagogue on the subject of race, as were some of his contemporaries. In some ways he was a bit unusual. As a young attorney, he represented African Americans when no one else would. And he fought hard for them, winning most of the cases. He also opposed the Ku Klux Klan in the 1920s, when doing so was seen by many as political suicide. And when the Republicans attacked him as a racist in the 1928 presidential campaign, numerous black leaders from across the state wrote defending him, saying he had always "enjoy[ed] the respect and confidence of the colored voters" of Arkansas.

If anything, his inconsistencies and blemishes prove him human; they underscore his many accomplishments and efforts. While not perfect, he did many things throughout his career that improved the lives of everyday Americans.

1 ANCESTRY AND YOUTH

Throughout much of American history people have moved continually westward. The 1840s were no exception. By boat, by ox cart, by horse, even on foot, settlers pushed the frontier ever closer to the Pacific Ocean. Within little more than half a century Americans had traversed the great mountain barrier of the Appalachians, pressing their civilization onto new lands. That generation could easily remember the opening of the Mississippi River Valley to pioneers. By midway through the 1840s five states lay west of that mighty stream. The United States was attaining its "manifest destiny."[1]

Unnoticed in this throng of migrants, twenty-seven-year-old James Madison Robinson possessed a story spare in details yet similar to that of many migrants. Born near New York City on November 14, 1816, he claimed that his family was related to Pres. James Madison, thus the explanation for part of his name. But being orphaned at age thirteen, he—and a brother Edward—actually knew little of their family heritage. Apparently Robinson studied medicine at Bellevue Hospital in Manhattan; later he would be referred to as "doctor." Looking for greater opportunities, he and his brother traveled inland, first to Illinois where he practiced medicine. Shortly thereafter, in the 1840s, they moved to St. Louis, where the brothers separated, never to see each other again. Edward left for "the west" (possibly for California), while James headed for Texas.[2]

In the mid-1840s James Robinson entered Arkansas, as yet a wild and somewhat untamed frontier. Even though the 1840 census showed that the population had nearly doubled to a "staggering" 97,754 since admission to the Union in 1836, Little Rock (the only "city") could boast merely 1,500 residents and just ten brick buildings. A few other towns were beginning, such as Fort Smith, Pine Bluff, Helena, Batesville, Camden, Washington, and Searcy, but most were rough places where dramatic duels were still more plentiful than theatrical plays. Nearly every man carried a weapon, ostensibly for self-protection, in most cases preferring a Bowie knife. Wildcats and razorbacks (wild boars) roamed freely throughout many areas. Resident Cherokee Indians, usually less violent and more prosperous than their white contemporaries, had only recently been forced off much of their Arkansas land and had moved to Oklahoma.[3]

While en route James Robinson stopped in Lonoke County (then eastern Pulaski County) and decided to stay in that beautiful area. The flat land and rich soil seemed perfect for farming. Water was plentiful and the climate excellent for cotton as well as food crops. A short distance to the east a rolling prairie emerged, ideal for livestock. To the north the farthest fingers of the Ozark foothills reached into the county; small grains such as wheat and oats dominated this upcountry. The several bayous turned the southeastern corner into a swampy breeding ground for mosquitoes, which would later become one of the premier rice-growing regions in the United States. Abundant timber could be found throughout the countryside. All it needed was settlers.[4]

While staying at the home of James P. Eagle, one of the first settlers in the region, Robinson opened a small school. Shortly thereafter he once again became "Doctor" Robinson, although unplanned and unexpected. In the mid-1840s a malaria epidemic spread from Little Rock to Des Arc to De Valls Bluff and everywhere in between. According to family tradition, Robinson, after being approached by Eagle, who offered to furnish a horse and medicine (quinine and calomel), agreed to minister to the sick and dying. He surprised everyone by pulling out his worn medical bag. He had not told anyone that he was a trained physician. During the crisis he even exhausted his horse by working so diligently. Until 1861 he continued his medical practice, making many house calls throughout the country and always taking his cupping machine (a counterirritant), lancet (to remove poisons from the blood by bleeding), and red-hot poultice (for all pains and stomachaches).[5]

During this same time period Robinson established a permanent homestead. He bought two sections of land seven or eight miles northwest of Lonoke between Bayou Two Prairies and the old military road which connected Little Rock and Memphis. He later sold the south section near the bayou, keeping the north one for his own farm, which he and, later, his family would work by themselves, since they never owned any slaves. Near the military road he built a cabin of hewn logs, pinned together at the corners to withstand, if need be, "hurricanes." In the fashion of the day this double-log cabin consisted of two large rooms on either side of an open dogtrot or breezeway. In the summer a family could gather comfortably on the porch and in the winter huddle near one of the two fireplaces. Beneath the house Robinson excavated a large cellar. Nearby he dug a well, even curbing it with brick. At the same time he built a second, single-room log structure for use as a school or as a guest house for itinerant ministers.[6]

Even after becoming settled, James Robinson revealed little of his past, although a few facts, some strong probabilities, and several speculative rumors have survived. Some deduced that he was fleeing from a violent past, citing his first years in Arkansas when he was prone to fights and brawls. Others theorized that he had escaped an overbearing family that planned a career in the celibate priesthood for him. Still others believed he was leaving some great tragedy behind, perhaps a bad marriage or a deceased spouse or child. Of his heritage, in addition to his claim of being the cousin of President Madison, some purported him to be a descendant of the puritan John Robinson. At the least he was of Anglo-Saxon heritage. But whatever the actual case, he never cleared the puzzle of his past.[7]

On one of his many medical trips Robinson met Matilda Jane Swaim, who came from an old and prominent family. The Swaims (pronounced "swim") traced their lineage to colonial Virginia. Some have even suggested that they were descended from Thys Barentsen Sweem, a Dutch immigrant to New Amsterdam in 1661. The Swaims migrated to the Piedmont region of North Carolina, near Greensboro, probably reaching the area before the end of the eighteenth century. Early in the 1820s they moved westward into Maury County, Tennessee (less than fifty miles south of Nashville), along with other friends. Here, Mary "Polly" Weatherly Swaim gave birth to her last child, Matilda Jane, on October 12, 1832. Finally about 1840 the Swaims settled in the new state of Arkansas not long before Robinson emigrated. Already they had become leaders in the area. And most of their thirteen children stayed nearby, mingling with the best clans. Three of the Swaim children married members of the Eagle family, who had also emigrated from North Carolina. And one of those, James P. Eagle, who had persuaded Robinson to "doctor" the vicinity, sired a future governor of the state. Robinson sought to join this prominent family by marrying the youngest daughter, Jane.[8]

After a highly emotional religious conversion, Robinson joined his future wife as a member of the Pleasant Hill Baptist Church near her home; the Swaims had been Baptists for generations. Soon, however, he began causing difficulty in the congregation because of his controversial beliefs. He believed that a person could strive continually to be more like Christ until some day he would reach a state of sinlessness, or perfection. This belief was anathema to Baptists. Several members tried to dissuade him of this "heresy." But his stubborn nature took control, and he refused to change his beliefs or even to quit publicizing them. Finally the congregation "churched" him, excommunicating him from the assembly. Not to be deterred, Robinson gave five acres of land for a cemetery and a new congregation, which later became the Concord Methodist Church; he never formally affiliated with any denomination, although he preached in several churches, including, most often, the Concord Methodist Church.[9]

On December 22, 1852, James Madison Robinson married Matilda Jane Swaim, beginning forty years together. Soon they began their large family. In 1854 Julia arrived, the first of eleven children. In addition they reared perhaps as many as six orphans as members of the family. Three sons, James, William, and Edward, all became prominent men. But on August 26, 1872, the ninth child, fourth son, and most famous offspring was born. They named him Joseph Taylor Robinson.[10]

In 1872 Lonoke County was rapidly losing its frontier qualities, becoming more tranquil and prosperous. Although never wealthy, the Robinsons also improved economically. They built a new six-room home from milled wood, not rough logs. On one side of the hall was Mother and Father Robinson's bedroom. Behind it was a dressing room and a large bedroom, with a bed in each corner for the four daughters. Farther back was an enormous kitchen. At the front of the house on the other side of the hall was the large living room, where James Robinson kept his voluminous library, perhaps numbering over two hundred classical and historical books—and a trophy or loving cup with the word

"Loyalty" inscribed on it. To the rear lay the boys' bedroom and the dining room, across from the kitchen. Behind the house was the apple orchard—so big that one grandchild remembered it as "the most famous thing there was around here," producing "millions" of apples. The Robinsons even had a grove of peach trees. They raised both cattle and hogs for meat as well as milk cows for dairy products. They also had a number of horses, so that in any emergency the doctor would have a fresh mount. On this cultivated land they raised mostly food crops—corn, sweet and Irish potatoes, and other vegetables—for home canning. Additionally they planted a few acres in cotton for a cash crop, though in later years some suggested that the family made more money from their fruit trees.[11]

James Robinson ruled his home like a benevolent dictator. Stern and unbending, the six-foot-tall preacher demanded complete obedience from his children; none dared cross him. He required that all live up to his high ideals—no drinking or card playing in the house, no deceiving someone in a deal, no talking behind a person's back, no disloyalty to a friend, and no lying under any circumstances.[12]

Yet a warmth pervaded the Robinson household. Every night after a plentiful dinner of garden vegetables, homemade corn bread, and fresh buttermilk, James Robinson assembled the family for Bible readings and prayers. Then they would all gather around the Mason and Hammond pump organ to sing favorite songs, usually old, familiar hymns. Each of the children played a musical instrument—Joe, the coronet. Eventually, however, the family joined in nightly discussions, sometimes religion, other times local or family problems, and occasionally politics, which was young Joe's favorite topic. As one family member put it, "[T]hey were all good talkers. They got that from their father." Guests coming from Lonoke, strangers traveling the military road, and hobos looking for a handout all visited the Robinson home; none were turned away, because Christian charity demanded hospitality. Often the family stayed up late into the night talking, while Joe and older brother Ed would hide in the corner to listen. What a lively household they became after dinner.[13]

Perhaps the most important influence in the family was religion. The older that James Robinson grew, the more single-minded in pursuit of Christian perfection he became. Each week more churches in the area asked him to preach, since regular clergy were rare in the rural areas. Few people could refute his well-reasoned sermons, his dynamic and magnetic personality, his personal earnestness and devotion. On one occasion a visiting farmer enthralled the children by explaining how he had gotten the better of an acquaintance in a horse trade, since his animal was ill and practically useless. Upon hearing the story, Robinson became furious, lecturing the man on why not to defraud a neighbor. As a result, the shamed visitor immediately negated this business deal. On another occasion a group of ministers gathered after dinner at the Robinson home. Gradually the conversation turned to a man who was not present, dwelling on his many problems and shortcomings. Suddenly Robinson stood up, looked each minister in the eye, and indignantly announced: "I will leave the room and let you talk about me." By the time he returned, each of the ministers was "repentant" and swore never to talk behind the back of another person. Perhaps more significantly, young Joe and Ed, who were sitting in a dark corner of the room, learned a valuable lesson which they would never forget.[14]

Young Joe's daily ritual was, in most ways, common for the rural areas. He arose early in the morning and ate breakfast with the family before going into the fields. His persistent nature developed early, as he took pride in being able to chop cotton at an earlier age than any of his brothers or sisters. He also hoed his first row while still a young boy of seven, just to prove that he was equal to his older brother Ed. He loved to hunt and to fish as well as to participate in most outdoor activities, spending large amounts of free time with his dogs. To the horror of his father, one of his favorite pastimes was racing horses—as fast as possible—down the military road. On Saturdays he often hitched a horse to a wagon and escorted his mother to town, where she sold vegetables and fruit, sometimes trading them for needed staples. The other children would ridicule young Joe—a chubby, redheaded, freckle-faced country boy, who wore rolled-up overalls with one suspender fastened over a shoulder. On one occasion some local bullies taunted him, yelling that their mother wanted a cabbage and was "his head for sale"? He jumped from the wagon and attacked his tormentors. After the battle, "Scrappy Joe," soon to become known for his violent, short-fused temper, had bested the city boys. Although his manner of assault would later change, his temper continued unabated until his death.[15]

Formal education in rural Arkansas was primitive at best, but young Joe made the most of his opportunities. He usually went to a one-room schoolhouse, but only during the summer months. He learned the rudiments of reading, writing, and arithmetic, with a little American history and geography thrown in when possible. While Joe took advantage of all the possible formal training, his studies did not stop there. At night he and brother Ed would each take a book from their father's library and read it until sent to bed. Then before going to sleep, they told each other the gist of their readings. Or the next day, while working in the fields, they recounted a number of details within their book. In this way they mastered more material. At times after work they went to their parents' bedroom to peruse some of the great literary works—Scott and Dickens, Cooper and Hawthorne, Bancroft and Gibbon, and, of course, the Bible. Sometimes Lincolnesque in their approach, they would lean their chairs close to the kerosene lamp. To their great embarrassment, one evening while the two were reading, the heavy pine plank supporting their chairs broke under the added weight, dumping them into the floor. Long after his father fixed it, young Joe would blush whenever anyone mentioned the broken board.[16]

Although a teenager, Robinson became well known as a local orator. He practiced for hours (where no one but the two old mules, Pete and Beck, could hear) and developed a persuasive style. His deep, resonant voice could be easily heard even under the worst circumstances. While speaking, he continually cut the air with his hands, gesturing almost as if directing an orchestra. And according to some witnesses he had a presence, a "magnetism" about him, which appealed to listeners. According to his niece, Maysell Walls Curry, he always "knew what he wanted to do and say." During his teens, for example, a speaker for the Agricultural Wheel (later absorbed by the Farmers' Alliance) began to harangue a gathered crowd when his Democratic opponent seemingly had not arrived for the debate. Out of the crowd Robinson jumped to challenge the "imported socialist." With an "impromptu" speech he so thoroughly defeated the Populist that a local newspaper recounted that the guest speaker "slipped away and never was heard from in Lonoke County afterward." Unknown to the crowd, Robinson had been selected by local Democratic leader Tom Trimble for the debate. But rather than advertise the fact, he had played his youth to an advantage; even a country boy could refute the Wheeler.[17]

On another occasion several years later Robinson defeated his brother Ed in a local forensic contest. In order to raise six hundred dollars for the local Epworth League, the Lonoke Methodist Church sponsored a debate on whether newspapers were an "abominable curse." At first Ed appeared to win the debate by his clear logic and use of poetry and quotations. Joe then responded, Ed fondly recalled, that "my brother . . . lies in the shade all day and reads Shakespeare while I have to do all the farm work such as milking the cows, chopping wood, and forking hay." Before Joe could finish his thought, the crowd erupted in laughter. Besides winning the debate, Joe learned an important speaking technique—identifying with an audience.[18]

But to improve on natural talent, Robinson needed to further his education, not easy for a family lacking cash. He, therefore, had to finance such pursuits alone. He soon prepared to teach, although having received only the barest of formal training—less than forty-six months total. In 1889, at seventeen, he passed the Lonoke County teachers' examination, earning a license to instruct first graders. For the next two years he taught all courses: reading, writing, spelling, arithmetic, geography, and United States history. While working in the nearby communities of Tanner's Chapel, Mount Carmel, Oak Grove, and Union Academy, he saved as much money as possible. Often he defrayed expenses by staying with relatives such as his sister Sally Walls. Although paying monthly room and board of eight dollars, he still saved most of his thirty-five-dollar salary. After two years he finally had enough money to enter the Arkansas Industrial University (later the University of Arkansas) at Fayetteville in the spring of 1891.[19]

Robinson used his collegiate career to expand personal interests and improve his talents. In class work he pursued a liberal arts program, enlarging on his knowledge with courses in Latin, French, Greek, physics, zoology, and geography. Extracurricular activities included the Philomathian Debating Society. During commencement exercises in December 1891, he even participated in a forensic contest, the subject for discussion being whether Arkansas should have an education requirement for voting.[20]

But upon the death of his father in 1892 Robinson's formal education came to an abrupt halt. Because of family commitments, Robinson immediately left the university and returned home to help support his mother. Although later enrolling in the University of Virginia Law School summer session of 1895, he never again would be able to devote himself to academics. His childhood had come to an end.[21]

2 LAWYER OR POLITICIAN?

After his father's death Robinson had to find a way to support himself as well as his mother. On the family land husbandry might have seemed the obvious choice—but not to Robinson. At an early age he had developed a definite dislike for the back-breaking, never-ending labor of farming. To handle a hoe had been a necessary way of existence in his childhood. And even though many urbanites romantically glorified the agricultural lifestyle, he knew it to be sweaty, arduous toil. Even his educational pursuits had originally been designed to keep him off the farm. Years later, when a nephew announced an intention to start farming, Robinson grew almost apoplectic, shouting: "Boy, are you crazy? That's one of the reasons I am where I am today. I was determined that . . . I would never put my hand on a hoe again."[1]

Instead Robinson chose the law, a career which had fascinated him for a long time. Years earlier, Judge Thomas C. Trimble of Lonoke had stayed overnight at the Robinson home, talking late into the night with Father Robinson, while young Joe listened attentively to every word about legal and political problems of the area. The next morning upon preparing to leave, Trimble announced that he would someday be happy to train Joe as a lawyer—much to the horror of Father Robinson, who felt that the legal profession was unsuitable for his son. Even so, whenever visiting Lonoke, Joe would stop at the law office. Now that he needed a job, and since his father could no longer fight his decision, he accepted a job from Judge Trimble in 1892.[2]

Robinson enjoyed his legal "apprenticeship." He moved into a small, but private, back room of the law office. During the day he became better acquainted with his profession by reading such works as

Blackstone's Commentaries. As his proficiency increased, he began researching cases and writing briefs. On occasion he attended court with Trimble. And whenever possible, he usually dined with his mentor's family. In fact, some noted that Mrs. Trimble treated Robinson as if he were "her own son."[3]

But caring for "Mother Robinson" still occupied a large portion of young Joe's time. Since his father's death he had managed the family farm. He also directed the renters or "tenants" by planning crops, scheduling planting, even suggesting fertilizers. In addition he oversaw all legal matters, including paying the taxes on the land. And whenever his mother needed help, he offered assistance. In October 1894, for instance, he insisted that she visit her daughter Betty Brewer, who lived at Kingsland, nearly one hundred miles away. Because she refused to ride on the train alone, Robinson took time off and accompanied her. He always felt a responsibility both for his immediate family and distant relatives.[4]

Robinson not only studied law, but became interested, enthralled, even involved in politics. Since Judge Trimble was the local leader of the Democratic Party, Robinson became intimately acquainted with partisan machinations. He learned that often in Arkansas the small, rural counties nominated a local citizen for just one state or national office. Then several of these candidates worked together to elect their slate at the state convention. Larger counties, including Lonoke, selected several people and tried to gain as many positions as possible. In 1893, against the advice of Trimble, Robinson campaigned throughout Lonoke County for Carroll Wood of Drew County, a candidate for associate justice of the state supreme court. But the Lonoke contingent was instructed to vote for a local candidate. Eventually Robinson convinced a majority of his fellow delegates to endorse Wood, who then won. (In 1902, when Robinson ran for Congress, his previous support of Wood helped swing Drew County to his side.)[5]

Arkansas Populists were one of the few groups after the Civil War that challenged the statewide hegemony of the Democratic Party. In 1894 Lonoke became a political battleground, and Robinson a Democratic soldier. Already recognized as an orator, he attacked the Populists, often calling them "political polecats." Then he decided to enter the race for the state legislature. Since Lonoke received two seats in the one-hundred-member House of Representatives, Robinson and distant relative W. H. Eagle secured the Democratic nominations. No doubt Judge Trimble, the acknowledged party leader in the county, aided his protégé. Yet also important was the support of his cousin, former governor (1888–92) Jim Eagle.[6]

To some, the twenty-one-year-old Robinson seemed to be a foolish choice. But at a speech in Cabot, Arkansas, the leading town in the northern portion of the county, Robinson proved the wisdom of his selection. The Populist candidates spoke first, outlining their program in great detail. The crowd began to listen attentively, thereby worrying some of the local politicians. Then Robinson began his speech. With a loud, deep, even bellowing voice that everyone in the large crowd could hear, he "roared" that the Populist candidate for governor had not even paid his one-dollar poll tax. If the "head of their ticket" did not even contribute that small amount to support the common schools of the state, he asserted, then "WHAT shall be said of the complexion of the TAIL?" The crowd erupted in laughter, signaling a triumph for the Democrats. Years later, Robinson's friends asserted that the Populists in Lonoke County declined in popularity from that moment on.[7]

Robinson campaigned vigorously through election day—and with gratifying results. Every spare moment of the campaign he espoused his platform: economy in government, uniformity in tax assessments, and increased state aid for charitable institutions. Untiringly he visited all of the communities in his district and then traveled to as many individual farms as possible. According to some family members, months after the election was over, his horse would stop automatically any time it approached a farmer by the roadside or a fellow traveler on the pike. In the final tally Robinson was victorious, leading all candidates with 1,685 votes out of 1,803 cast.[8]

So in January 1895, Robinson embarked on a political career as the youngest member of the state legislature. Little Rock, although less than thirty miles from Lonoke, was a vastly different setting and ambiance. While Lonoke was growing rapidly and could boast of over eight hundred residents in 1890, Little Rock had a population of twenty-five thousand (and over thirty-eight thousand in 1900). It also had broad streets and a few buildings of three or four stories that some residents called "skyscrapers." The city was a bustling port on the Arkansas River, with trade reaching the Mississippi River and, from there, "the world." The business community ruled the town, being sophisticated enough to allow a Republican, H. L. Remmel, to head the local board of trade, because of his proven entrepreneurial acumen. Without question Little Rock was a "New South" city, culturally and politically, serving as the center of the state. Since territorial days it had served as the capital, except for a few years during the Civil War. Not surprisingly, local society hinged on what happened at the capitol and in the city at large. For example, the *Arkansas Gazette*, the only statewide newspaper, printed not just the news but also the political gossip and social events of the entire region. To Robinson, therefore, Little Rock and Lonoke were far different, having little in common.[9]

At the Arkansas capitol the most captivating, thrilling, and suspenseful spectacle every two years was the election of a Speaker of the state House of Representatives. Robinson, due to his youth and inexperience, plunged recklessly into the fracas. On January 14, 1895, he nominated M. J. Manning of nearby Monroe County for the speakership. In order to save time, no one gave nominating speeches—a disappointment for Robinson. On the first ballot, however, his candidate finished last (seventh place), receiving only eight of the fifty-one votes needed for election. On the second vote, he had dropped to only five supporters; therefore, Robinson withdrew his name and scouted for someone new to favor. At first he supported Jerry South of Baxter County in north Arkansas, but to no avail. Eventually on the fourteenth ballot, Robinson switched to J. C. Colquitt of Columbia County (near the Louisiana border). He chose well; ten roll calls later Colquitt won the post.[10]

Despite his youth, Robinson soon achieved recognition in the legislature. Although receiving minor appointments to the Committee on County and Probate Courts and the Committee on the Militia, he secured a position on the important Judiciary Committee, probably for his support of Colquitt. And his old friend Manning was appointed chairman. In fact, three colleagues who had just campaigned to be Speaker served on the committee. As a member of this powerful group Robinson debated the most important laws coming before the session, as well as met the state's prominent politicians. Early in February 1895, his increasing political stature again became apparent when the

Democrats held a caucus to decide whether the state and national elections should be consolidated. Chairman Thomas Newton of Pulaski County appointed Robinson secretary. A short time later, Speaker Colquitt named Robinson to the important Special Committee on Corporations, especially since it considered all laws dealing with business. Late in February he opposed the Speaker of the House (as well as Lonoke's other representative, Eagle) by supporting a primary instead of a caucus for statewide officials. Then to the shock and horror of many Democratic leaders, the primary bill passed.[11]

Robinson's greatest effort thus far, his most noted work, yet least successful struggle, concerned railroads. On January 23, 1895, he introduced a measure that allowed limited rate regulation of state transportation companies. After securing its approval from the Judiciary Committee, he guided it to passage through the House. But the Senate neglected, sidetracked, then killed the bill. As a consequence Robinson introduced a few days later a new and more stringent proposal, which would establish a state panel similar to the Interstate Commerce Commission. Diligently he guided the measure through committee against only token resistance. But on the floor of the House it received a harsh greeting. The railroads, in particular the powerful Iron Mountain Railroad Company, united the opposition under the leadership of Dan Jones, a former state attorney general and the next governor. According to reporters, Robinson spoke eloquently in behalf of regulation, yet with little success. When the final vote was taken, the bill failed forty-eight to thirty-nine. Surprisingly, eight members of the Judiciary Committee, although having recently approved the bill, voted against it, while only four, including Chairman Manning, supported it.[12]

Because of alleged railroad corruption, the Robinson bill did not die. Gov. James Clarke began intimating that the Iron Mountain Railroad had "bought" the House of Representatives. Then the *Memphis Commercial-Appeal* began denigrating the legislators almost to the point of questioning their parentage. Rep. G. W. Yancey of Phillips County told Robinson and Governor Clarke that Rep. W. C. Roberts of Madison County had introduced him to lobbyist T. L. Cox of the Iron Mountain Railroad, who in turn offered to buy his vote for two hundred dollars and a free railroad pass. Yancey, Robinson, and Governor Clarke then tried to trap the would-be briber—but to no avail. Finally, on April 6, 1895, less than a week prior to adjournment, Yancey brought the issue before the general assembly.[13]

Agitation, frenzy, even hysteria permeated the capital. According to the *Arkansas Gazette*, "nothing had ever created more excitement" in the state. Tensions mounted and tempers flared as members impugned the character of fellow representatives. Some politicians even began carrying weapons with them. Perhaps the most volatile situation occurred when Governor Clarke and Representative Roberts became embroiled in a fistfight in a downtown hotel and were separated by several onlookers after the governor brandished a pistol.[14]

Robinson soon took a leading role in the scandal. After being appointed to a committee to investigate the charges, he stated on the House floor that he never "publicly or privately" asserted that bribery had defeated his railroad commission bill. He did not, however, want to see the charges "kept quiet" just because the session was about to end. If anyone had taken a bribe or any lobbyist offered one, Robinson asserted that the member should be "found out and stamped with final shame and disgrace; tracked by sleuth hounds, hunted down and arraigned; consigned to . . . a dungeon in prison or a place in hell." Later that day the committee selected Robinson as chairman and began its investigation.[15]

The political turmoil had several positive outcomes for Robinson and railroad regulation. Over the next week most state newspapers carried various accounts of the scandal; those people who had not already heard of the commission bill now learned of Robinson's fight against government corruption. The gallery packed with curious spectators, House members anxiously, nervously, even worriedly awaiting the investigation results, newspapermen scurrying around trying to uncover any information, a silence as "quiet as a graveyard" abruptly enveloped the chamber as Robinson read the report. Unable to find any proof of corrupt practices in the limited time before the end of the session, the committee officially exonerated the members of the legislature. It did, however, urge that the bribery charges against Cox be turned over to the prosecuting attorney and brought before a grand jury. Even though some called the inquiry a "whitewash," the legislature had limited the political damage by investigating the matter promptly; Robinson's committee report pleased most of the representatives, since it condemned only Cox. The next governor, Dan Jones, was elected on a platform which promised a railroad commission similar to Robinson's proposal. Finally, the next general assembly approved an amendment to the constitution, authorizing the creation of a railroad commission; the voters overwhelmingly approved it in the 1898 election, 63,703 to 16,940.[16]

Robinson—although only twenty-two—had earned an excellent statewide reputation through his stint in the legislature. He was recognized as an outstanding orator, the *Arkansas Gazette* calling him perhaps "the very best speaker of the assembly." Both "brilliant and effective," his speeches "thrilled" the galleries. Unlike some members, Robinson always took routine work seriously. He never missed a roll-call vote and, according to one report, was "wide awake" to the proceedings, always knowing the issues before the legislature. But most importantly he had gained wide recognition as a friend of the farmers and a protector of small-town residents—he had fearlessly opposed the most "notorious" force in Arkansas, the Iron Mountain Railroad. As the *Gazette* observed, he had a "political future of great possibility, if he so wills."[17]

Already characteristics were surfacing in Robinson that would follow him throughout his career. He had proven himself an astute politician, even at his young age. He had made numerous influential friends, including many of the leaders of the state Democratic Party. He had earned a reputation as a "winner" by backing successful candidates and legislation. He had even used the press to champion his causes.

Yet, even while building a reputation as a loyal party member, Robinson also exhibited a streak of courageous independence. While always loyal to the Democrats, he was unafraid of bucking the leadership when he believed they were wrong or too conservative. For example, when most of the leaders opposed a state primary, he had supported it as a means of taking democracy closer to the people. And with most of the pols fighting a railroad rate commission, he fearlessly advocated a board to regulate freight charges. Eventually the Democratic Party would support both measures. Both of these traits—political wisdom and fearless independence on issues—resurfaced throughout his life.

During the next several months, after the legislature adjourned early in April 1895, Robinson was extremely busy. He briefly returned home, at which time he organized the family farms before his summer absence. Then in June he attended a nine-week summer Law School at the

University of Virginia. For approximately one hundred dollars (including tuition, room, and board), he immersed himself in the study of law, even if only for a short time. "Copious" lectures supplemented *Blackstone's Commentaries*, his only textbook. Courses included personal rights, domestic relations, corporations, personal and real property, contracts, probate, and courts of equity. Designed for the individual who could not spend several years in Law School, the summer term classes were intense, yet broad enough to cover as many practical matters as possible.[18]

After this rewarding summer, Robinson returned home to begin a successful law practice. In September 1895, although having already argued cases in justice of the peace courts, he passed an examination that allowed him to practice before the Seventeenth Judicial Court. Once again working for Judge Trimble, he now had prospects for a lucrative career. His first major case involved murder. Seven black men had been arraigned for killing another black man. No lawyer in Lonoke would represent them, perhaps because the case seemed hopeless, perhaps because of their color. Finally they approached young Robinson and each offered him one hundred dollars, if he got them acquitted. After a short trial in which he bested the prosecution, the jury returned a verdict of "not guilty." His courtroom ability thus spread throughout the county.[19]

While busy with his budding legal career, Robinson still made time for Miss Ewilda Gertrude Miller, a local beauty. Four years his junior, "Billie," as he called her, came from a prominent family. Her father, Jesse Miller, had been wounded while fighting for the South in 1862 at the Battle of Shiloh. About 1873 he and his wife, Sarah Evelyn Grady, had emigrated to Lonoke, where he opened a general store. Just a few years later, in 1876, their second child, and only daughter, Ewilda, was born. Soon thereafter with his business prospering, he built a two-story, multigabled, frame house on Court Street (near the railroad tracks), which enabled his wife to host a number of events as well as participate prominently in local society affairs, such as card parties and meetings of the "Four Leaf Clover Club." The Millers were unquestionably one of the leading families of Lonoke.[20]

Throughout 1896, Robinson's affection for Ewilda Miller steadily grew. They first met on a picnic at Hill's Lake. The railroad offered fifty-cent excursion tickets for the twelve-mile trip to the local "resort," making it a favorite spot for the young people of Lonoke. R. H. Grady, Ewilda's uncle, introduced the couple, who liked each other immediately. During the next few weeks, they began meeting at the local drugstore to become better acquainted. Soon thereafter they started dating, perhaps ending some evenings on the Millers' front-porch swing. Within the year, they were engaged.[21]

On December 15, 1896, the wedding of Robinson and Billie Miller was an auspicious occasion. The Methodist church overflowed with family and friends, roses and chrysanthemums enshrouding the chancel, the "Wedding March" billowing from the organ. The beautiful bride, dressed in a long, puffy-sleeved white dress and cathedral-length veil, slowly walked down the aisle on her father's arm. Slender, dapper Joe, his dark hair in a pompadour, waited at the front for Billie, with Grady Miller, the bride's brother standing next to him as best man. After the "beautiful and impressive" ceremony the couple, along with family and guests, retired to the Miller home for a "sumptuous repast." The union of the prominent "lawyer, statesman, and orator" to one of "Lonoke's fairest and most accomplished daughters," the *Lonoke Citizen* announced, was the social event of the year.[22]

Within a short time the Robinsons moved to the Millers' home, which was only a couple of blocks from the growing law firm. Judge Trimble and Robinson made an ideal team. Trimble was a legal genius with an astounding memory. He could recollect precise details of cases tried twenty years earlier. In addition, he knew every local politician and attorney in the area. Yet he had his problems. He spoke poorly in public, apparently with some form of speech impediment. He was also absentminded; once he used a one-thousand-dollar check for a bookmark, all the while complaining that he had never been paid for his services. And as for grooming and personal appearance, he was often comical, with none of his clothes matching. Fortunately the young and inexperienced Robinson was a good counterbalance. Although new in the legal profession, with much less knowledge than his partner, he was one of the finest orators in the state. He could sway juries and win seemingly hopeless cases. Well dressed and impeccably groomed, he frequently helped select Trimble's clothes. And he often spent hours finding articles, which his partner had misplaced or had put away for "safe keeping."[23]

In 1898 Robinson achieved an envious reputation as a trial lawyer in the Eagle-Booe murder case. Here is what happened. At England, Arkansas, about fifteen miles south of Lonoke, Charley Booe, a lawyer, was ambushed, shot in the back, and rushed to a hospital in nearby Little Rock for treatment. Booe, as well as many members of his family, assumed that Bob Eagle of Lonoke had shot him. The Eagle and Booe families had operated adjoining stores in Lonoke for several years. Often fights had broken out between different members of their families, leading many people, especially the Booes, to suspect Eagle of the attempted murder. Fearing retaliation and revenge from the "hot-headed" Booes, W. H. Eagle (Bob's father) offered to pay all of Charley Booe's expenses in starting a new law practice for a full year if he would just move to Texas. Instead, Charley's father, Will Booe, said only a duel could settle the feud. When Charley recovered enough to return home, his father and brother traveled to Little Rock to bring him back. Upon returning, the three men stepped off of the train and walked out of the Lonoke station. Suddenly W. H. Eagle and his sons stepped from behind the building and shot all three in the back, killing them instantly.[24]

Amidst general hysteria and terror, including an incident where one of the armed Eagle boys burst into the court chamber during deliberations, the grand jury returned indictments only for second-degree murder. The spectacle then began. In oven-like heat, citizens packed the stifling courtroom, hand-held palm fans providing the only breeze. The local judge, afraid of offending either side and possibly being killed, disqualified himself, leaving the case to someone from outside Lonoke. Then the prosecuting attorney selected an old, one-armed Civil War veteran, a Colonel Vaughn, to aid in arguing the case. Trimble, Robinson, and a Little Rock attorney, Colonel Murphy, represented the Eagles. The show continued for several days, with the crowds arriving early each day to get a good seat. Both sides filled the air with verbose oratory.[25]

Robinson gave an effective closing argument for the defense. He claimed that Charley Booe was an outlaw. More dangerous still was the "fierce, unrelenting, uncompromising" Will, who had refused every effort at mediation. Accordingly, the Booes had determined "to kill all of the defendants." In fact, the shooting was destined to take place because of their bad nature. In actuality, he asserted, the Eagles had acted in self-defense—even if the Booes were unarmed at the time of the murder.[26]

Robinson was pleased with the outcome. Although the prominence and wealth of the Eagle family had not hurt the defendants' chances, Robinson's stirring final argument had helped convince the jury to acquit all of the men. And he added to his growing reputation as an attorney and an orator.[27]

Since 1892, Robinson had matured and improved his station in life. He had served in the legislature, gaining a statewide reputation. Perhaps most importantly for his future, he had proven himself a knowledgeable, astute, even shrewd politician. Yet, as would be true throughout his career, he had also demonstrated an independence on issues favoring the common man, such as the direct primary and the railroad rate commission. Characteristics for which he would later become famous were already being forged.

Professionally and personally his life was expanding. After attending a short session of the University of Virginia Law School, he had been admitted to the local bar. And his legal career was acknowledged as one of the fastest rising in the state. He had even found time for personal happiness in marrying Billie Miller, who would become his life-long partner. For a twenty-six-year-old his achievements were surely impressive, if not remarkable.

3 POLITICIAN

The law might have been Robinson's profession, but politics was his avocation. In every election, for example, Robinson had hurled himself headlong into the fight. Then during the summer of 1896 he succeeded his partner, T. C. Trimble, as county chairman of the Democratic Party, although only twenty-four years old. Because of his outstanding oratorical ability, and with the support of the Lonoke delegation (the largest in the Sixth Congressional District), Robinson was chosen as the Democratic presidential elector. He was thus scheduled to speak for William Jennings Bryan throughout the district, which stretched from the Mississippi River delta of Arkansas County to the Ozark mountain region of Marion, Baxter, and Fulton counties along the Missouri border. But when the Populists also selected Bryan as their candidate, members of both parties urged their colleagues to join together and submit a fusionist list of electors. Robinson, consequently, withdrew in favor of a Populist.[1]

Robinson did not hurt his future political chances by this decision. In fact, he may have helped himself since many leaders would later remember his sacrifice for the good of the Democratic Party. But in 1896 he turned his attention to other races, making numerous impassioned speeches for different candidates. For instance, while campaigning in his congressional district for Democratic gubernatorial candidate Dan Jones, he attacked the Populists. The price of their many programs or "schemes" would cost over twenty-six billion dollars, which was much more than "all the money in the world." Their principles were those of the "socialist" and the "anarchist" who, in "selfishness," betrayed the poor and branded as "liars and fools" anyone who would not blindly follow their lead. Then with great vituperation and vindictiveness he assailed the Populist candidate for governor, A. W. Files, who had a political record as "black as hollow hell." Further, Robinson accused him of being "discarded" by the Democrats and joining the "populites," not as a matter of principle, but to win a position. Files was just one more example of leaders, Robinson asserted, who had "violate[d] their pledges and trample[d] upon the rights of the public." Because of this type of campaigning, several newspapers dubbed Robinson the "boy orator of the prairies," a takeoff on Bryan's sobriquet, "boy orator of the Platte." And, when most of the Democratic candidates won, Robinson took pride in his, albeit small, contribution.[2]

Over the next four years Robinson continued to expand his political base, becoming well known throughout the state but particularly in the Sixth Congressional District. He continued as Lonoke County Democratic chairman until 1900. In addition, he served as secretary of the state senate district committee, composed of members from Lonoke and Prairie counties. He also debated Republicans and their policies whenever and wherever opportunities arose.[3]

Robinson gained even more favorable public exposure through his nonpolitical speaking engagements. In the summer of 1896 he addressed the Southern Teachers' Association in Texarkana on "Patriotism in the Public Schools." The main reason for maintaining free schools was, he pointed out, "to make good citizens" of students by "inculcating patriotism." In fact, the hope of the nation rested with "education." This stance obviously pleased the teachers. And throughout his career he enjoyed the support of most educators. On another occasion in June 1899, he spoke to a large assemblage of Masons in Clarendon, an important community in his congressional district. Robinson won the crowd to his side by relating a story about the Civil War. His father had become stricken with a fever, he told his attentive audience, and was confined to bed in a delirious state when a band of drunken "yankee" soldiers burst into the family cabin looking for liquor and loot. When unable to find any treasure, they lit torches to burn down the home. Suddenly one soldier, wielding a sword, ordered the "ruffians" to leave; he would defend this farm to the death, since he had discovered the Masonic regalia of Robinson's father. By the end of the speech many in the audience wept openly; some applauded thunderously; others yelled their praise. But all approved of their young speaker.[4]

Consequently, by 1900, Robinson was formulating plans for a congressional race in the Sixth District. He, therefore, immersed himself even more in regional Democratic politics. First he secured a place on the Lonoke County Democratic Executive Committee. Then he garnered a slot for the local judicial convention, a powerful position, since that small group of men chose all of the Democratic candidates for judge in the district. More importantly, though, he became one of Lonoke County's eleven delegates to the state convention in Little Rock. During that meeting in July 1900, Robinson nominated John W. Crockett of neighboring Arkansas County for secretary of state, the second most important position in the state. Although U.S. senator James H. Berry had supported another candidate, even speaking for him at the convention, Crockett won the election by acclamation. In turn, Robinson won the post of presidential elector.[5]

Robinson made the most of his position as elector. He traveled extensively throughout the district, attacking the Republicans and praising the Democrats. While speaking across most of the state, he spent the last three weeks in almost every hamlet, village, and town in his district, making eighteen major addresses, as well as often sparring with opponents who were brought in just for the occasion. He stopped in all but the smallest county in the district (Stone). He even visited more of the area than three-term Democratic incumbent congressman Stephen Brundige. Each speech met with success as, according to the local newspapers, the "brilliant young champion of Democracy" held his audiences "spellbound" by his "matchless eloquence." At times he excoriated the Republican Party "with scathing denunciations," attacking it, the *Lonoke Democrat* reported, "without gloves" and leaving opponents at his "mercy." Other times he reviewed and praised the accomplishments, platform, and programs of the Democrats. And no matter what the circumstance he won every debate, entertained the audience, and made the crowd his friends. Bryan, as well as the other Democrats, carried the district overwhelmingly.[6]

After the election Robinson began preparing for 1902, intending to run against Congressman Stephen Brundige. But he had to alter his plans. After the 1900 census, Arkansas gained a House member, and Brundige saved his seat by redrawing the boundaries and leaving Lonoke out. Robinson thus found himself in a new and varied district containing only one familiar county (Arkansas) besides his own. The eastern and southern section was a vast farming region known mostly for cotton, grown by sharecroppers and tenants. Large rivers and small bayous crossed the land, generally flowing from northwest to southeast and eventually emptying into the Mississippi River. The commercial, social, and political center of this area was Jefferson County, with its largest city being Pine Bluff, an agriculturally oriented town on the Arkansas River, forty-five miles south-southeast of Little Rock. To the west lay the Ouachita Mountains and the second largest town, Hot Springs, notorious for ill-tempered gamblers, "fallen" women, and corrupt political bosses. A national park sliced through the middle of the town, causing jurisdictional and law enforcement problems. Many people in this region earned their living in the timber industry, either working as lumberjacks in the pine and hardwood forests or as machine operators in the many sawmills dispersed over the area. And, off by itself, sticking up as if it were a lone finger pointing north toward Missouri, Lonoke was on the fringe of the district.[7]

Robinson also faced a new, yet formidable, opponent, attorney Sam M. Taylor of Pine Bluff. Active in the Democratic Party for over fifteen years, he had traveled to Chicago (1896) and Kansas City (1900) as a delegate to the national conventions. He had even been temporary chairman of the state convention in 1900. For five years Taylor had served as the prosecuting attorney for a region that included five of the twelve counties in the new congressional district. And for the previous seven years he had presided over the Pine Bluff school board. He was, without a doubt, a leading citizen of Jefferson County and the early favorite to win the Democratic nomination, which was tantamount to election.[8]

At first, Robinson's campaign drew only condescending notices. The *Pine Bluff Commercial* ridiculed his candidacy, urging him to stay home and "teach Greek" to students. Then the *State Republican* stated that he was running merely to keep Taylor from winning uncontested; and if former congressman Clifton R. Breckinridge of Pine Bluff joined the struggle, then Robinson would withdraw. In order to stop this rumor, Robinson formally announced that he was staying in the race, no matter who announced for the office. When no one else entered the contest, most political pundits pronounced Taylor as the obvious winner.[9]

Although not expected to win, Robinson forged ahead and organized for the election. During the fall of 1901 he enlisted supporters in each county, including many local officeholders. Then he assigned prominent citizens of Lonoke to coordinate each county; in turn, they spoke in each of the communities and even polled leading residents as to their preference. In January 1902, local Democratic leaders held a meeting in Pine Bluff to organize the congressional district convention and to approve the rules for electing the next congressman. Thomas C. Trimble, representing Lonoke County, found the meeting stacked in favor of the Sam Taylor forces. Two counties had given their proxies to men from Jefferson County; five had no representatives at all. Trimble quickly moved that a quorum was not present, but the acting chairman overruled him. Following Robinson's announced preference, he then tried to force a district primary, but he was defeated four to three. All three of the men from Pine Bluff voted against a popular election. Instead they called for a convention to decide—presumably to help Sam Taylor. Robinson would be fighting on his opponent's terms.[10]

During the spring of 1902 Robinson and Taylor campaigned together, yet applied quite different political techniques. Remaining on cordial terms, they hired a carriage and traveled from one speaking engagement to the next, usually arriving for the first day of each county's circuit court, when most residents would be in town. They stayed in the same hotels, often in adjacent rooms. But the next morning they employed dissimilar tactics. Taylor slept late, ate a leisurely breakfast, and then walked through town, greeting people at the courthouse, the square, and finally at the livery stable—a local gathering place in most of the small communities. Robinson, however, arose early, often skipping breakfast in his hurry to visit the countryside. He rode from farm to farm, stopping at every crossroads store to talk with the rural public. He then returned to town in the early afternoon, where he joined his opponent in passing out campaign cards and talking to the residents. Not until after the election did Taylor find out that Robinson had been visiting the outlying areas on their joint tours.[11]

Robinson did not manage his campaign alone; instead, he depended on several others for their insight, influence, judgment, and organization. Trimble, his law partner and political mentor, worked with local Democratic leaders, shoring up support in weak areas and allocating resources where they could best be used. But older brother Ed was especially effective throughout the district; his main push was among local teachers, since he had been one, as well as a superintendent of schools. He was popular with this group, having organized "teachers' conventions" across much of south Arkansas, encouraging better educational systems, higher salaries, and greater public financial support. Robinson's wife, Ewilda, acted as a clearinghouse, disseminating information to her husband and other campaign workers. Yet she wanted to do more than early twentieth-century society allowed women; she wished that "it were proper for ladies to campaign," to "enter the field" in hopes of "doing a little good."[12]

Robinson often admitted that only small differences separated him from his opponent. Both he and Taylor advocated a Nicaraguan canal, support of the Monroe Doctrine, limited immigration, low tariffs, and levees and navigation systems on Arkansas rivers. Yet one issue, one distinction, emerged in this campaign. Robinson urged abolishing all trusts and businesses which restrained trade. He pointed out that Taylor had served as an attorney for the Iron Mountain Railroad, the dominant carrier in Arkansas. Robinson continually reminded voters in his campaign literature that this corporation, a part of the Jay Gould Railway system, had defeated the railroad commission bill when Robinson first proposed it in 1895. In addition, Taylor had used free passes for most of his travels, something the common citizen could never hope for. How could Taylor possibly protect the people, he asserted time and again, from "the greedy, unjust and vicious demands of these arrogant, heartless, and powerful corporations," if he represented them in legal matters. Everywhere Robinson or his supporters went, cards and leaflets trumpeted his campaign slogan: "Never served a railroad corporation; always serves the people."[13]

Still the election seemed in doubt. Robinson then decided to unleash his greatest political weapon—cousin James P. Eagle, who had served two terms as governor. Respected by many political groups who did not otherwise know Robinson, Eagle convinced many undecided community leaders to support his kinsman. In addition, he was perhaps the best-known Baptist in Arkansas. He had been the leader of the state evangelical organization for several years and in 1902 was elected president of the Southern Baptist Convention. His letter to ministers attesting to Robinson's "strict integrity and good morals" guaranteed their support. As one partisan wrote: "Gov. Eagle is a power. Use him." And Robinson did.[14]

In 1902, convention delegates, who were selected by separate votes in each county, chose the nominee for Congress, rather than the people through a popular primary. This placed an emphasis on winning counties, and thereby the most delegates, rather than garnering the greatest popular vote. Robinson, therefore, stressed different causes, issues, or even personality traits in each locality. Having spoken to Democratic groups many times over the past eight years, he was well known and well liked in Arkansas County, which had been in his old congressional district. He only needed to solidify his popularity there. In Drew County, however, he reminded voters of his crucial support of native son Carroll Wood for the Arkansas Supreme Court, thus imploring the residents to return the favor. In several localities Robinson applied still another tactic; he decried Jefferson County's attempts to control every major office in the region. In fact, several of the smaller counties harbored a jealousy, rivalry, even bitterness toward their more influential and much larger neighbor. Some newspapers reminded voters that every major judicial post in their district had gone to a Pine Bluff resident. Now was the time, Robinson announced, to share positions. Perhaps most important in each case, though, was his oratorical skills. At every stop he bested Taylor in debate. As a result, many believed him much more suitable for Congress.[15]

When the election finally took place on March 29, 1902, Robinson triumphed. He carried eight of the twelve counties. He won the five westernmost counties of Dallas, Garland, Grant, Hot Spring, and Saline. In addition, he took the outlying counties of Drew on the south, Arkansas on the east, and Lonoke on the north. Taylor captured only Cleveland, Desha, Jefferson, and Lincoln counties, which were in the center of the district. At the forthcoming convention in Fordyce, Robinson had forty-nine delegates to nineteen for his opponent.[16]

Even though given little chance of winning, Robinson had succeeded and had earned even the grudging respect of his former adversaries. In analyzing this election the *Stuttgart Republican* announced: "Naturally, logically, geographically, in age and experience," Taylor should have been elected. Yet Robinson, "the beardless kid in comparison, poor in purse but full of the persimmon juice of the native brand and the vinegar of hopeful audacity," defeated the "solid phalanx of old schemers" arrayed against him in Pine Bluff. After winning the general election overwhelmingly on November 4, 1902 (5,195 to 622), Robinson received an endorsement from the *Stuttgart Republican*, the organ of the opposing party. The editors predicted "a brilliant career in Washington—a long one in fact" which they would watch "with the interest of a friend." How true their forecast would prove.[17]

4 CONGRESSMAN

In 1903 when Robinson began his ten-year service in the House of Representatives, a new important wave of thought and action was sweeping to the forefront in the United States—the progressive movement. Reformers, in most cases starting in the cities and then moving to the statehouses and finally onto the national scene, tried to answer the country's vast problems with political solutions. In the municipalities they fought outrageous utility company charges by advocating "gas and water socialism" (the city ownership of basic services). To fight local corruption they championed innovative methods of administration such as the Galveston Commission Plan and the city-manager form of government. In large urban areas they also espoused settlement houses, such as Jane Addams's Hull House, to better the lives of the poor and the immigrants. Some cities even began night classes to teach the illiterate to read and write. At the state level these crusaders endorsed grass-roots democracy through such measures as direct primaries, the popular election of United States senators, and initiative, referendum, and recall. Here, too, they fought public malfeasance, by outlawing free railroad passes for state legislators and by passing corrupt practices acts. In many cases they foreshadowed goals of the national movement by supporting the income tax, antitrust measures, strict railroad regulation, and state banking controls.[1]

On the national level Pres. Theodore Roosevelt, robust, aggressive in nature, and optimistic in outlook, typified the movement. Although assuring conservatives that he would continue the policies of slain president William McKinley "absolutely unbroken," he pursued, in actuality, a moderately progressive program. He attacked large monopolies, filing antitrust suits against first the Northern Securities Company and then the "beef trust." Next he created a cabinet-level Department of

Commerce and Labor, which included a Bureau of Corporations (a forerunner of the Federal Trade Commission) to investigate monopolistic practices. And before his two terms were completed, he started suits against forty-four corporations, including such industrial giants as Du Pont, American Tobacco, and Standard Oil. In addition, he had pushed the Elkins Act through Congress in an effort to strengthen the Interstate Commerce Act by eliminating unfair discrimination between shippers on the railroads.[2]

Even with a progressive president at its head, the government was not controlled by the reformers. In 1903, when Robinson entered the House of Representatives for the first of his five terms, he faced an ossified structure with little practical hope of him being able to make an impression. The Republicans, with a large majority mainly from the Midwest, Far West, and industrial North, dominated the body during his first eight years. They had a majority on every committee as well as all chairmanships. More importantly, though, "Uncle Joe" Cannon of Illinois was the Speaker of the House. Using the rules established over decades and perfected by an earlier Speaker, "Czar" Thomas B. Reed of Maine (1889–91, 1895–99), he often dictated which bills had an opportunity to pass or were destined for oblivion. In much the same way he frequently determined the success of an individual member, especially newcomers. He was the leader of the Old Guard or "stand patters," those Republicans who opposed change. And from this powerful position he fought the reformers on each issue. Nor were the Democrats much more receptive. Drawing most of their support both from the former Confederate states and big-city political machines, many of their members were elected over and over again, thus making it difficult for a newcomer to advance, since more senior members had the first choice of committee assignments. And these same congressmen could determine the program of the Democrats, often without heeding the concerns of freshmen legislators. Indeed, few first termers ever gained any notice, much less any legislative success.[3]

Washington greeted Robinson as it did all newcomers from the hinterlands—with overpowering beauty and grace. From the train station, still located in the mall, he could look straight ahead to the magnificent Capitol Building, which dominated the entire area from its lofty perch on the hill. Behind him stood the dramatic Washington

Monument, rising heavenward, capturing the imagination of travelers as it seemed to pierce the sky. Between these two structures lay the wide vista of green, a natural boulevard bordered by large trees, many almost one hundred years old. Within walking distance a red sandstone "Norman castle," home of the Smithsonian Institution, anachronistically loomed, as if transported from an earlier, more regal age. And also not far away the palatial home of the president, the White House, glistened invitingly. Nearby large, ornate buildings held the various offices of the executive branch. Throughout the district's intricate road system, circles abounded, highlighted by statues of such notables as Daniel Webster as well as of oft-forgotten, yet once-prominent, men such as Arkansas's Albert Pike.[4]

Washington was more than just magnificent structures; it was a city facing the multifarious problems of a growing urban living. By 1903, its population was approaching three hundred thousand, nearly ten times larger than Little Rock. Yet, for the moment, it did not have the poor, immigrant neighborhoods of other large coastal communities. Instead, the city was divided between the mansions of the wealthy and the large homes of middle-class and government employees on one side and, on the other, the poor "alleys"—small, unofficial, and unnamed streets winding behind large edifices. And in hovels, shanties, and even tenements along these crowded walkways, perhaps the largest urban black population in America tried to survive. Even the massive Park Commission Plan for the city, unveiled in 1901, ignored the problem, addressing only ways to improve public areas.[5]

But such slums were not Washington's only shortcomings. Culturally, the city seemed barren. No official orchestra existed, with one experiment having failed after only six performances. Art galleries were not yet prominent, although the government already owned many paintings and sculptures, either loaned out to museums or stored in warehouses. Theater, outside of a few burlesque shows, was also practically nonexistent. Society itself seemed stratified and out of reach of new congressmen. Less than two dozen elected officials were ever invited to the most prestigious local gatherings. And many Washingtonians looked with disdain on transient senators and representatives.[6]

Even though Washington had many problems, Robinson, like many other congressmen, began immediately to ensure his return by addressing the needs of his constituents. His weakest political base had been in Jefferson County and Pine Bluff, the home of Democratic opponent Sam Taylor. The greatest concern of the area residents was the need for a federal building to house the growing postal business. Repeatedly in previous years Congressman John S. Little had introduced a measure in the House to construct a new and larger facility, and each time it had been defeated. Finally, early in 1903, he had amended an appropriations bill to include seven thousand dollars to buy land for a future government building. But after congressional redistricting in 1901 Robinson, not Little, represented Pine Bluff. So in his first term he introduced a bill appropriating one hundred thousand dollars to build a post office. At first it met with little success. Robinson persisted, however, showing that the present building at Pine Bluff was too small for its burgeoning business and that the rent would continue to rise, making the leased quarters less and less frugal. Over the next few years he thus secured several allocations for its construction.[7]

Robinson continued to concentrate on matters that would help his constituents. For instance, in 1903 he spoke for federal aid to combat the boll weevil—a destroyer of cotton—a crop on which his constituents predominantly depended. Then he, along with several visionary farmers from the area, urged the Department of Agriculture to experiment with growing rice in two locations in his district, one near Lonoke and the other by Stuttgart. By 1906 a crop had been raised successfully, convincing many farmers that rice offered a better opportunity for profit than cotton. Within a short time rice was the leading commodity of the area, making depleted fields once again productive, as well as turning much of the swampy low-lying areas into rich agricultural lands. In addition, at the request of small-town residents of his district, he struggled unsuccessfully for ten years, trying to locate post offices in almost a dozen communities where the government rented space.[8]

For Robinson, Hot Springs, the second largest town in his district, posed particular problems and needed special attention. A national park divided the community nearly in half, practically surrounding one section of the town. Roads, therefore, either wound long miles out of the way or, with congressional approval, cut across a small section of park land. Even finding locations for schools, firehouses, and other civic buildings often needed assent from Washington. Throughout his tenure Robinson shepherded many local bills through the House of Representatives that facilitated growth and improvement in the area. Other concerns, unique to Hot Springs, also needed resolution, usually with his help. The resort center, which featured refreshing, healthful baths and massages, catered to some unsavory types, because of its illegal, yet profitable, gaming houses and small casinos. Legal jurisdiction among city, county, state, and federal courts was jumbled and unclear, so Robinson guided measures through Congress, delineating who would hear cases arising from incidents in the park. He even found himself as the point man for such agencies as the Knights of Pythias, the Masons, and B'nai B'rith when they wanted to build offices, sanitariums, or hospitals at Hot Springs. It must have seemed as if everything concerning the town had first to pass Congress, with the aid of Robinson, of course.[9]

Robinson was also keenly interested in developing Arkansas waterways; but being in the minority party, he was hard pressed to accomplish anything for his district. He always backed legislation for the improvements of rivers and harbors. In 1907, for instance, when the Republicans led a fight against allocating enough money to improve Arkansas rivers, Robinson explained that the state had always "suffered from [a] lack of transportation facilities" which had not been abated with the rise of monopolistic railroads; he thus vehemently accused Republicans of "discrimination" and "favoritism." At the same time he envisioned navigation of the Arkansas River from its mouth to Muskogee, Oklahoma, as an inexpensive alternative to the railroads. (But not until the 1970s was such a project completed.) He also demanded appropriations for dredging operations at the shoals south of Pine Bluff; in fact, he called for the maintenance of the banks, channels, and levees of such rivers as the White, Cache, Black, and Red. The Republicans, however, were unmoved by Robinson's efforts; they defeated these measures.[10]

Not everything Robinson proposed was forward looking; two measures he repeatedly introduced were rooted in the Civil War and Reconstruction. While neither ever really had a chance of passing, he still championed both causes because of the sentiment in his district. The first concerned an internal tax on cotton of fifteen dollars a bale. Although the levy was assessed for only a short time before the U.S. Supreme Court declared it unconstitutional, Robinson argued that the collected money should have been returned to the people (or their heirs) who had paid it. And if they could not be found, the federal government should allocate it to the states for use in the public schools. His second bill called for a special Civil War Claims Commission to hear complaints against federal soldiers who had wantonly committed acts of outrage from 1861 to 1865. According to Robinson, Union troops had needlessly burned many buildings, such as churches and schools. In a drunken frenzy or for no apparent reason they had also destroyed homes, torched crops, and slaughtered livestock. Robinson contended that the federal government should reimburse innocent southerners for such losses.[11]

During his first year in Congress Robinson became known as a fearless defender of the average man, especially after protecting the interests of a small Arkansas newspaper owner. Here is what happened. Pres. Theodore Roosevelt had scheduled a message to Congress, a copy of which the Associated Press had sent in advance with the notice "released on delivery." The president, however, did not give the address when planned, and a small Arkansas newspaper ran the speech inadvertently. Melville Stone, president of the Associated Press, levied a one-thousand-dollar fine on the paper and forbade its using the wire service, thereby dooming it. Stone, upon being asked to reconsider the matter, realized that the punishment was too severe, but would not rescind the heavy penalty unless the president so requested.[12]

A delegation of Arkansans, led by the senior senator James Berry and which included Robinson, pleaded the case for the newspaper. The men, however, did not accomplish their goal. Roosevelt, possibly tiring of the interview, irritably interrupted: "If you were not such estimable gentlemen I should say you were a set of asses." Berry jumped to his feet, withdrew his request, and hurriedly left the White House, followed by the entire entourage—except Robinson. Roosevelt then turned and shouted, "Well, what do you think of it?"[13]

Although perhaps slightly awed at the surroundings, freshman representative Robinson did not cower at the remark, but stated his observations and opinions—with surprising success. Calmly he replied: "I think, Mr. President, that your treatment of that old, Confederate soldier was a gross act of discourtesy." Then, unflinchingly, he asserted: "You did not give him an opportunity to fully explain the case."

Robinson then related that Stone had suggested having Roosevelt ask for leniency, since the speech had been mistakenly printed when the owner was sick and not at the paper. Roosevelt quickly reacted and, with a big grin, announced: "You are right, my boy!" He then dictated a telegram to Stone and, before Robinson left the White House, the Associated Press responded that it was happily lifting the sanctions.[14]

Robinson enhanced his popularity even more by his continual support of progressive legislation—in particular, railroad regulation. In 1905, while still a freshman representative, he introduced a bill (H.R. 18595) enabling the Interstate Commerce Commission (ICC) to regulate private freight cars. According to Robinson, business managers, through "amazing skill and great intelligence," had acquired a virtual monopoly over many transportable commodities, including many items used daily, such as food stuffs. Robinson thus asked his colleagues rhetorically: "Is it not oppression when by unlawful or, at best, questionable means a corporation can fix the price of almost every product consumed by the public?" But his proposal never made it out of committee. Then when the House was debating the Roosevelt-endorsed Townsend-Esch bill for further railroad regulation, he encountered another roadblock. Because of the rules adopted for considering the bill, he could not introduce his plan, since no amendments could be submitted. Even minority leader John Sharp Williams of Mississippi tried and failed to have the proposal added. Robinson thus attacked the Republicans for passing the bill, which they knew would be killed by the conservative Senate. Prophetically he warned, even threatened, that unless something was done to relieve such injustices, the people might "find it necessary to own them [the railroads] in order to prevent them from oppressing the very power that created them."[15]

Even after losing this battle, Robinson was not deterred. Instead he fought for greater regulation. In 1906 he supported the president by voting for the Hepburn Act, which allowed the ICC to fix rates (which would remain in force until the railroads proved that the charges were too low) and to restrict free passes for travel. The next year he introduced several new regulatory measures. The first proposed that the ICC determine the actual value of all railroads involved in interstate commerce, as well as all of their property holdings, in order to establish equitable rates. Robinson found that railroads often sent goods via a third, distant, out-of-the-way location as a means to inflate prices. To combat this abuse, he introduced a bill to limit transportation charges to only the lowest fare between two points, unless the shipper specified a more circuitous route. In still a third bill Robinson recommended that the railroads be charged interest on deferred payments of claims. But in the Republican-controlled House of Representatives none of these bills ever reached the floor for debate, much less a vote. Then in 1911, he supported an unsuccessful bill that, by inspecting locomotive boilers, would have lessened the number of accidents and protected railway workers.[16]

Robinson actively supported other progressive legislation as well. In June 1906, during his second term, he and several other Democrats publicly broke with minority leader Williams and advocated the Pure Food and Drug Act. Having never before voted against the Democratic leadership, and still being a relative newcomer to the House of Representatives, he believed that he needed to defend his actions. In one of his earliest major speeches, he announced that his "convictions" favored the measure; therefore, he outlined his reasons. First, he disagreed with the Democratic minority's report which said that the federal government did not have the authority to enforce the proposal. He had reviewed over twenty-five court cases, concluding that such power existed in the commerce clause of the Constitution. Then he asserted that the states did not have the legal means to regulate food and drugs involved in interstate commerce, and therefore Congress was forced to take action. In fact, he argued that, when the public was "oppressed, defrauded, deceived, [or] robbed," the government must strive to prevent such abuses. "Why should the doctrine of State rights," he demanded, "be invoked in justification of indifference to the public welfare?" He would "yield to no man" in his regard for local government, but this issue did not concern states' rights. Robinson then charged that, since no state could adequately regulate these goods, the public was "left at the mercy of avaricious manufacturers and dealers, who are constantly poisoning the springs of existence by adulterating the food we eat" by selling unsafe drugs and by bilking the consumer. He branded such producers as "commercial brigands who rob the citizen of both his health and his money." In fact anyone who supported such people "must be cross-eyed in his moral vision to see merit in their claims." The next week, with Robinson's support, the Pure Food and Drug Act passed with bipartisan support.[17]

Guaranteeing the integrity and honesty of the government was an equally prominent cause for Robinson. In 1903 Roosevelt had instructed fourth assistant postmaster general Joseph L. Bristow to investigate charges of impropriety in the postal service. Toward the end of the year Bristow submitted his report, including a published summary. Several officials lost their positions, but the administration suppressed most of the evidence, reportedly because over 150 members of Congress, including such well-known Republicans as Senators Albert Beveridge of Indiana and Henry Cabot Lodge of Massachusetts as well as Speaker Cannon, had participated in schemes to charge higher rental rates for post offices throughout the country. On March 9, 1904, during his first major speech on the floor, he attacked the scandalous activities and apparent corruption in the post office department, demanding a complete inquiry by a special House committee. In his speech a righteously indignant Robinson announced that this "greatest scandal known to modern times" was a "stench in the nostrils" of every citizen. If the report was inaccurate, or full of only circumstantial or inconclusive evidence, as seemed to be the case, he could not understand why the impugned members did not push for a thorough examination, as would any "gentleman who regards his honor sacredly." He concluded that Congress, "out of respect for itself," must make a public inquiry into the post office scandal.[18]

Robinson continued his struggle for probity, but this time with mixed results. During 1907 in the Fifty-ninth Congress he introduced a bill limiting the expenses for which representatives could be reimbursed while traveling to and from their districts. According to his proposal, members would receive money each session only for the actual, necessary costs incurred on one trip. Thus he hoped to deter congressmen from padding their salaries with extravagant visits to their home districts. Yet his bill never left the Appropriations Committee. In 1907, however, he supported an eventually successful measure which prohibited certain corporations from financing campaigns. Of these businesses, the insurance companies irritated Robinson the most. They robbed "widows and orphans" by contributing money entrusted to them by men who had been "paralyzed by the power of death." Not only should a law be passed, but it should also be made retroactive, forcing the companies to reimburse policyholders and beneficiaries for the political gifts. But that would be unnecessary if only the president would tell the Republican national chairman, George B. Cortelyou, to refund the money. According to Robinson, Roosevelt had not berated the man responsible for such tactics, but instead had "promoted" him, thereby proving that the Republicans were not serious about addressing the problem.[19]

Other progressive issues further attracted Robinson's interest. For instance, he continually supported the concept of a graduated income tax as a means to lower the tariff, a traditional Democratic platform plank. When Republicans pushed to have the Sixteenth Amendment submitted to the states in July 1909, he initially fought it, arguing for a more rapid method, such as simple congressional action authorizing such a tax. He declared that if such a proposal were passed, no court would strike it down as it had in 1895. Congress should then "express itself fairly and fully" on the issue, by voting the tax without wasting the time necessary to send it to the states for approval. Realizing, however, that only the amendment could pass the Republican-controlled House, he urged that the submission be to state conventions and not to legislatures in order to quicken adoption. Unsuccessful in his attempts to speed up the process, Robinson finally voted for the amendment.[20]

While still in Washington, Robinson redoubled his efforts for a graduated income tax because of a confusing situation in Arkansas. In 1911 both branches of the state general assembly passed the Sixteenth Amendment. But then Gov. George Donaghey vetoed it, saying that Arkansas needed the revenue from a state income tax and that he feared the voters would not approve one if this federal imposition became law. In a Capitol Hill speech Robinson attacked the governor for exercising a power that did not exist, since state executives have no voice in the amendment process. Only the legislature could approve or reject a national amendment. Once a state body approved it, no option, such as a state legislature reversing its decision or an executive vetoing it, existed, because approval was the sole action which the U.S. Constitution acknowledged. To allow a veto would set an undesirable precedent. Even more importantly, he assured his colleagues that "90 per cent" of Arkansans favored a national income tax and had for many years. He believed it unfair for one man—no matter how powerful or important—to thwart an entire state. To an applauding, sympathetic House, he then announced that, at his prompting, the Arkansas secretary of state was sending an official copy of the resolution ratifying the

Sixteenth Amendment to Washington. That ended the controversy, since Congress ignored Governor Donaghey's unauthorized and meaningless veto.[21]

Robinson supported still other progressive legislation. Claiming that "the day of 'government by superior people' has passed," he urged Congress to send to the states for approval the proposed Seventeenth Amendment for the direct election of senators. He suggested that the public could select their surrogates "much more skillfully" than through state legislatures. At times he assailed the trusts, urging measures either to regulate or dismember them. Those great combinations of wealth often "robbed" citizens, who had no recourse to protect themselves. And he advocated postal savings banks and an inexpensive parcel-post system in order to improve life in rural areas where banks were often small, unsound, or nonexistent, and where merchandise was overpriced.[22]

Regarding unions and labor, Robinson was a strong and outspoken supporter of both. In 1907 he expressed this by voting to abolish child labor in the District of Columbia. That same year he also endorsed employer liability laws to protect workers injured on the job. But most importantly he committed himself to proposals for the common laborer, which in many cases would not be enacted for twenty years. Perhaps his best statement was a 1911 speech at the small town of Corning in northeast Arkansas. Besides acknowledging the "necessity" of unions in preventing "tyranny and oppression of the weak," he endorsed many programs, even though several Arkansans considered them "tainted with socialism." He asserted that each toiler was entitled to "the highest reasonable wage" that "each industry could afford," not just a minimum or starvation rate. In addition, workers had the "right"—not the privilege—to "enlightenment and recreation," which, according to Robinson, included the "boon" of an eight-hour day. While conceding that some in the audience might condemn this suggestion, he insisted that "in your souls you know that the man who yields eight hours every day to honest toil is entitled to pay for a day's labor." He then urged not only the abolition of the "intolerable" sweatshops, but the protection of women in all businesses, trades, and occupations. In closing he went even further, predicting protection for workers in future "'industrial crises' which they [could] neither bring about nor . . . prevent." He foresaw a "pension system for old and disabled workers," which would be "equally consistent" and perhaps "more justified" than annuities for servicemen. And although the time was not "yet ripe" for such proposals he assured his audience that the "pension roll of the . . . laborer [would] exceed that of the soldier." He even advocated a "tribunal" to arbitrate disputes between unions and businesses, similar to the National Labor Relations Board. While many of these measures never came before the House of Representatives during his ten-year tenure, Robinson had outlined a position which he followed throughout the rest of his career.[23]

Although having a consistent policy toward laborers, Robinson dealt differently with various minorities. Toward blacks, in 1909 he stated that they were capable of self-government—a right "inherent in all races." But when pressed by a northern Republican congressman, he angrily acknowledged that he did not "proclaim the doctrine of negroe supremacy in the South." He charged that his colleague did not favor it and would not "stand for it." While perhaps more tolerant than most southerners of the day, he never pushed for equal rights; nor, for that matter, did the Republican Party in Arkansas. Toward other groups, however, Robinson took a more egalitarian stand. For instance, in one speech he attacked the discrimination of Jews both abroad and in the United States. He recounted a list of abuses they had endured throughout their history, saying that perhaps they had become famous for "financial actions" as a means of overcoming persecution. And throughout his career he fought all scurrilous attacks on Roman Catholics and their beliefs.[24]

From 1905 to 1912 Robinson gained respect and prestige by serving on the Public Lands Committee. In 1909 he was the ranking minority member, thus making him the Democratic spokesman on the floor during debate as well as a member of most conference committees with the Senate concerning public land bills. Then in 1911 he became chairman when the Democrats gained control of the House of Representatives. He also introduced or authored many bills and reports covering germane issues.[25]

Throughout this time Robinson supported the Roosevelt and Taft conservation programs, even when many Republicans bolted. An avid, accomplished hunter and fisherman since childhood days, he loved the outdoors. He always voted to protect beautiful, wild areas. In fact, he often castigated Republicans (for example, committee chairman Frank

Mondell of Wyoming), who claimed to be naturalists, yet usually voted for the western mining and cattle interests instead of safeguarding undeveloped lands. Oftentimes such acreage had proven mineral resources; in others, enormous potential.[26]

Of all the sites under committee purview, Alaska fascinated Robinson the most. Undisturbed land spreading for miles in all directions, snowcapped mountain peaks stretching high above the terrain, gold-filled streams cascading toward the sea, massive veins of coal winding under the soil, beautiful inlets hiding hamlets of sea-going people, that vast northern territory seemed a mystery waiting to be unraveled. On one occasion in 1908 he supported a Roosevelt proposal to limit individual or corporate holdings of coal lands to 2,560 acres, thereby preventing monopolies and holding companies from gaining control. He acknowledged that the geological information was inadequate, since Alaska was "a new country." Thus Congress could not expect men who "take their picks on their shoulders, . . . go into that wild country, [and] take the chances that all explorers take" to send research data back to the government. The nation should aid such intrepid searchers, not hinder them, Robinson argued, by demanding time-consuming surveys which the Congress had failed to authorize in its last session. In 1907 Robinson had been one of the chief, yet unsuccessful, proponents for such an expedition. Consequently in 1911, he was honored for his efforts when the Speaker appointed him one of five House members of the Alaskan Commission; and later that year he finally traveled to the place which had enthralled him for so long.[27]

Perhaps unlike some representatives who worried only about domestic legislation and reelection, Robinson took an active interest in foreign policy. In 1906, during his second congressional term, he attacked the tariff placed on Philippine goods coming into the United States. If the United States was going to rule that territory, its exports should be free of any imposition. But, more to the point, he despised the Republican Party's handling of the islands. He vehemently argued that the United States had broken faith by not granting independence. He implied that the administration would never admit that the Filipinos were capable of self-government, thereby subjecting them to American dominance indefinitely. Over the next six years he verbally excoriated his opponents for their calloused and tyrannical rule of the Philippines.[28]

Robinson also championed the cause of international peace through intergovernmental action. In 1904, during his first session in Congress, he and several other representatives formed an "interparliamentary group" to advocate world understanding by meeting with elected officials from other nations. That same year he furthered his knowledge on the subject by attending the Lake Mohonk (New York) Conference on International Arbitration. Then in 1910, and again in 1911, he introduced resolutions calling for a "joint assembly and meeting of the parliaments and national legislative bodies" of the world to improve relations through personal friendships. But both bills died in committee. In 1910 Robinson fought for financial support to settle international disagreements peacefully. The Republicans recommended building several new battleships; to make the proposal more palatable, they authorized one-twentieth of 1 percent of the total for arbitration. Robinson, who normally supported most defense measures, was incensed. The idea that the $60,000 appropriation for peace should be tied to a $120,000,000 military package was ridiculous. Instead he suggested striking out the battleships and substituting money designated strictly for international arbitration, since "every dollar spent that way" would "produce more good . . . than hundreds of dollars spent for . . . armaments." Once again his efforts were fruitless.[29]

The building of the Panama Canal became another major interest for Robinson. At first he appeared concerned with the progress of the construction, since so much money was being spent with little visible improvement. In 1906 he introduced a resolution to investigate its development. At the same time he charged that the government had not purchased necessary supplies from the lower Mississippi River Valley—and especially Arkansas; instead it had bought goods from other regions further from the canal, thus robbing southerners of needed business. Perhaps because of this early involvement, he joined nearly four dozen congressmen, including Speaker Cannon, on an investigative journey to Venezuela and Panama. While en route on board ship, he met George Goethals, who directed the American operations, and they became good friends. During his stay in Panama, he met the Arkansans involved in the venture, promising to relay their greetings when he returned home. At the conclusion of his first trip outside the United States, Robinson wrote several articles about his visit for Arkansas newspapers. He expounded on the actual digging, as well as the great improvements in sanitation, the beauty of the tropical area, and the high caliber of men involved in the project—especially the transplanted Arkansans. Thereafter, Robinson always supported legislation or appropriations for the canal.[30]

During ten years in the House of Representatives, Robinson continually safeguarded the interests of Arkansas and its citizens. Following an earlier precedent, he advocated numerous efforts to limit the power of railroads. At the same time he voted for most progressive proposals, although few of his specific bills became law. He also supported many domestic measures which would not be enacted for over twenty years. And in foreign affairs he advocated the inter parliamentary movement, trying to create worldwide goodwill through friendship and understanding. Robinson had developed his basic philosophy which he would follow throughout his long career—support of progressive and internationalist ideals.

But in 1912 Robinson put all of this aside for the moment; because of important political issues back in Arkansas, he redirected his efforts away from the national scene, concentrating on state problems. That year, 1912, would change the focus of his career.

5 GOVERNOR AND BEYOND

Arkansas has had a tradition of fluid political alliances throughout most of its history. Voters have usually supported candidates for such reasons as the proximity of their counties, the religious background of the aspirants, and the local influence of regional leaders. Rarely, however, has an issue divided the people into two camps for more than one election. And many who opposed each other in one campaign, sided together two years later. Since the Democrats won every statewide contest for over ninety years after Reconstruction, all of the battles were within the same party. Thus in November, or in many cases September, some of the most bitter adversaries reunited to defeat state Republicans.[1]

Yet for over a decade, from 1900 through 1912, Jeff Davis divided the electorate. Known as the "tribune of the haybinders," he campaigned vigorously throughout the rural and backwoods areas, attacking the "high-collared" city crowd. With oftentimes demagogic speeches, he stirred his followers, known as the "wool hat and one-gallus boys," while assailing trusts, Wall Street, and foreign bankers. His vitriolic orations—although usually considered progressive—were more coarse in language and invective than substantive in nature. He built a potent political machine of small farmers and backwoodsmen, called the Old Guard, which normally voted according to his wishes. His greatest support came from the highlands of the northwest, as well as a few sparsely populated southern counties. His adversaries included most Arkansas newspapers and many former state officials whom he had vilified in his early campaigns. The cities and larger towns, although few in number, usually went against him, as did many of the "plantation" counties along the Mississippi River. But in nearly every community his faction within the Democratic Party emerged.[2]

In 1902 Robinson supported Davis for reelection as governor, although never specifying the reasons. He may have favored the progressive, antitrust program of the governor. Perhaps he thought that Davis deserved the second term, which most Arkansas chief executives traditionally received. Possibly his friendship and admiration for former governor James P. Clarke, who was running for senator as a "pro-Davis" candidate, brought the endorsement. And Robinson might have believed that such backing would aid his own campaign, although his opponent, Sam Taylor, carried those counties with the greatest Davis majorities.[3]

Political circumstances, however, soon shattered any possible alliance or good feelings between the two men. Shortly after the election Davis demanded that ex-governor James Eagle, Robinson's cousin, resign his membership on the state capitol commission; Eagle refused. In the ensuing, vicious fight Davis resigned as vice-president of the Arkansas Baptist Association after the Second Baptist Church removed him from its membership—for public drunkenness and gambling. Since Eagle was president of the Arkansas Baptist Association, as well as a deacon in the Second Baptist Church, Davis accused him of political persecution.[4]

Consequently, during the next ten years Robinson opposed Davis at every opportunity. In 1904 he backed his old friend state supreme court justice Carroll Wood in an unsuccessful effort to prevent Davis from winning a third term. In 1906 he supported aged United States senator James H. Berry, whom Davis decisively defeated. Then in 1908 he supported progressive contractor and political neophyte George Donaghey for governor, instead of Atty. Gen. William F. Kirby, a member of the Old Guard. When his candidate won, Robinson and his friends helped organize the 1908 state Democratic convention. After some secret negotiations he became permanent chairman of the meeting. He then helped strip the "pro-Davis" forces of all their positions. To humiliate Davis further, the convention voted against making him one of the four "at-large" delegates to the national convention, an honor usually bestowed on both senators, the governor, and a leading party worker. In 1910, Donaghey was reelected with Robinson's support; Jeff Davis's strength seemed to be waning.[5]

In 1910 Robinson further distanced himself from Davis during a hearing before the House Public Lands Committee. Controversy surrounded the ownership of a six-hundred-square-mile area in northeast Arkansas known as the "sunk lands." During the violent New Madrid earthquakes of 1811–12, the St. Francis River Valley had fallen as much as thirty feet, making the area swampy and undesirable for farming. In 1850 Congress had granted the land to Arkansas, but because of "legal technicalities" the state had never officially possessed it. Although two separate secretaries of the interior had agreed that Arkansas had the lawful title, the Roosevelt administration announced in 1908 that the disputed lands were federal property. Many poor citizens had then hurriedly established homesteads. Davis, however, supported the St. Francis Levee Board, which wanted to remove the settlers and disavow their rival claim.[6]

In the House Public Lands Committee hearings on the "sunk lands" Robinson attacked Davis's reputation as the "tribune of the haybinders" and spokesman for the common man. He pointed out that, surprisingly, the senator, as a legal representative for the St. Francis Levee Board, was opposing the poor farmer on behalf of some of the richest, most influential citizens of northeast Arkansas. For instance, Judge E. A. Rolfe had speculatively bought more than sixty thousand acres of the disputed land from the levee board for $1.50 an acre. Robinson noted that the courts, including the Arkansas Supreme Court, had sided with the homesteaders and that Davis, therefore, was, trying to circumvent the judicial process by having Congress vote to confirm the land gift to Arkansas. In turn, this decision would give the St. Francis Levee Board the land, thereby validating its earlier sales. In defending the small farmers, Robinson forced Davis to admit that the proposal would "work some hardship on the little fellow."[7]

With his animosity toward Davis undiminished, Robinson weighed his political prospects as the 1912 election approached. He surely desired advancement, which meant one of two races—governor or senator. At first he decided to oppose Davis in his reelection bid. To G. W. Hendricks he wrote: "I will have to beat him for either office, and it will be more satisfactory to me and my friends to have the issue with him direct rather than collateral." But after traversing the state to gauge public support, he became disheartened. And then when six-term congressman Stephen S. Brundige of Searcy, a leader of the anti-Davis movement, entered the race, Robinson realized his chances of victory were shrinking. He therefore decided to run for governor. Most political observers believed that

Gov. George Donaghey, whom Robinson had supported in 1908 and 1910, would not run for a third term. Since no other formidable candidate had yet appeared and because of many statewide contacts in the Democratic Party, Robinson felt certain of success.[8]

On July 4, 1911, Robinson formally announced for governor at Osceola in northeast Arkansas, just a few miles from the Mississippi River. Before an estimated crowd of thirty-five hundred people, he outlined his progressive platform. Basing the campaign on a government unencumbered by political pledges and uninfluenced by special interests, he championed a corrupt practices act to curtail sharply the influence of lobbyists at the state legislature. He further espoused a limit on campaign expenditures; the high cost of winning offices prohibited some people from running and indirectly encouraged others to accept income from questionable sources. For greater voter participation Robinson specifically advocated the initiative, referendum, and recall. To lower the indebtedness of the state, he promised to change the budget process by limiting expenditures to income and thereby end the practice of paying for operating deficits with long-term debts. Of equal concern was prison reform; he suggested placing state penitentiaries under an appointed commission rather than a committee of elected officials who had little time to oversee them. And he proposed abolishing the convict-lease system in which many inmates, although guilty of only minor crimes, were in virtual slavery.[9]

Apparently Atty. Gen. Hal Norwood of Mena—who also had an impressive record—would be Robinson's opponent. In 1893 he represented Sevier County (southwest Arkansas) as the youngest member of the general assembly. In 1899 he served as an assistant to Atty. Gen. Jeff Davis, becoming part of his "inner circle." Then from 1901 to 1905 Norwood spent four years in the state senate, followed by the first of two terms as attorney general in 1909. He was well known for his progressive views and appeared to have the backing of the Davis machine. That support, and his popularity in western Arkansas, encouraged him to begin planning a gubernatorial race as early as May 1910.[10]

Governor Donaghey, however, seemed to be considering another bid for reelection; during two terms, he had not yet accomplished all of his goals. Although a successful Conway contractor, he had entered public life in 1899 as a member of the first capitol commission, a body charged with erecting a new building to house the state government. In 1908 Donaghey had promised, if elected, to complete the building as soon as possible. Yet in 1912 the capitol remained unfinished. The governor had also pledged to run the government on a sound financial basis. He had thus championed the Turner-Jacobson bill to equalize tax assessments, which required voter approval. As the party nominee, he could perhaps aid the proposal at the polls. And because of his militant leadership in the prohibition movement, he also hoped to establish a statewide ban on all alcoholic beverages.[11]

Yet in the autumn of 1911 Arkansans wondered if Donaghey would run again, especially since his advisors disagreed over a third term. He was finishing his second stint as governor, which was the traditional limit; only Jeff Davis had served longer—six years. Donaghey had already hinted on several occasions that he would not consider a third race, thus leading many to speculate that either retirement or a run for the U.S. Senate was possible. Politicians, such as state senator Charles Jacobson of Little Rock, urged him to oppose Davis and thus accomplish more for Arkansas as a senator, especially if a Democrat became president; shortly thereafter Jacobson wrote Robinson that he believed Donaghey would challenge Davis, although nothing was certain. Others noted that Donaghey, because his relationship with the legislature had deteriorated, would probably be unsuccessful in passing any new proposals. They also noted that Brundige might perhaps withdraw from the election, if he announced his candidacy. Several of Donaghey's political appointees, however, urged him to seek reelection in order to oversee completion of the capitol.[12]

Finally on October 21, 1911, Donaghey settled all doubts by announcing for a third term; he then issued a vituperative statement which would set the tone of the campaign. Although claiming the contest would be run on a "high plane" of "principles" and based on "issues" and not men, he attacked an unnamed "machine" of state senators which had killed every proposed measure "possessing real merit." He asserted that these men were controlled by the ruinous "whiskey interests" who promoted divisiveness in the legislature in order to deter action on statewide prohibition. By this method, the governor charged, these "machine" lackeys had derailed all his efforts to balance the budget. Since the adjournment of the legislature, they had fought the Turner-Jacobson revenue bill in behalf of "tax dodgers" and "large corporations." Donaghey thus appealed to Arkansans to "stop sending men to . . . the General Assembly who ought to be sent to the penitentiary instead."[13]

But Robinson soon became the leading contender. Early in January 1912, he received a major boost when Norwood withdrew from the race. After explaining that Donaghey was a wealthy man who could easily outspend him, Norwood attacked the governor for making the contest too costly. He also berated him for supporting the Turner-Jacobson bill, which, he claimed, would raise taxes. And he further castigated the governor for breaking tradition and seeking a third term. In closing, he announced his support for Robinson and urged all of his backers to do likewise. In fact, he wrote many of the leading politicians in western and southwestern Arkansas, stating that Robinson would be a better governor.[14]

In the ensuing campaign Robinson and Donaghey disagreed over the major issues. Perhaps the most controversial difference concerned state indebtedness. Arkansas had frequently incurred operating deficits, which the legislature had paid by issuing long-term bonds. To alleviate this yearly problem, Governor Donaghey had thus pushed the Turner-Jacobson proposal (to equalize tax assessments) through the general assembly. While rates would remain steady, collections would rise with higher appraisals. And within a few years Arkansas would eliminate the deficit. Donaghey assured voters that the bill would not affect most farmers and businessmen. Only "tax dodgers"—mainly the large landowners and big companies—needed to fear the law. In fact, Donaghey was willing to let his political future be decided on that proposal. Robinson, however, attacked the proposal as a tax hike in disguise. It would hurt farmers, he asserted, since the evaluation would occur in February instead of June, when many still had unsold agricultural products. Equally distressing was a provision which vested most of the review power in a state commission, not in local officials or boards. Residents would be forced to appeal all decisions to a committee in Little Rock. Robinson thus predicted that the proceedings would be more expensive for a small farmer or businessman than a tax increase. Large landowners and corporations, however, would probably win their cases and pay lower assessments.[15]

The two candidates also differed on prohibition. Donaghey, a Baptist, favored absolute abolition of all alcoholic beverages and supported a referendum for a statewide ban. From his opening announcement until election day, he charged that his greatest opponent during his two terms had been the "whiskey ring." Since the anti-prohibitionists were determined to destroy him, the governor reasoned that anyone who opposed him must be in league with the liquor companies. Robinson fervently fought the slur; he pointed out that John Hinemon, one of his campaign managers, had been one of the earliest and most active leaders in the anti-liquor movement, having run for governor in 1908 on a prohibitionist platform against Donaghey, who, at that time, had cheerfully accepted the support of the "whiskey ring." Following a more traditional approach, Robinson endorsed local option rather than a statewide ban.[16]

Donaghey's work on the state capitol provided yet another important issue. For over a decade he had claimed that he could construct the building more cheaply than the firm of Caldwell and Drake. But as governor from 1909 to 1912 he had spent more money than originally promised. Many people began to speculate that his actions were simply to justify his campaign accusations against the former contractor. For instance, he had ripped out floors, even though they had passed several stress tests far in excess of their specified loads. He had also dismissed the original construction company as well as architect George Mann. Robinson argued that Donaghey had been given four years to finish the capitol and had failed. The voters should now replace him. Many people, especially the Old Guard, must have remembered Jeff Davis's accusation that the project would be the "most infamous steal" in state history. Throughout the campaign Robinson used this issue extensively.[17]

Candidate endorsements affected many voters as much as, if not more than, issues. Many of the leading politicians of the state backed Robinson, thus strengthening his efforts. In addition to Attorney General Norwood, former gubernatorial candidates Carroll Wood (1902) and Hinemon (1908) openly favored Robinson. Sen. James P. Clarke, a powerful political leader in eastern Arkansas, wrote letters to his followers, encouraging them to support Robinson, a friend of longstanding. Many people speculated that if Donaghey won a third term in 1912, he would then run for Senate two years later; however, a defeat would ruin his chances. Finally, after several months of silence, Davis, who was in his toughest election, began attacking Donaghey, urging the Old Guard to join the Robinson forces. Helping each other in their strongholds—Robinson in rural eastern Arkansas and Davis in the mountainous northwest and southwest—they hoped to improve both their chances of winning.[18]

In February and March 1912, the political campaign became more personal. Donaghey advertisements, sometimes filling an entire newspaper page, attacked Robinson as a stooge, a "do nothing," a tool of the "machine." If he did not know of the efforts by the senate gang, whiskey interests, and the railroad lobby, Robinson had to be "uninformed"—oblivious to what was happening across the state. Or perhaps, he suggested, Robinson was obediently following their orders, a willing participant in their chicanery. Donaghey further accused the "ring" of forcing Norwood out of the race to help Robinson. (Norwood vehemently denied this charge, once again citing monetary restraints as the reason for withdrawing.) Toward the end of the race Donaghey claimed that Robinson had misled many of his supporters by secretly allying with the anti-prohibitionists. He even castigated him for his record in the 1895 general assembly and finally charged that during five terms in Congress Robinson had been ineffective, passing no legislation aiding Arkansas.[19]

The attack on his congressional record may have actually helped Robinson. Early in March 1912, Speaker of the House Champ Clark of Missouri, popular in Arkansas as a contender for the Democratic presidential nomination, defended Robinson and praised his contributions in Washington. He could not believe that anyone would "belittle" Robinson's work, calling him one of the "strongest and ablest" as well as "most promising" members of the House. He lauded his good attendance, "intelligent and effective" committee work, and his excellent debating skills. With "no hesitancy" Clark commended his career.[20]

At the same time Robinson supporters heatedly assailed Donaghey. For instance, Judge P. H. Prince of Conway denounced him as a "tax dodger," who had paid no personal taxes in 1911 in Faulkner County, his home; he also accused Donaghey's campaign manager, Joe Frauenthal, one of Conway's richest merchants, of cheating the state by reporting personal property worth only $130. In an advertisement, Rep. C. P. Newton of England (Lonoke County) upbraided the governor for lying to the state legislature and for vetoing necessary appropriation measures strictly to further his political career. Newton then charged the governor with joining the anti-liquor fight to gain votes. Having supported such measures for years, he knew who the "friends of prohibition" were and Donaghey was, he emphatically wrote in an advertisement, "NOT NUMBERED AMONG THEM." Other campaign literature reiterated the "flip-flop" of the governor on alcohol. After each new accusation, Robinson offered to debate Donaghey in a public forum. But since Robinson was the "greatest orator in the state," the governor never accepted, although trying unsuccessfully to show up unannounced on one occasion; a missed train connection prevented the joint appearance.[21]

The two candidates did see each other once during the campaign, although away from any crowds or newspapermen. Surprisingly, their mutual vilification in the press had not embittered the two men. Twenty-six years later Donaghey recounted their chance meeting in a hotel in northern Arkansas. After a "hectic" campaign day they passed in the corridor. Robinson greeted Donaghey, who was about to take a bath, and asked him what he was doing. He then gave a "musical chuckle" and said: "I guess we both need a bath terribly, George. We're pretty dirty, aren't we?" They shook hands warmly, remembering their old friendship, and then departed.[22]

During March 1912, both sides predicted victory. Donaghey campaign workers bought ads throughout the state, announcing that the voters had swung to the governor over the previous three weeks, and thus predicted a triumph over the "sinking" Robinson. They even projected specific margins of victory in most counties. Just before the election Robinson asked for conservative predictions from each of his county leaders. When these were tallied, he forecast a 45,000-vote margin, that campaign workers exaggerated to 60,000 votes.[23]

On March 27, 1912, primary election day, Robinson won by more than 40,000 votes—90,520 to 46,701. The combination of several factors fueled the enormous Robinson landslide. He had judged the mood of the people correctly on the two most important issues of the campaign, the Turner-Jacobson bill and statewide prohibition. In September, voters defeated both measures in a referendum. Robinson had also damaged his opponent by continually asking for a joint debate. Some people questioned whether Donaghey was able to defend his record. Perhaps most detrimental to the governor was the decision to run for a third term. Only Jeff Davis had won three terms, and many citizens feared the domination of Arkansas politics by one person. At least a few voters must have begun to question Donaghey's competence after not completing the capitol in four years. Donaghey had blamed Robinson for the problems in the legislature, but most voters disregarded these charges, since he had been in Washington. The aid of some of the best politicians in the state also undergirded the campaign. And unquestionably the strong endorsement from Champ Clark also helped.[24]

With his nomination assured, Robinson began organizing for the state Democratic convention at Little Rock. Above all else he wanted harmony and unity at the upcoming April meeting. As the gubernatorial candidate, he named all major party positions, most of which went to staunch supporters and allies. Immediately he chose his brother-in-law, Judge A. J. Walls of Lonoke, one of the best political strategists in Arkansas, for the most important post—chairman of the state central committee. To promote goodwill among various factions, he picked Atty. Gen. Hal Norwood to nominate him. One of the most important functions of the gathering was the selection of the "big four" at-large delegates. In a move to include as many people as possible, Robinson suggested eight people be given one-half vote each. As a result, five party workers could be honored in addition to the governor-elect and the two senators. In fact, the convention was surprisingly quiet, especially considering the recent, bitter primary.[25]

Robinson also used the meeting to repay Speaker of the House Champ Clark by securing a delegation to the national convention pledged to him. The main competition for Arkansas delegates came from Gov. Woodrow Wilson of New Jersey. His campaign manager, New York lawyer William McCombs, was an Arkansas native with close ties to the southeastern part of the state. He helped organize Wilson clubs throughout the state and hosted the governor at Little Rock early in 1912. In addition, Wilson received endorsements from Governor Donaghey and popular University of Arkansas professor Charles Hillman Brough, who would later serve two terms as governor from 1917 to 1921. (Brough had been an early graduate student of Wilson's at Johns Hopkins University.)[26]

But Wilson's efforts were inadequate. Clark had organized his neighboring state well. For several months chief clerk of the House of Representatives J. C. South, an Arkansas native who knew the intricacies of state politics, had successfully directed Clark's local campaign. At the same time many congressmen, such as Robinson, strongly endorsed the Speaker. And, as the Wilson supporters complained, many Arkansans joined his campaign out of regional pride. At the county meetings around the state, Clark held a commanding lead in delegates to the state convention.[27]

Robinson then orchestrated a Clark victory. He urged his followers at the Little Rock meeting to vote for Clark. Next he stopped a rumored move by Sen. James Clarke to have the delegates "go" uninstructed or uncommitted. Instead the state convention agreed to support Clark as long as his name was in nomination. And, finally, Robinson headed the entourage to Baltimore, which was bound by the unit rule and pledged to cast all eighteen votes for Clark.[28]

At the same time Robinson busied himself with many political interests until his gubernatorial inauguration in January 1913. At the Democratic National Convention in Baltimore he served as one of Clark's floor leaders in an unsuccessful attempt for the presidential nomination. In addition, he kept the eighteen Arkansas votes firmly in the Clark column until the last ballot. Afterward, he returned home to campaign against the Turner-Jacobson revenue act, a statewide prohibition proposal, and a "grandfather clause" that limited black participation in elections. In September 1912, the voters defeated all three measures. Soon thereafter he launched a speaking tour on behalf of Democratic presidential nominee Woodrow Wilson. Then in December he returned to Washington for the last session of the Sixty-second Congress, resigning in time for his swearing in as governor.[29]

But on January 3, 1913, the Arkansas political atmosphere changed dramatically. Early that morning Sen. Jeff Davis died of a heart attack. For more than a decade every candidate and issue in the state had either been for or against him—but never neutral. His Senate seat would now be open, with the state legislature deciding on an occupant for the next six years. And because of his death the members of the general assembly were not bound to support any particular candidate, as they had been by the state primary law.[30]

Many state politicians hoped to succeed Davis for a variety of public and personal reasons. The next day Brundige announced his candidacy. He believed that his close second-place finish in the primary made him the logical choice as did many former supporters. Attorney General Norwood, a member of the Davis "machine," declared his readiness to carry "Little Jeff's" banner to Washington for the Old Guard. Almost immediately he began soliciting votes from legislators, especially those from southwest Arkansas. He also benefited from having served terms in both branches of the general assembly and four years as attorney general, where he encountered most members daily. Within the week, Supreme Court justice William F. Kirby became another contender. He, too, had been a leader of "Jeff Davisism," before losing in the 1908 governor's race. Meanwhile, many people speculated that Donaghey might enter the contest. And John Hinemon told the press that, while many people had urged him to run, he would not oppose his good friend Robinson, who was also considering the position. Instead he would seek the governor's seat if Robinson were elected senator.[31]

Yet, throughout the first days after Davis's death, Robinson refused to commit himself to the campaign, avoiding the press by bird hunting in southern Lonoke County. Then, upon arriving in Little Rock, he declined to comment until after the senator's funeral. Nothing, however, could keep other people from speculating as to his decision. Each day the newspapers carried articles declaring that the race "hinged" on his decision. In addition many of his personal friends had run for the legislature on a ticket with Robinson, thus strengthening his position in the general assembly. Besides most politicians knew that his ultimate goal was a Senate seat. If he waited, Robinson would be forced either to oppose his friend Senator Clarke in 1914 or not to seek the post until 1918, two years after leaving office. Some authorities, however, predicted that he would serve his term as governor rather than vacate the "trust" the people placed in him. After several days with no declaration, some even suggested that the governor did not have time for the race because inauguration preparations and the approaching legislative session.[32]

Finally on January 8, 1913, Robinson announced his candidacy and explained his reasons. Without question, his "usefulness to the state" would be increased in the new position. While acknowledging the "obligations imposed on [him]" as governor, he contended that, after the end of the legislative session in March, his duties would be largely ceremonial and "administrative." He would have accomplished any "constructive" work before the proposed special session of Congress convened "probably" after April 15. The major topic would be tariff revision, a subject he had mastered during his five terms in the House of Representatives. He was thus prepared for this "broader sphere" of service.[33]

From this point onward, the *Arkansas Gazette* noted, the Senate race was "the field against Robinson." Because of his strength in the state legislature, opponents demanded a primary to select the next senator, Brundige being the first aspirant to espouse this idea. In a letter to Robinson, with a copy sent to Arkansas newspapers, he argued that, without a vote, the people could never express their opinion. He also reminded the readers that the last Democratic National Convention had demanded the direct election of senators. All party members, therefore, should endorse popular selection. Norwood soon joined in asking the general assembly to call a plebiscite. And within a short time several politicians from around the state sent petitions to Little Rock demanding a popular vote.[34]

The first political test for Robinson, that of organizing the legislature, had mixed results. In the House of Representatives several Robinson supporters vied for the Speaker's post. After a fierce fight, all of them withdrew in favor of Judge Joe Hardage of Arkadelphia. While not a member of the Robinson forces, he was acceptable to everyone because of his reputation for impartiality. In the race for president of the Senate, William. K. Oldham of Lonoke County, a distant relative of Robinson by marriage, easily won in caucus over several candidates. One adversary, A. C. Martin of Conway, quickly congratulated Oldham and pledged his support to Robinson in the upcoming senatorial contest. All of the other contenders, however, did not join in this "love feast." On Monday, January 13, 1913, however, the Brundige-Norwood partisans won a skirmish in the Senate; they gained the floor as the session opened and refused to end their filibuster until adjournment. Since the law required that the election for senator be held on the second Tuesday after the legislature was organized, the debate postponed the selection for a week (January 21–28). During all this time they hoped to incite the voters against the rapid promotion of Robinson to the Senate. And in the minds of the undecided legislators, this important delay proved to many that Robinson was not an automatic winner.[35]

Next, several Brundige supporters vainly tried a new approach. In a resolution they asked the state central committee of the Democratic Party to call a special primary, thereby allowing voters to express their will and binding the legislators to the successful candidate. But Robinson supporters, selected at the previous state convention, filled the committee and opposed the proposal. Even more importantly, his brother-in-law, A. J. Walls, chaired the body and refused to call a special meeting of the committee, much less urge a primary. On January 20, 1913, after bitter debate the Robinson forces barely defeated the resolution in the Senate by an eighteen to seventeen vote, presaging a close fight. As the *Arkansas Gazette* observed, since the "lines [were] drawn clearly" over the primary, Robinson's lieutenants declared the continued battle for a popular election "the frantic grasping at straws" by already doomed adversaries.[36]

While all pundits agreed that Robinson would receive the highest number of votes, the complicated constitutional rules made the outcome uncertain. On January 28, 1913, each chamber of the general assembly would vote for United States senator. If, as was expected, no one received a majority in both bodies (fifty-one in the House of Representatives and eighteen in the Senate), the representatives and senators would meet jointly on the next day and would continue to vote until a candidate received a majority of those present. Many predicted that if Robinson did not win on one of the first ballots, a "dark horse" would emerge and capture the seat, especially since the governor would probably have the strength to prohibit any of the other announced candidates from winning. He must be successful early or his chances would diminish considerably.[37]

As the appointed election day approached, each of the candidates predicted victory. Less than a week before the vote, the *Arkansas Gazette* released a Robinson poll of legislators that predicted a close but clear victory on the first ballot, with fifty-eight representatives and eighteen senators pledged. The next day Norwood announced closer results for the combined chambers (Robinson forty-nine, Norwood thirty-six, Brundige thirty-four, and Kirby seven). When second choices were counted, however, Norwood had a clear majority of ninety-eight. Since the campaign would be deadlocked at first, he was certain to win in later votes. Brundige "scoffed" at the polls, insisting that he would be the eventual winner because the "people" backed him. Kirby lobbied the legislators and avoided the papers, but his supporters predicted a victory after a protracted battle.[38]

At this same time a family emergency interrupted Robinson's personal campaigning. One of his brother Edward's sons, five-year-old Alvin, accidentally shot and killed his sixteen-year-old sister Mae with a shotgun. Shaken by the loss of one of his favorite nieces, Robinson returned to Lonoke immediately to comfort his brother and nephews and to help with funeral arrangements. He did not return to Little Rock until late Sunday night, January 26, less than forty hours before the balloting would begin.[39]

On January 28, 1913, the closely contested battle began in both houses of the general assembly. In the jam-packed Senate chamber, President Oldham walked to the dais and asked for nominations. At first no one interrupted the tense silence. After several moments Oldham broke the eerie calm by sarcastically stating: "No nominations . . . I'll take it." The spectators laughed and the process began. Following several long speeches the lawmakers cast their ballots—sixteen for Robinson, nine for Brundige, six for Kirby, two for Norwood, one for "Bull Moose" candidate James A. Comer, and one "complimentary vote" for Judge E. A. McCulloch—no majority. At the other end of the capital the tension was even greater and the race just as close. Speaker Hardage cleared the floor of everyone except members, clerks, and reporters, sending the rest to the already overflowing gallery. A hush filled the room as representatives cast their votes. Robinson again nearly won with forty-seven votes, but four short of the necessary number. Interestingly, the four Republican members pledged their support to Republican Andrew Russell and could, therefore, hold the balance, if the Democrats remained unchanged.[40]

By the next day, when the two groups met in joint session with sixty-seven votes necessary to elect a senator, the level of interest and excitement reached a new high. The gallery was packed with visitors—mostly supporters of Robinson; one reporter mused that the entire town of Lonoke had descended on Little Rock for the proceedings. First the Senate voted: Brundige . . . Robinson . . . Robinson . . . Norwood. At the end Robinson had only sixteen votes. Then came the House. The stillness was so great that most members spoke in soft tones, barely above a whisper, which, even so, resounded to the top of the domed chamber as if shouted. After everyone had voted, Robinson still had only sixty-two votes, five short. As the *Arkansas Gazette* reported, "[T]he silence of death prevailed for a minute and the hundreds of people in the gallery sat breathless." Suddenly, one by one, the four Republican representatives came forward and changed their ballot to Robinson, leaving him just one vote shy. Noise and confusion increased as campaign managers tried to stop this momentum for the governor. "A mighty shout went up" as M. T. Shackleford rose to change his vote. Supporters of Brundige and Norwood mobbed him, pushing him back into his seat. Across the room, however, Louis Josephs jumped up and was recognized by Oldham. Before being quieted, he voted for Robinson—and victory. The onlookers began cheering, shouting for the new senator-elect, and disrupting the proceedings. In the pandemonium many representatives tried to join the Robinson "bandwagon," but after a few additional changes, Oldham declared Robinson the next senator from Arkansas. The battle was over.[41]

In the meantime—on January 16, 1913—Robinson had taken the gubernatorial oath of office. Soon thereafter he had set the tone for his two months in office when he delivered a brief message, concisely outlining his various proposals to the general assembly. To place Arkansas on a sound financial basis, he had suggested borrowing $750,000 to liquidate the short-term debt. The state would then issue bonds for that amount and pledge a portion of its yearly income to retiring the notes. Furthermore, he had argued, the legislature had to stop spending more money than it collected. The old method of annually anticipating future revenues he had labeled as "amateur politics, not wise statesmanship." Just as important to the process was the establishment of a budget commission, consisting of the governor, the secretary of state, the attorney general, the president of the Senate, and the Speaker of the House, that would submit a balanced, compromise budget. He also proposed taking higher education out of politics by giving the University of Arkansas, the four state agricultural schools, and the normal school a set percentage of all taxes collected, rather than making two-year appropriations each session.[42]

At the same time Robinson had suggested a number of progressive reforms. He had proposed a tough corrupt practices act which would severely limit campaign contributions and expenditures. He had also advocated a reorganization of the penitentiary board, removing the elected officials and appointing commissioners to oversee the prisons on a daily basis. As a further help he had called for an investigation into past abuses of prisoners and for an end to leased convict labor. For the worker he espoused a Workmen's Compensation Act, placing the responsibility for injuries on employers for the first time. And he had endorsed the Seventeenth Amendment for the direct election of senators, although not urging its application until ratification. Equally important he had supported a revision of banking laws, the paving of state roads, and the creation of a highway commission to oversee expanded construction.[43]

His organizational ability and pragmatic approach to government were even more important to his success. With each proposed bill he sent a short message delineating his reasons for support. As soon as the clerk finished reading his letter, a representative or senator introduced the measure, which was read twice before being sent to committee. Shortly thereafter it returned to the floor for a vote. After approval by both chambers, Robinson signed the bill into law and then moved to the next one.[44]

By such methods Robinson soon succeeded in passing his progressive programs. At his insistence the legislators established several regulatory boards. They created the state banking board to govern and investigate financial practices in Arkansas. Because of a smallpox outbreak in Oklahoma, they enacted a bill organizing the state health board, which oversaw all matters of public health—from quarantining areas of epidemics to inspecting possible causes of disease. Bowing to his pressure, they also formed the Arkansas Highway Commission to plan a system of state roads. But perhaps his most important achievement dealt with reforming the prison system. In conformance with his wishes the legislators established a paid penitentiary board, appointed by the governor, to design and administer the Arkansas correction facilities. They also outlawed the convict-lease system and appropriated money for a new prison farm.[45]

Robinson also successfully lobbied for other progressive measures. Besides securing the ratification of the Seventeenth Amendment, he signed acts establishing workmen's compensation, a state department of labor and a corrupt practices act. Rather than increase the state property tax, he suggested a levy on insurance companies to lower the deficit; the legislature therefore passed a surcharge of 1.5 percent on their gross receipts.[46]

Despite such accomplishments, Robinson soon damaged his reputation and angered many Arkansans. On Saturday, March 8, 1913, he resigned as governor, less than a week before the legislature adjourned. Many people harshly denounced this move, since he had promised not to leave his post until after the end of the session. To them, his actions proved that he was just another politician looking for a higher office. While most of his proposals had already passed, he could have personally lobbied for a better budget system, they argued. He also failed to make appointments to many state boards, thereby frustrating some loyal supporters who desired state positions.[47]

His resignation caused a constitutional crisis. Since the position of lieutenant governor did not exist, the president of the Senate was next in line. But the language of the state constitution was confusing and ambiguous. Senator Oldham would be chief executive only until the legislature adjourned, many argued. Whoever succeeded him as president of the Senate would then become governor. In less than a week Arkansas would have two gubernatorial claimants. By waiting just one week, Robinson could have averted this problem.[48]

Robinson left for Washington with many people bitter over his rapid advancement. Within a two-week span he had left the House of Representatives, had taken the oath of office as governor, and had been elected senator. And little more than a month later he resigned as governor—before the legislature adjourned.[49]

But Robinson was determined to stay in the U.S. Senate. Shortly after arriving in Washington, he rejected an offer to become the American ambassador to Brazil. He declared that he planned to stay in the Senate for a full six years. After the previous hectic three months, few observers could have foreseen his long tenure and great leadership in Washington as those six years eventually became twenty-four, and he went from freshman member to majority leader.[50]

6 SENATOR

In March 1913, when Robinson returned to Washington, the political climate on "the hill" had undergone a metamorphosis; the Democrats were in control. For the first time in a generation they had captured the White House from a split Republican Party. As a result, hordes of jubilant office seekers had arrived, hoping to fill numerous posts in government, jobs which had been out of their grasp since the end of Grover Cleveland's administration in 1897. Making the victory even more pronounced was the fact that the Democrats had also swept both the House of Representatives and the Senate. Now they would chair the major committees and enlarge their staffs with deserving campaigners from home, since all of the patronage prizes were theirs to award.[1]

For his small office staff, Robinson turned first to his family—as he would continue to do throughout his career. Although having no children, he and Billie doted on their many nephews and nieces; but above all others they loved her younger brother Grady Miller. Before entering Congress, and even afterward during recesses, they had lived in Lonoke with the Millers and became increasingly attached to them. When they moved back to Washington, young Grady went with them to work as a legislative office aide. For the next quarter-century he would be Robinson's closest and most trusted advisor, spending large amounts of time setting up an Arkansas network which would be responsible for four reelection victories. But more importantly, he became a surrogate son for the childless couple, intimately involved in every family matter. Whenever Grady was absent, both Robinson and Billie wrote long, rambling letters to him, covering everything from political events to agricultural crises and from romantic encounters to family problems.[2]

During his first term as a senator many of his personal characteristics and traits, already known in Arkansas, became apparent and notable even in Washington. One of the most acclaimed was his temper. Robinson usually appeared calm and jovial. But when anyone questioned his integrity or actions or when someone challenged him personally, he could become livid. Almost immediately his face would flush a bright crimson; his voice would grow louder and louder, at times reaching an ear-shattering level. In a quick stiletto attack he would try to destroy the opposition with pointed barbs. To the galleries he was most entertaining during his extemporaneous episodes, excoriating his opponents with rapid-fire emotional charges which thrilled the crowds—and often embarrassed Robinson afterward. At times he would strike a pose with raised fists, as if daring someone to oppose him. After a short time, during which most adversaries studiously avoided a confrontation, he would calm down, usually apologizing in a soft, almost bashful voice. On several occasions the victim of his barrage became a good friend, defending him despite such outbursts.

Robinson also earned a reputation for thoughtful preparation and careful argumentation. Before introducing a measure he would study it at length. He usually submitted written statements to a committee considering one of his proposals. If sponsoring the legislation, he would become conversant in all aspects of a bill, as well as its history, usually disseminating such information to the full Senate in a formal report. When the measure finally came to the floor, Robinson often would make the opening speech, inundating his colleagues with data. He tried to anticipate any questions, then meticulously answered them in the first round of the discussion by citing numerous legal scholars and judicial opinions. But in closing he would digress from his scholarly approach with a rousing emotional appeal directed as much toward the crowds in the galleries and the reporters in the press box as toward his associates.

At other times, when viewing the ills of society, Robinson became a paladin, in most cases championing the underprivileged. When a group or individuals were oppressed, he defended them. He fought for the Yakima Indians in Washington, even though they were not constituents. He opposed bigotry based on religion, often speaking in favor of religious tolerance, freedom, and equality. He defended both Catholics and Jews in predominately Protestant Arkansas. And in Washington, D.C., few things could bring his temper to the boiling point faster than an assault based on religion. He even attacked the Ku

Klux Klan in the 1920s when few southerners dared defy the organization and its anti-Semitic, anti-Catholic rhetoric. Yet he never supported increased participation of black Americans in the electoral process. Nor did he try to dismantle the discriminatory system which existed throughout the country. On the issue of civil rights he, like most of his colleagues, was always quiet.

During his first term Robinson also mastered the rules and procedures of the Senate—a talent which would be extremely beneficial for more than two decades. An outstanding parliamentarian, he often derailed legislation, delaying or defeating it without having to mount a frontal attack. If, however, someone tried to filibuster a favored measure, Robinson would locate unused, forgotten, even antiquated rules in order to force a vote. By 1918 he had become one of the premier strategists of the Senate, guiding a number of President Wilson's legislative measures through to completion. He developed the parliamentary skill of "counting noses"; yet when necessary he used strong-armed tactics to acquire the necessary votes. And he learned how to force the Senate to act without jeopardizing the many friendships he so assiduously cultivated.[3]

With aid from his wife and Grady Miller, Robinson immediately began formulating a first term of accomplishments which would ensure his reelection, especially since several disgruntled state Democrats had already announced their candidacies for 1918. He thus intended to continue his progressive stands, supporting many necessary reform measures which had won him five terms in Congress and one as governor. Next, he wanted to serve President Wilson unswervingly. Not only would this aid Democratic policies, but it would also help him with government patronage for his supporters. If a dispute arose in Arkansas, he wanted his lieutenants in federal positions, not his enemies. (Perhaps more significantly Robinson always considered loyalty—especially to the Democratic Party—of paramount importance.) And, finally, he would continue his internationalist outlook, by advocating a lower tariff as well as a worldwide arbitration panel.[4]

One of the first battles of the Wilson administration concerned the tariff, an issue which had challenged Congress for years. Since the Civil War the Democratic Party had, in the main, supported low import duties, while the Republican Party had favored higher ones. In Congress, however, this fight had become complicated. Representatives and senators who usually supported low tariffs would make exceptions when considering goods manufactured or grown in their districts. Because of this attitude, fluid coalitions, such as supporters of wool and sugar imposts sided with advocates of steel and iron, to defeat each attempt to lessen import duties.[5]

During the summer of 1913 Robinson voted with the president consistently for the Underwood Tariff despite regional sentiments. At each juncture, whether in Democratic caucus, in legislative committee, or on the Senate floor, he fought to lower the fees on imports as promised in the 1912 Democratic Party platform. He even opposed a protective impost on rice—one of the major products of Arkansas and his former congressional district. He also struggled against favorable treatment for cotton, another cash crop in the South. The importance of party regularity outweighed the temporary, bad publicity he received in Arkansas for "opposing" cotton and rice farmers. For these efforts Wilson commended Robinson for supporting the "interests of the nation and the party" over sectional desires.[6]

Perhaps the most important legislation passed during Wilson's first term was the Federal Reserve (Owens-Glass) Act. Approved in December 1913, this bill reorganized the national banking system. Robinson had only a minor role in this legislative fracas. He favored the proposal, as did many other progressives, but, as a new senator, he only spoke briefly for the bill, avoiding the sparring of debate. First in the caucus and then later on the Senate floor, he voted to create the Federal Reserve system.[7]

Concerning the regulation of business, another important issue for Wilson, the Senate specifically addressed two separate, but related proposals in 1914. Although considered a strong supporter of the administration's Clayton Anti-trust Act, Robinson was absent from the Senate on the day of the vote because of illness. But regarding the Federal Trade Commission (FTC) act, he took a leading role in passing the measure. (By this proposal, the new commission would replace the Bureau of Corporations as the body regulating large businesses and monopolies.) As a member of the Senate Interstate Commerce Committee, he served as chairman of a subcommittee to draft the "trust legislative program" of the FTC in the spring of 1914. From that position Robinson argued that the new body could investigate "interlocking directorates, holding companies, stock watering, and . . . price discrimination." He foresaw a "an independent body with liberal powers" for controlling monopolistic businesses.[8]

Robinson encountered some problems with Republican senator Albert Cummins of Iowa over the wording of an initial draft of the subcommittee report. In exasperation, he told Cummins to "dictate exactly" the wording he would like. If possible Robinson would include it. The next day when he delivered the report to the entire Interstate Commerce Committee, Cummins announced that he could not agree to the language of the report. Growing angrier by the minute, Robinson fumed: "Well, Senator, you dictated it and if you can't be satisfied with your own language I presume our task is hopeless." Now somewhat embarrassed, Cummins reread the report and accepted it.[9]

When the Senate considered the Federal Trade Commission report, Robinson contributed to an often heated debate. His primary task was the defense of the "vague" phrase "unfair competition." In a well-researched speech, citing both federal and state cases, he convincingly argued that the courts had, since the passage of the Interstate Commerce Act, defined "unfair competition" on numerous occasions. At one point an opponent of the measure then questioned the need for the clause at all, if the courts knew what the phrase meant and had declared it illegal. Robinson asserted that, while many jurists acknowledged "unfair competition," only a few ruled it against the law; this clause would now make such endeavors illegal. He thus concluded by arguing that to be successful, the Federal Trade Commission must have powers "broad enough to prevent . . . again having to consider the same subject within a short time." In the end, this proposal and the entire measure became law in 1914.[10]

At this same time Robinson became known for a zealous probity which, at times, bordered on the humorous, but sometimes irritated his colleagues. For instance, when the *Washington Post* reported in December 1914 that financial records of the Mexican government listed "seventy-five thousand dollars in gold" paid to "two United States Senators for their influence in bringing about the evacuation of Vera Cruz by American forces," Robinson demanded that the Senate Foreign Relations Committee investigate the incident. Other senators were "plainly amused" by the report. When Foreign Relations Committee chairman Democrat William J. Stone of Missouri begged to have his committee relieved of this inquiry because of their overcrowded calendar, Republican Boise Penrose of Pennsylvania comically asked that it be sent to his unused Committee on Additional Accommodations for the Library of Congress, since it had not yet had a reason to meet. At such derision Robinson became incensed; he therefore unleashed a diatribe against those who did not desire to defend the honor of the Senate. But even as he quixotically argued for the investigation, others moved to end the discussion, thereby preventing any inquest.[11]

On another occasion he seasoned his forthrightness with humor. As a means to save money, he suggested placing a limit of $600 per year on the franking privileges of congressional members. He claimed that many senators abused the free-mail-and-telegram provisions. Consequently he urged that only material "of great interest to the public" be mailed. When Republican senator Albert B. Fall of New Mexico questioned who would decide what material met this criteria, Robinson admitted that he did not know and had in the past not always followed such practices. But, if a limitation were placed on material sent through the mails, he replied with a big grin: "I shall send only my speeches and remarks, which are always of great interest to the public." People in the chamber laughed loudly, but the measure never passed.[12]

Robinson was usually quite serious when attending to official business. For instance, as a member of the committee on Indian Affairs, he became a champion for Native Americans, a position he would continue for the rest of his life. One of his earliest crusades occurred in 1913 when, as chairman of a Joint Commission on Indian Affairs, he investigated problems at several reservations. At the Yakima Indian Reservation in Washington Robinson found that the Interior Department had deprived Native Americans of irrigation water, diverting it instead to nearby white settlers. Robinson forcefully argued that by an 1855 treaty the Indians were entitled to everything necessary to make that land productive—including water rights. He therefore appealed for an impartial and equitable settlement for the Yakimas. Since federal officials had urged Indians to become farmers, surely the government could provide the necessary resources. On the Senate floor he movingly remarked: "There is a stain of shame upon our flag. We have not kept faith with the Indians." He lamented the many "unfulfilled promises, [the] violated treaties." He thus demanded a new Indian policy based on "simple justice, common honesty, honest restitution."[13]

In the course of these investigations, Robinson and his committee also uncovered poor medical conditions on many reservations and therefore advocated improved public health provisions. An outrageous number of cases of tuberculosis (three times higher than the surrounding white population) accounted for a high mortality rate among Indians. An unusually high incidence of trachoma, a highly contagious, incurable, yet easily preventable, eye disease which eventually leads to blindness permeated as much as one-half of the Indian population. Because of these statistics Robinson proposed the immediate erection of temporary tuberculosis hospitals on all reservations where the disease was common in order to bring needed treatment to all Indians within five to ten years. He also recommended that the Bureau of Indian Affairs hire public sanitation and health professionals to help abolish the causes of tuberculosis and trachoma as well as other infectious diseases within a decade. After a six-month battle his proposals were passed in June 1914.[14]

In perhaps his most important battle during the Sixty-fourth Congress, Robinson led the Senate fight for child-labor legislation. In fact, his ardent support of this bill demonstrated his deeply held progressive beliefs and his earnest desire to improve the everyday life of fellow Americans. At first this measure appeared doomed. Originally introduced early in 1914 by Democratic representative A. Mitchell Palmer of Pennsylvania, it languished in the Senate without any prospect of passage. Many congressmen agreed with the president that the bill was a usurpation of states' rights and therefore unconstitutional. With an election approaching, Wilson finally announced his support for the measure on July 18, 1916, and began pressuring the Senate to pass the measure.[15]

At this point Robinson became floor leader for the measure. As early as April he had introduced a twenty-three-page report from the Interstate Commerce Committee supporting child-labor legislation. On August 4, 1916, he opened debate on the bill before a packed Senate. Nearly every Democratic senator attended, as did many Republicans, all listening with "great interest" to his defense of the bill; the many advocates of the proposal who filled the galleries loudly applauded his efforts.[16]

As had become his usual manner in debating a bill, Robinson delivered a well-crafted speech. First he pointed out that the Senate measure was, in actuality, a tougher bill than the House proposal; it outlawed the interstate commerce of all goods mined, quarried, or manufactured by a company employing youth under either age fourteen or sixteen (depending on the item) rather than simply prohibiting the transportation of specific items produced by children. Government prosecutors would only have to prove that children had been employed while the goods were manufactured. Robinson next delineated the opposition's arguments, answering each one—especially the question of constitutionality. He cited numerous court cases supporting his view that the Supreme Court would not invalidate the proposal. And he argued the case philosophically. He admonished that "government . . . is a progressive science else revolutions would be continual."[17]

Over the next four days Robinson successfully steered this bill past the opposition. He opposed amendments to slow down implementation or to emasculate the proposal. Consequently on August 8, 1916, the Senate overwhelmingly passed the bill, fifty-two to twelve. Then in the House-Senate conference committee Robinson helped effect a compromise, which was passed in August.[18]

Throughout the Wilson administration (1913–21) foreign affairs and national defense were troublesome topics. But no matter what the issue Robinson was an ardent, loyal Democrat. In 1914 at Vera Cruz, Mexico, when troops landed to protect American citizens and property, he defended the president's actions. In 1916 he approved of the Jones Act by which the Wilson administration laid out independence for the Philippines. And after Pancho Villa attacked Columbus, New Mexico, in 1916, he praised the president for sending the army after the bandito.[19]

All of these events paled in importance, however, when compared to the conflict in Europe and its effects on the United States. Robinson at first opposed becoming entangled in the European conflict through the expansion of the United States military. In April 1916, he assailed efforts to enlarge the standing army to 250,000 men, at first favoring an amendment to limit the size to 150,000. After the original bill passed, he supported an unsuccessful measure to shrink the size to 100,000. On yet another occasion in July 1916, Robinson voted for four amendments to reduce the number of naval ships scheduled for construction. He also advocated lengthening the time over which the ships would be built, stretching the completion dates from 1919 until 1921. After all of these efforts failed, however, he voted for the final naval appropriations bill.[20]

But Robinson soon became more receptive to war preparations. On February 2, 1917, as he was leaving the capitol for home, a presidential aide summoned him to a White House conference where Wilson read aloud a German declaration for unrestricted submarine warfare against all shipping; he then asked the assembled leaders for advice. While some urged a note of protest to the German ambassador, Robinson became convinced that war was inevitable and urged the president to break diplomatic relations. After several minutes, Wilson announced that "the hour to act has come." Robinson was pleased with the apparent impact of his argument; in actuality, Wilson had already decided to break diplomatic relations and was testing the views of several congressional leaders.[21]

From that point onward Robinson became an outspoken proponent of war preparedness. In February 1917, a fierce debate erupted in Congress and across the nation over the presidential proposal to arm American merchant ships. Shortly thereafter the State Department released the infamous Zimmermann note, by which Germany offered aid to Mexico in return for war against the United States; this plot infuriated Americans, thus solidifying public opinion in favor of armed neutrality. A substantial and vocal minority, however, vehemently denounced this plan as militaristic. On March 1, 1917, the House of Representatives overwhelmingly passed the Armed Ship Bill, 403 to 13. But in the Senate, with its tradition of unlimited debate, the measure became bogged down in a filibuster. Since the Sixty-fourth Congress would end at noon on March 4, such a delay would defeat the bill.[22]

At the climax of this imbroglio Robinson aggressively assumed a leadership role. Early in the morning of March 4 he introduced a "round robin" in the Senate signed by seventy-four senators who supported the Armed Ship Bill and wanted a chance to vote for it before the session ended. If the isolationists, led by Republican Robert La Follette of Wisconsin, would not let senators go on record by voting, at least they could "say how they stand" in this manner.[23]

Immediately turmoil erupted. One of the signers, Republican W. L. Jones of Washington, complained that he did not sign the "round-robin" for publication, intimating that a confidence or trust had been breached.

Robinson, according to the *New York Times*, became infuriated at "the accusation of bad faith." Then, "raising his voice to a pitch rarely heard in the Senate, . . . he threw his body back and forth" as he thunderously and vehemently rebutted Jones by reading from the resolution, "We desire this statement entered in the *Record*." Then amidst interjections by Jones, who continually tried to interrupt him, Robinson continued unabated. With diplomats and their wives peering over the railing of the visitor's gallery in surprise at the heated exchange, he brought his extemporaneous, yet impassioned, plea to its climax. "Let men of courage rise now to speak. The hour has arrived when . . . [senators] ought . . . to say how they stand on this question. It is a fateful hour, an important issue."[24]

After this dramatic interlude the "weary" Senate filibuster settled back into a dull routine. But if the administration forces could not get a vote before adjournment, Robinson was determined at least to frustrate the leader of the opposition, La Follette, who intended to give the last speech opposing the Armed Ship Bill—before a large crowd in the gallery. Robinson and several colleagues, aware of his plans, instructed whoever held the chair not to recognize La Follette. Since the opponents had determined not to allow a vote on the issue, instead planning to talk the issue to death, Robinson decided to keep them from ever gaining the floor. Indeed, the supporters of the bill spoke all morning, only taking time out to ask for the unanimous consent of the Senate to vote on the bill. At each interruption, La Follette would object to a vote and demand the floor.[25]

As the morning progressed La Follette realized what was happening and became livid. Exasperated and indignant, he demanded to be given time to speak. At one point he vowed he would toss a spittoon at the temporary presiding officer, Robinson, if not recognized. As soon as a new senator came to preside, La Follette demanded, under the guise of a parliamentary inquiry, to know when he would be allowed to address the issue. When Robinson pointed out that La Follette was not making an inquiry, he "shrieked" that he would finish his statement "unless somebody carries me off, and I should like to see the man who will do it."[26]

Robinson accepted the challenge. He immediately "leaped to his feet and stamped down the aisle" toward the clerk's desk. Red faced and fuming, he outshouted his adversary. He demanded that his point of order be enforced and that La Follette take his seat—by force if necessary. When the chair sustained Robinson's parliamentary maneuver, La Follette appealed the ruling to the full Senate, demanding a roll-call vote. By a margin of fifty-two to fifteen Robinson won, and the debate proceeded. Although La Follette continued to protest that his senatorial rights were being denied, he had been beaten in his efforts to make the final speech. The bill died when the session ended at noon, March 4, 1917, without a vote—and without an address by La Follette.[27]

Yet this acrimonious Senate debate did bring about three important changes. Shortly before the next special session of Congress, Robinson and several other senators supported a rule allowing the Senate to limit its debate—the first cloture rule in the history of that body. This new procedure allowed senators to stop filibusters from derailing needed war measures. Secondly the battle moved Robinson into the Democratic leadership as his colleagues and the president became aware of his mastery of Senate rules and procedures. And finally Wilson decided to arm merchant ships without any action by Congress.[28]

Soon all this posturing became irrelevant. On April 2, 1917, Wilson asked for a declaration of war against Germany. Two days later the Senate approved his request, as did the House of Representatives on April 6. As Robinson had noted a month earlier, "the fateful hour" for the United States had arrived.[29]

7 WAR AND PEACE

World War I had a profound effect upon the United States. For instance, it signaled the end of the progressive political movement; people were more concerned with battles and bombs than child labor and trust busting. Business boomed. Agriculture reached its most profitable level, as the farmers fed foreign friends and allies. This world conflagration brought the nation into a military alliance with European states. Although the nation might try to disentangle itself from future engagements, never again would the United States be completely isolated. And those soldiers who traveled across the sea would return, some disillusioned, others wounded, still others forever silenced.[1]

World War I had a no less important impact on Robinson. As the conflict drew near, he became an outspoken backer of Wilson and preparedness. Once the United States entered the fighting, he was a leading proponent of all measures necessary to win the crusade, damning all who opposed the war efforts. He soon became a leader in the Senate, receiving an important wartime position on the Foreign Relations Committee. And the 1918 reelection battle with Stephen Brundige, which had promised to be both close and bitter, turned into an easy victory, as many Arkansans equated Robinson with the war effort. Then, after the armistice, he prepared to skirmish, scrap, and struggle for the Paris peace treaties. Throughout each of these instances he continually advanced in the Senate, gaining access to the power centers, although still a relatively new member. By the end of 1920 he was a recognized leader of the Democratic Party.

Another aspect of Robinson's character—loyalty—also came to the fore during the war. He had always emphasized this trait in regard to family and friends. Often he found jobs for unemployed relatives and backers. With some regularity he "loaned" money to nieces and nephews to help them attend college; rarely was any money repaid; never did he ask them for it. And whenever anyone close to him was attacked, he responded swiftly, even when such defense was unpopular. His fidelity went further, including institutions. As an example, his faithfulness to the Democratic Party and its leaders became legendary. He vehemently castigated anyone who, in his opinion, slandered colleagues or the national organization. At times this partisanship clouded his judgment; but if an issue divided along party lines, Robinson's personal belief in, and loyalty to, the Democratic Party usually dictated his actions.[2]

In the spring of 1917 the most important issues concerned the war, and on each occasion Robinson supported Wilson's mobilization efforts. In urging his colleagues to support conscription legislation, he asserted: "Congress . . . [must] provide an aggressive policy which will make victory certain." Thus during the first session of the Sixty-fifth Congress he supported, advocated, indeed championed a diverse number of bills, all aimed at improving America's war efforts. For instance, he spoke for passage of the Lever Food and Fuel Control Act, which gave the administration almost dictatorial powers over the production of certain necessities. Robinson also joined the majority in voting for the Trading with the Enemy Act, which empowered Wilson to establish an embargo against American adversaries and censor materials entering or leaving the United States. He even introduced and passed a bill which authorized the government to condemn and seize lands for military training camps. And since the war effort was expensive, he backed the War Revenue Act, which introduced an income tax, an excess profits impost, and other money-raising measures.[3]

The war also brought about one of the angriest exchanges in the history of the United States Senate. On the closing day of the first session of the Sixty-fifth Congress, Sen. Robert La Follette, the leader of the antiwar faction in Washington, battled a resolution for his own ouster from the government. In an earlier speech at St. Paul, Minnesota, he had declared that the nation had entered the war to protect munitions manufacturers who supplied Great Britain, to save the House of Morgan which had loaned large sums to the allies, and to safeguard "venturesome" citizens who sailed on armed ships in war zones. As a consequence numerous groups petitioned the Senate, asking for his removal from office. By the closing session a committee had already been appointed to investigate the charges and make recommendations to the next session concerning whether La Follette should be seated. In an impassioned plea to his Senate colleagues, he defended his right of free speech. He noted that others before him, including Abraham Lincoln and Daniel Webster, had voiced their disapproval of the United States going to war. Uncharacteristically, he read his speech in almost penitent tones, using none of the boisterous passion for which he was famous. Yet at no time during his two-and-a-half-hour presentation did he apologize for opposing the war effort or, possibly, for undermining morale, as some of his colleagues had accused him. Instead he closed by addressing the galleries, courting their favor and support.[4]

Infuriated by this answer to the charges, Robinson, because of his loyalty not only to Wilson but also to the entire war effort, launched a "caustic" attack on the Wisconsin senator, according to the *New York Times*. In a lengthy, fiery speech on the chamber floor he volatilely denounced La Follette, his temper flaring and unchecked. At first he carefully obeyed the Senate rules which prohibited direct attacks; he heatedly announced that "if I entertained those sentiments . . . I would apply to the Kaiser for a seat in the Bundesrath." Robinson then overstepped the limits of official decorum—some observers believed—by continually linking the German emperor with La Follette. If both had their way, he asserted, "liberty would become a memory, honor a tradition, and tyranny the ruling power throughout the world." Standing directly across the aisle from his adversary, he pointed his finger accusingly as his anger raged forth. He blamed the war on La Follette for orchestrating a successful filibuster against a bill to arm merchants' ships. If it had passed, Germany would have realized that the States were unified and the Central Powers would have backed down, thus keeping America out of the war. He even accused La Follette of running for the presidency by organizing the "disgruntled, semidisloyal elements" into a political coalition. (After the close of the session, and after Robinson calmed down, the petition to have La Follette removed from the Senate was allowed to die.)[5]

During 1917 Robinson also addressed other important issues. He successfully fought for stringent railroad regulation by advocating the enlargement and the reorganization of the Interstate Commerce Commission (ICC). He, along with several other senators, introduced a measure to increase the number of ICC members from seven to nine. The commission could split equally into three divisions, thereby making it more productive. Then after submitting a favorable committee report, Robinson led a floor fight for ratification and defeated two efforts to derail the measure. Thus, with the support of the president, the Senate also approved the bill.[6]

At the beginning of the second session of the Sixty-fifth Congress, Robinson advanced in the Senate hierarchy. In December 1917, perhaps because of his espousal of the war effort or because of his loyalty to the Democratic Party or even because of his defense of President Wilson, he filled a vacancy on the powerful Foreign Relations Committee. Several months later he received an appointment to the Finance Committee, thus having to surrender his seat on the important but less influential Appropriations Committee. At the same time he also achieved a position on the Democratic Senate Steering Committee, which formulated legislative strategies and policies.[7]

Despite such successes, Robinson still had to attend to important business at home—his reelection battle of 1918. Several groups had been planning to oppose him for some time. The most likely adversary was former representative Stephen Brundige, who persistently announced that the people should be given a chance to decide upon their champion. In 1912 Jeff Davis had barely defeated him; therefore, when Davis died prior to taking office, Brundige claimed that he should automatically become the Democratic nominee, since he had finished a close second in the primary. But Robinson won the legislature's vote and went to Washington. Since that setback Brundige had sworn to oppose and defeat Robinson in 1918. Former governor George Donaghey also intimated to several supporters his desire to enter the fray. He, too, seemed most animated by a hope for revenge; he held that Robinson had merely run for governor as a stepping stone to the Senate, making him an unnecessary victim of "unbridled ambition." He pointed to Robinson's two-month tenure in Little Rock as proof of his greed for higher office. Still another group, the former followers of Sen. Jeff Davis (led by his son, national committeeman Wallace Davis, and Frank Pace), appeared equally ready to field a candidate. They hoped to revive the old Davis machine, especially in the rural southern and mountainous northwestern parts of the state. They believed that Robinson had not considered enough of their supporters when suggesting federal appointments to Wilson; the Davis machine was, therefore, rapidly dying from neglect. A few lesser politicians viewed Robinson as a roadblock to advancing their own political careers. If he were defeated, perhaps then they could fill the obvious power vacuum. All such rumors and talk led Robinson to expect at least one, if not many, opponents.[8]

As the filing deadline approached, Robinson used all of his influence, and that of his "friends," to avoid any opposition in the Democratic Primary, which was tantamount to election. He set up an organization headed by "Judge" A. J. Walls, his sister's husband who, besides being a U.S. marshal, was campaign chairman for his 1912 election, and by Grady Miller, his brother-in-law as well as Washington aide. With other leading Arkansas politicoes, such as Charles Jacobson of Little Rock and Earl Hardin of Fort Smith, these men tried to pressure potential candidates. Within a short time Pace and Davis nominally assured their support, while secretly trying to arrange a primary opponent. To lessen the election frenzy and the divisive ballot battles, Robinson urged his allies to support the reelection bid of Gov. C. H. Brough, thus officially binding the "progressive" candidates and close personal friends.[9]

In spite of such preparation Stephen Brundige still announced his candidacy—and all previous strategy changed. Robinson now emphasized his importance to the war effort. Because of important committee assignments and official responsibilities in behalf of the American military, he could not leave Washington. At first some of his supporters urged him to return home and make a strong campaign. But Robinson, reading the electorate correctly, declined. During the first months of 1918 he continually asserted that the public was more concerned with the successful execution of the war than a primary election; therefore, he was staying in Washington and foregoing any personal campaigning. Even the taunts of Brundige could not force him into joint debates. As a consequence, the only state appearances by Robinson were in behalf of a liberty loan drive. And in this patriotic endeavor he even urged Brundige to join him, thereby emphasizing that a nonpartisan war effort was more important than any election. Upon completion of this brief tour he again refused to campaign, instead returning to Washington to "resume my duties in the Senate."[10]

Robinson was right; the public responded well to his reelection strategy. But his most important ploy centered around endorsements. While receiving commendations ranging from labor unions to Treasury secretary William Gibbs McAdoo, he used one from the president to his greatest advantage. In a letter dated February 6, 1918, Wilson wrote that he was "distressed" to hear that Robinson might not seek reelection. "I should deem your retirement . . . a real national loss," he asserted. "My close and confidential association with you has taught me to value your counsel . . . in these trying times in a very unusual degree." Urging that they "should stand together," Wilson "appeal[ed]" to him to stay in the Senate. Robinson waited until the campaign was well under way before releasing the letter to the press. In reality, he won the election as soon as that correspondence was reproduced throughout the state; Arkansans overwhelmingly returned him to office later in the year.[11]

Back in Washington, Robinson again attended to the war effort. Without question he supported administration proposals such as the Sedition Act, the prohibition amendment to food and fuel legislation, the operation of the War Finance Corporation, and alien property laws. At the same time he advanced his standing in the Democratic Party and secured a pro-administration reputation by his deft handling of transportation legislation. A member of the Interstate Commerce Committee and considered by many as an expert on railroads, he became the Senate floor leader for a measure to set compensation for railroads, which had been nationalized for the duration of the war. He advocated giving businesses the same return on their investments which they had earned prior to the war. This moderate approach angered those who wanted strict limitations on profits as well as those who believed that the corporations were entitled to as much money as the system could bear. But Robinson emerged victorious. He avoided crippling amendments, the Senate approving or voting down changes according to his instructions. He then served on the House-Senate conference committee to work out all differences. Because of a parliamentary maneuver, the Senate rejected the first conference report on March 13, 1918. Robinson then submitted a new version with only a slight change, which passed both houses of Congress and was signed by Wilson.[12]

In 1918 Robinson continued his progressive stance of fighting for women's rights—but with no success. The House of Representatives, after a long and bitter fight, finally approved a suffrage amendment; however, several senators were determined to block it, either through dilatory tactics or by parliamentary procedures. Numerous efforts to bring up the measure failed. Late in the spring of 1918, Robinson moved to make the amendment the "special business" of the Senate, thus keeping it on the floor until a decision was made. The motion needed a two-thirds majority to pass. In a close, roll-call vote, his efforts failed by one—forty to twenty-one. When the Senate eventually voted on the proposal, a majority supported it (fifty-three to thirty-one) although it fell short of the two-thirds needed. Robinson then urged his colleagues to reconsider their votes, but to no avail. He was also interested in helping women who were unable to afford maternity and infant medical care. He therefore proposed a joint federal-state project, focusing on rural women who traditionally received the worst care; however, this visionary proposal died in the Committee on Education and Labor.[13]

In November 1918, Robinson suffered significant political reversals. In the general election the Republicans regained control both of the House of Representatives and the Senate, which meant that the Democrats lost seats on committees as well as all chairmanships. Robinson thus forfeited his place on the Foreign Relations and Finance committees, although keeping his place on the Interstate Commerce panel. As a result, he had to cut his staff, since Republicans selected their committee workers. Then on November 11, World War I came to a close in Europe; therefore, Congress focused on the peace treaties and the retooling of the economy, but from his minority position Robinson had difficulty affecting legislation.[14]

Shortly after the armistice, the president traveled to Europe to negotiate for the United States himself and, except for a brief sojourn to Washington, stayed until the summer of 1919. Upon returning home from the Paris Peace Conference, Wilson found many members of Congress already adamantly opposing the treaty for a variety of reasons. Officials at the meeting had agreed not to publish any materials before final approval; because Wilson scrupulously adhered to this plan (while others did not), lawmakers received versions of the proposals from the press instead of the president, thus infuriating them. Nor had senators been asked to lead the American delegation or assume prominent positions in the talks; such slights had upset many solons who jealously guarded their constitutional prerogatives. And even though the Republicans now controlled the upper chamber, Wilson neglected taking any leading party members with him to Paris. In addition, several traditionally isolationist leaders attacked the proposed League of Nations, claiming that it would force the United States into future wars. Then Wilson, upon his return, enraged the senators even further, with speeches favoring the League at Boston and New York City before consulting with them.[15]

Late in May 1919, Robinson moved back to the fore of Senate leadership by vehemently counterattacking for the administration. First he criticized James A. Reed of Missouri, the only Democratic senator who openly opposed the treaty. He suggested that they should both resign their seats and run for reelection as a referendum on the League of Nations. He confidently declared that he would win by a "two-to-one" margin, while Missouri would "favor the league by the same ratio." Rather taken aback by the surprising offer, Reed could only answer that the suggestion was "impractical." Robinson then berated the Republicans. He suggested that their arguments against the League were similar to those "urged by cave men in opposition to any social order." Those senators, by fighting the treaty before discussing it with Wilson, had stabbed the president "from behind," he asserted. In fact their continual charges against him were "unfair, unjust, and unpatriotic." As Democrats would do throughout the League battle, Robinson concluded with an attack on Republican leader Henry Cabot Lodge of Massachusetts, who had endorsed an international union before the United States entered the war. He thus hinted that Lodge had "shifted ground" and was now denigrating such a proposal because of base partisanship.[16]

Three groups quickly emerged during this struggle. On one side a relatively small number of senators, known as the "irreconcilables," opposed the treaty in any form. On the other extreme Democratic loyalists, led by several senators including Robinson, sided with the president, vowing to vote down the agreement if any amendments or any reservations (a country's explanations of how it interprets certain treaty sections) were added. In the middle were a majority of the Republicans, known as "reservationists," who favored some changes in the treaty which would guarantee American rights and traditions, such as the Monroe Doctrine. They also wanted a reservation which guaranteed that American troops would not be sent into battle without the authorization of Congress, even though Wilson had already pointed out that the League could not deploy a nation's troops. Yet overall these men supported joining the League of Nations.[17]

By autumn 1919, Wilson and Lodge, who bitterly despised each other, controlled the fight. On one side Lodge orchestrated the Republicans' dilatory tactics. As chairman of the Senate Foreign Relations Committee, he held extensive hearings which allowed anyone who disliked provisions of the treaty to attack it publicly. He even read the entire treaty aloud, word by word, during the proceedings. He also solidified enough votes against an unamended pact so that the president would be unable to find the two-thirds needed to approve it. On the other side, Wilson countered by holding numerous White House meetings with reluctant Democratic senators. He also began a cross-country trip, taking his message directly to the people. But on September 25, 1919, while speaking at Pueblo, Colorado, he suffered a breakdown; upon his return to Washington, a massive stroke downed him, thus disabling and demoralizing the pro-League forces at a critical time.[18]

Back in the Senate the emphasis shifted to the League amendments with Robinson taking an aggressive position in support of the president. Early in November 1919, the "Lodge Reservations," which had been approved by the Foreign Relations Committee, became the major focus; Robinson opposed each of them, arguing angrily against the actions of the Republican majority. When nominal Senate minority leader Gilbert Hitchcock (D-Nebraska) tried substituting amendments approved by Wilson, Robinson supported each effort, but with no success; practically all of Lodge's changes were adopted. Afterward Robinson did help defeat an isolationist reservation offered by Hiram Johnson (R-California), as well as numerous minor amendments. Even so, the pact contained most of the measures advocated by the Republicans.[19]

On November 19, 1919, the Senate finally rejected the treaty. Only thirty-nine senators (out of the sixty-three needed) voted for it—mostly mild reservationist Republicans. Of the fifty-five opponents, fourteen were irreconcilables. The others were Democrats, such as Robinson, who followed Wilson's wishes. Just one day earlier the president had issued a statement calling the amended pact a "nullification of the treaty." After several parliamentary wrangles, a second ballot proved just as futile; the proposal was rejected forty-one to fifty-one. Finally the Democrats pushed a vote on the treaty without any reservations; this failed thirty-eight to fifty-three.[20]

Yet nearly four-fifths of the senators, and the vast majority of Americans, favored some sort of American participation in the League. Many people, therefore, still hoped that a compromise could be worked out; but no middle ground could be found. On March 19, 1920, the Senate took one last vote on the amended treaty. Once more Wilson urged the Democratic senators to stand firm and reject the proposal. Some, however, realized that the only hope of the United States joining the League was with the Republican reservations; therefore, they switched their votes and joined the majority which voted for it forty-nine to thirty-five. Still the measure fell seven votes short of the necessary two-thirds. Robinson, because of personal loyalty, could not forsake the president. Although having advocated an international peace organization since his earliest years in the House of Representative nearly two decades before, he voted to sustain his leader and friend.[21]

Robinson vainly tried one last ploy. Without the aid of Minority Leader Hitchcock, he proposed that the Senate return the pact to Wilson without taking any action. He suggested that such an action would not be a rejection of the treaty, but a postponement of a decision. It would also allow the president to consider compromise reservations. Suddenly several senators joined his arguments. After a few bitter exchanges, the chair ruled that Robinson had not made a valid motion and the Senate adjourned. (Not until 1921 would the United States officially be at peace with Germany.)[22]

But politics would continue; therefore, Robinson began to focus on the upcoming presidential election. As the undisputed leader of the Democratic Party in Arkansas, he headed the state delegation to the national convention at San Francisco in June 1920. Once more his infamous temper was on display. Apparently he went to the convention site to pick up the credentials for his delegation. But the man holding Arkansas's badges refused to hand them over; instead he loudly asked whom Arkansas would support. Robinson calmly but firmly replied: "That's none of your business." Still the official refused to deliver the credentials, once more demanding a candidate preference. This time in a determined, angry tone Robinson shouted: "None of your business." When for the third time the official refused to distribute the badges, Robinson struck him in the face, knocking him to the ground. As a crowd gathered, he bent over the official, took the Arkansas credentials, and muttered once more "none of your business," before walking away.[23]

This same type of animosity pervaded the Democratic convention. But Robinson had to mediate such hostility; he was elected to the nationally prominent position of permanent chairman—and not by accident. Some senators resented Wilson's humiliating, dictatorial rule over Democratic solons; they thus refused to support a cabinet member for the job—and demanded one of their own. The president therefore turned to one of his staunchest admirers, a "thorough-going administration man" according to the Associated Press, who had proven his fidelity by consistently supporting administration policies, even the vote against the Versailles treaty in March 1920. Furthermore, the convention chairman needed to be an excellent parliamentarian who could rule quickly and fairly on any questions as well as be an outstanding speaker who would dramatically outline the Democratic principles in the upcoming election. On both counts Robinson had ably demonstrated such skills in the recent Senate debates. As a consequence, he was the unanimous choice for chairman on June 28, 1920.[24]

Several controversial issues immediately loomed as disruptive. In a fight over credentials, Sen. James Reed of Missouri, who had opposed the Versailles treaty, was attempting to be seated at the convention, while the administration forces, led by Sen. Carter Glass of Virginia, were trying to have him expelled. Then problems arose over the platform. Specifically, prohibition divided delegates both by region and religion. Whether to join the League of Nations, even if it meant accepting Republican reservations, was equally volatile. But, not surprisingly, the most fractious bickering occurred over the presidential nomination. Former Treasury secretary William Gibbs McAdoo, Atty. Gen. A. Mitchel Palmer, Ohio governor James Cox, and several others were all vying for the post.[25]

But as permanent chairman, Robinson first had the responsibility to deliver an electrifying speech which could be used as a campaign document afterward. Yet, despite all efforts, he had some difficulty at first in rousing the crowd. With the band playing "Dixie," spotlights leading his path, movie operators preparing to film the speech, crowds cheering and waving, Robinson strode to the podium accompanied by such friends as Gov. Charles Brough of Arkansas and Sen. Pat Harrison of Mississippi. Although the demonstration was "not remarkable" according to the press, he passionately began by declaring that the Democrats were "entitled to victory," but the crowd barely applauded. When he attacked the Republican platform as "an astonishing and amazing jumble of inconsistencies, ambiguities, evasions, misrepresentations, straddles, and slanders," a line the *New York Times* called "a first rate welkin ringer," the audience did not respond at all. He revived the moribund delegates slightly when mentioning the prosperity during the Wilson tenure. Even the progressive accomplishments of the previous eight years left the crowd unresponsive. Nothing seemed to work.[26]

In desperation Robinson decided to speak extemporaneously, to enunciate the feelings of Democrats everywhere. The Republican nominee, Warren G. Harding of Ohio, was not his kind of man. He had denounced California senator Hiram Johnson (the Progressive Party nominee for vice-president in 1912) as a "faker and blackguard" and had termed Theodore Roosevelt a "Benedict Arnold." At this point the delegates went wild with their applause. In fact, Harding was like the "sphinx," unwilling or unable to comment on any campaign issues. Instead he "sits on his front porch . . . and watches the stately ships go by." Each of these and other similar comments brought laughter and applause from the crowd. As often happened, Robinson spoke best when he attacked without prepared prose. His facile mind and sensitivity to the audience once more proved essential to his success. By the end of his address, the delegates cheered loudly for him; he had reignited their enthusiasm.[27]

The convention next began the process of ratifying a platform and choosing the presidential nominee. For several days, therefore, Robinson directed all delegate business enjoying his different roles as traffic supervisor, timekeeper, and even history maker. After candidates were nominated, he allowed their workers to hold floor demonstrations for thirty to forty minutes before gaveling the proceedings to order. Often he had to clear the podium and aisles, asking specific delegation leaders to end the candidate parades. During A. Mitchel Palmer's nominating speech he turned the gavel over to Mrs. George Bass, leader of the women's committee of the Democratic National Committee, making her the first woman to chair a session of a national convention. Once the fourteen Democrats had been nominated, the convention switched to the platform; in conjunction with administration spokesman and platform committee chairman Carter Glass, and William Jennings Bryan, who had five minority reports to deliver, Robinson pushed through a motion to limit debate to three and a half hours, followed by an immediate vote on all of the minority reports. After the convention had turned down all amendments and approved the platform, Robinson ordered the balloting to begin for the Democratic nominee on Saturday, July 3. Sixty hours later on Tuesday, July 6, the convention chose Ohio governor James Cox on the forty-fourth ballot, then later that afternoon picked Assistant Secretary of the Navy Franklin Roosevelt as vice-president, thus bringing the convention to an end.[28]

But such efforts were to no avail. The 1920 election was a disaster for the Democrats, with Harding sweeping to victory in November. Yet for Robinson those years since the outbreak of World War I were extremely important. He had advanced from a junior senator to one of the most respected men in the Congress. His defense of the war effort and his attack of those opposing Wilson had, at times, placed him in the national spotlight. Through his staunch, partisan efforts he had earned the admiration of President Wilson and his colleagues, who, in turn, brought him into the leadership of the Senate. As a consequence he had proven to be an able parliamentarian and debater, skills which would help advance his career in the future. And he had gained national recognition as the chairman of the 1920 Democratic National Convention.

8 MINORITY LEADER

The 1920s were a time of enormous change in the United States. Industrial output boomed as America became an urban society. The stock market bulled ahead to unheard of highs, making millionaires out of humble investors. Often workers earned greater wages for fewer hours, opening up leisure pursuits such as golf, tennis, and bowling. As automobile production more than tripled during the decade, people became more peripatetic, venturing across town for entertainment, across county for shopping, even across country for vacations. With the advent of KDKA in Pittsburgh, radio became an integral part of daily life, tying Americans closer together with common programs. Jazz replaced other music as the norm, while movies transformed as "talkies" replaced silent films.[1]

Yet at the same time many Americans experienced a darker side to the apparent prosperity of the postwar years. Farmers experienced a severe depression which would not end until the beginning of World War II. Crop prices fell as equipment costs rose. More and more tenancy and sharecropping became harsh ways of life for once independent men and women. Across the nation religious, racial, ethnic, and political intolerance became commonplace, accentuated by the Scopes "Monkey Trial," the Ku Klux Klan, the "Red Scare," and the Sacco-Vanzetti Case. Vast numbers of people violated the Constitution by disobeying prohibition laws. And to quench their thirst, bootleggers such as Al Capone rose to prominence and power.[2]

In the 1920s a generation of progressivism was halted and a reactionary regime came to power. Warren G. Harding won the presidency by pledging a "return to normalcy." Soon thereafter he repudiated American participation in the League of Nations, thus ending the ongoing and bitter Senate fight. He also brought leading industrialists, such as Andrew Mellon of Pittsburgh, into the government, thereby squelching the regulatory impulses of the past two decades. Not since the days of William McKinley had such a pro-business administration controlled the White House and the Capitol.[3]

Yet in these difficult years for Democrats, Robinson successfully advanced his career. He moved into continually more important roles in the Senate until he was elected minority leader in 1923. Consequently, he became an outspoken critic of the Republican administration, especially regarding the many scandals such as Teapot Dome. In addition, numerous admirers pushed him as a favorite-son presidential candidate in 1924. And in Arkansas he solidified his paramount political position, even winning the governorship, and later a federal judgeship, for his closest supporters. Even his legal practice, which was pursued only during congressional recesses, brought him additional income, allowing him to buy one of the showplace homes of Little Rock.

But in 1921 the political ambiance at the Capitol looked grim. Harding and Coolidge had all but destroyed Democratic hopes. In the Senate, Republicans took even more seats. Robinson and his progressive ideals seemed out of sync with the new, conservative times. The Treaty of Versailles, the leading issue for the previous two years, was now discarded. His role in the Democratic Party, enhanced by his leadership of the 1920 convention, appeared almost inconsequential, since the opposition had more than enough votes to pass any legislation by themselves. These years might well have reminded Robinson of his first terms in the House of Representatives two decades earlier when none of his proposals made it to the floor for debate, since the committees were dominated by reactionary and often despotic Republicans.

The earliest battles of the Harding administration centered on foreign policy. The president easily persuaded the Republican-controlled Congress to declare that the First World War was over—without ratifying the Paris Peace treaties. His next series of proposals centered on the fruits of the Washington Naval Conference, a move for world stability and security separate from the League of Nations; of these, the Four Power Pact was the most controversial. It said that the major powers in Asia, France, Great Britain, Japan, and the United States, would "respect" the possessions of the other signatories in the Pacific Ocean. In addition, those countries would consult among themselves during any crises in order to "meet the exigencies" of any emergency. It superseded the earlier Anglo-Japanese treaty and prohibited any of the four countries from building new Pacific bases or fortifications.[4]

Rising once more to an important, high-profile position, Robinson led the Senate opposition in a caustic, bitter, even vengeful battle. He began by employing the tactics used by the earlier adversaries of the Versailles treaty. For instance, he began Fabian moves, not overtly filibustering but, rather, raising numerous questions in order to embarrass the Harding operatives. First he simply asked who wrote the original provisions. Since no one could claim authorship, he hinted that the treaty was Japanese in its source; further, it would guarantee their hegemony over the Far East, while limiting American efforts to protect the Philippines. Then following the example set by "bitter-enders" two years earlier, he submitted two reservations which were in many ways reminiscent of the efforts by Sen. Henry Cabot Lodge (R-Massachusetts) against Wilson. Thus he hoped to make the Republicans, who now supported the treaty, as uncomfortable as possible. The meaning of this action was not lost on anyone.[5]

On March 9, 1922, obviously angered by the demise of the Versailles treaty, Robinson lashed out personally at Lodge, who had toiled arduously against the League of Nations. With syrupy sarcasm he noted that this new pact was heralded in Wilsonian terms as "the greatest achievement of modern times for the preservation of world peace." Yet its chief proponent had fought other recent attempts to foster global harmony. He then attacked Lodge for describing the proposal in a "poor paraphrase" of the glowing terms that Wilson had used of the League. (In fact, during the dialogue on the floor, other senators followed Robinson's lead and termed it "unconscious cerebration" and even "plagiarism.") Next he announced, in a slam on the senator's intellectual vanity, that Lodge was "a great scholar and great statesman," since "he admits it." Mockingly he further declared that in "beautiful and meaningless poetry" Lodge had now pronounced the treaty "inseparably linked with the fate and destiny of mankind," while earlier dooming the vastly more important League of Nations. Evidently Robinson savored this moment of revenge.[6]

Surprisingly, however, Robinson did not limit his attacks to Republicans. In trying to avoid the errors of Wilson, Harding had appointed the minority leader as a delegate to the Washington conference; Democrat Oscar Underwood of Alabama now defended the Four Power Pact unswervingly. Robinson, who had often served as a deputy leader, now assaulted his nominal boss. Interrogating Underwood as vehemently as Lodge, he forced his colleague, on several occasions, to admit his ignorance of several portions of the treaty, since he had been out of town on a family emergency during much of the negotiations.[7]

On March 24, 1922, Harding, Lodge, and Underwood prevailed. Each of Robinson's reservations was voted down by a two to one margin; however, all the Democrats, except four, supported his amendments. Later that day the treaty received the necessary two-thirds vote for ratification.[8]

One of the biggest concerns of the 1920s was the continual worsening farm conditions. Even as the rest of the nation gloried in ever-increasing prosperity, the agricultural economy fell to new depths as prices plunged for several reasons. With the end of World War I, the government no longer guaranteed a minimum amount for crops. Prices then tumbled to a much lower, free-market level. In addition, crops from new lands in Australia, Canada, and South America, often having lower expenses and lower costs, began competing with American exports around the world, thereby pinching off American markets. Then European farms, which had either been fallow or underworked during the conflict, began harvesting again.[9]

Another facet to the predicament was overproduction at home. Indeed, after the armed struggle subsided, the United States continued to plow as many acres as during the war, including marginal lands with high costs. Then as the farms mechanized more and more, the productivity went up, causing ever-greater surpluses. And as Americans became more dependent on automobiles and farmers on tractors, perhaps as much as twenty million acres of land, heretofore used for hay and oats to feed horses and mules, now began competing in other crops, once more increasing supply without increasing demand. And if that were not enough, cotton, in particular, suffered from the opening of new fields in West Texas and Oklahoma, which were flat and more conducive to large-scale tractor farming.[10]

To combat the crisis, several members of the Senate and the House of Representatives formed the nonpartisan Farm Bloc in 1921, pushing two measures to help agriculture through the Sixty-seventh Congress.

The first initiative, the Capper-Volstead Act, exempted agricultural cooperatives from antitrust laws. Passed early in 1922, it allowed farmers to work together in buying and selling goods without government interference. Then in 1923, Congress passed the Agricultural Credits Act, which opened up government subsidized credit for short terms of six months to three years—the time frame needed most by livestock farmers.[11]

In both instances, on the initial bill and on the final act, Robinson supported the Farm Bloc's legislation. Throughout his career he often tried to improve the plight of farmers, for whom he had deep empathy. In fact, he had numerous brothers, sisters, nieces, and nephews involved in agriculture. As he told a nephew and aide who decided to return to Arkansas and become a farmer, "Back-breaking farm work made me the success I am today. After picking cotton as a young man, I determined never to have to work that hard again. Everything I have done, started when I decided to do anything to get out of farming."[12]

Although it lost formal structure after its initial two-year session of Congress, the Farm Bloc, or rather its former members, continued to work together for agricultural legislation throughout the remainder of the 1920s, with Robinson supporting their efforts. For instance in the mid-twenties Robinson voted for the McNary-Haugen bill which would have required the government to purchase surplus crops and keep them off the domestic market in order to inflate prices. Then the bureaucracy would sell the products when the price rose, or dump it on international markets for whatever price it could get. Any loss would be made up by an equalization fee on producers. Twice this measure passed the Congress only to be vetoed. Then at the end of the decade Robinson supported the Agricultural Marketing Act with the Senate's export debenture plan. The plan would pay a "bounty" of approximately half of the tariff rate to farmers of agricultural products which were exported. When Hoover announced he would veto any bill with the measure included, the Senate eventually dropped the export debenture plan in order to get a marketing act. In all ways, Robinson tried to support legislation to improve the life of the common farmer.[13]

Other issues divided the congress. And on each one Robinson attacked forthrightly, announcing his positions even on controversial topics. For instance, he fought the Fordney-McCumber Tariff of 1922, unsuccessfully working with fellow Democrats and notable Republican progressives such as Robert La Follette of Wisconsin and George Norris of Nebraska. (He did break with these colleagues—and with the consistency of his argument—to support a continued high tariff on rice, which was produced in Arkansas.) He also endorsed adjusted compensation for veterans of World War I, better known as the soldiers' bonus, leading the fight for immediate consideration; the Republican majority, with the support of Underwood, tabled discussion on the measure on June 20, 1922. Less than a year later he would lead a fight against a Republican-sponsored tax cut, urging that the excess money coming in each year be spent on poor veterans instead of wealthy businessmen. Like many of his colleagues in both parties, he was offended by the profligate spending of Senate candidates; therefore, he advocated strictly limiting campaign expenditures. And like many progressives, he supported the Twentieth Amendment to the Constitution, which ended the "lame duck" session of Congress and started sessions on January 3 instead of March 4.[14]

In this continuing progressive stance, Robinson sided with the working men of the nation on several occasions during the Harding administration. When the coal miners struck in 1922 and brought some industries to a standstill, he agreed that the government had the authority to operate the mines on an emergency basis. But rather than have troops dig the coal, he proposed an investigation by a commission which would include a member suggested by the union. Then later in the year, when Atty. Gen. Harry Daugherty filed a temporary injunction against railway workers and unions in order to stop a strike, Robinson excoriated him for trampling on the constitutional rights and freedoms of workers. The issuance of more than one thousand writs, which were to be delivered by over fifty-five hundred deputy marshals (with the army held in reserve if needed), caused Robinson to rail against the courts for the usurpation of power. As often during his career, he supported organized labor against big business—even though few Arkansans belonged to unions.[15]

Robinson also protected his constituents. When rice farmers wrote that the milling price had dropped precipitously, he demanded, and got, an investigation of the situation. He even served as the ranking minority member of the Congressional Joint Commission of Agricultural

Inquiry. He continued his support of local voters by speaking out against an effort to slash the tariff on imported rice, even though this position went against his other low-tariff arguments. Then for urban interests he shepherded a proposal through the Senate to construct a building for the Little Rock branch of the Federal Reserve Bank of St. Louis.[16]

Robinson also defended the South in general and Arkansas in particular against attacks from northern senators. Concerning illiteracy among blacks, he endorsed the prevalent regional view that whites, by paying for separate but equal educational facilities for minorities, were actually pushing the South to a "condition of enlightenment and glory, and leading upward the men, women, and children of the black race." In addition, he opposed the Dyer Anti-lynching Bill, arguing that it was just an election-time ploy of Republicans to gain the vote of African Americans. While Robinson would often attack the bigotry and hatred of the Ku Klux Klan, he did not believe in total racial equality.[17]

Late in 1922 Robinson had an unexpected opportunity to advance his career. In November, Minority Leader Underwood announced that he would not be a candidate for another term as floor leader. Democratic senator Gilbert Hitchcock of Nebraska was next in line, having tied with Underwood in balloting the previous time the position had been open, but he had just been defeated for reelection. Quickly, senators maneuvered for the position. Speculation for a replacement included Robinson, Furnifold Simmons of North Carolina, and David Walsh of Massachusetts.[18]

Simmons would be Robinson's toughest opponent. Having served in the Senate since 1901, the sixty-nine-year-old Democrat believed that he had the best claim on the post. During the Wilson administration he had served as the finance committee chairman, ably guiding the many wartime finance measures through the Senate. Known as a superb parliamentarian and behind-the-scenes worker, he had even led the Democratic opposition against the Fordney-McCumber Tariff earlier in the year. He thus entered the race believing that he would be unopposed for the position.[19]

Yet Simmons was at a distinct disadvantage. Because of a massive fire which swept through his home town of New Bern, North Carolina, he did not personally campaign; instead he stayed at home rather than return immediately to Washington. Then, he contracted influenza which halted any personal politicking. He, therefore, relied on his friends, especially Claude Kitchin and Senators E. D. Smith of South Carolina, Lee Overman of North Carolina, and David Walsh of Massachusetts, to solicit votes on his behalf. And his aide, Frank Hampton, while acting as a clearinghouse for all of the others, kept him informed of the election and corresponded with most of the uncommitted and freshmen senators. As the secretary/treasurer of the Democratic National Senatorial Campaign Committee in the 1922 election, he held an advantage over other staff members.[20]

Unlike his opponent, Robinson involved himself in the campaign. Early in December he returned to Washington with Sen. Pat Harrison of Mississippi to organize his forces. With the aid of John Sharp Williams of Mississippi, Thomas Walsh of Montana, and Key Pittman of Nevada, he began lining up votes. Robinson portrayed himself as an aggressive leader who would fight the Republicans, not join them. While overtly meant to show the difference between himself and outgoing leader Underwood, this stance led several senators to see Simmons as another quiet individual who would go along with the opposition rather than lead a tough charge. (In fact Hampton may have damaged Simmons's chances because he portrayed him as deliberate, thoughtful, and "not belligerent.") Robinson also pointed to his relatively young age, fifty years old, as a plus, since he would have greater stamina than Simmons, who would turn seventy before the end of the next Congress.[21]

At first the outcome was uncertain. Both sides believed the election was winable. Simmons drew his greatest support from the East Coast; Robinson pulled well in the West and border states. The deciding factor would be the freshmen senators. Although Hampton tried to build support for his absent boss, since most of these men did not know either candidate before coming to Washington, Robinson personally swayed several votes. In addition Simmons's attack of influenza in January made him appear physically weak. If too ill to campaign for a party post, then he might be unable to fulfill the arduous tasks of floor leader. Finally on February 8, 1923, Simmons withdrew from the contest, ostensibly to promote party unity. But his doctor had also prescribed extensive rest to recover from the flu. Many people believed, however, that Robinson had finally solidified enough votes to win.[22]

Prior to assuming this new position in December 1923, Robinson concentrated on foreign affairs. Late in February 1923, Harding proposed joining the Permanent Court of International Justice (World Court)—a branch of the League of Nations; quickly Robinson and several Democrats came to his aid, but the Republican majority refused to bring the matter to a vote. While terming such action "surprising" since the court could not interfere with any issue to which the United States did not agree, he castigated Harding for not guiding American foreign policy. He also attacked Senate Republicans for sidestepping the issue and refusing to allow a vote on membership. (Already he was taking on a more belligerent tone.)[23]

Later in August 1923, shortly after Harding's death, Robinson traveled to Geneva as an American representative to the Interparliamentary Union, an international body formed to promote world peace through understanding among governmental officials. Having been a member for many years (he had traveled to Vienna for the meeting in 1922), Robinson renewed old friendships and enjoyed a respite away from hot and humid Washington, while representing the policies of the United States. He and Billie loved to travel, meeting elected officials wherever they went; on one of these European visits he first became friends with Winston Churchill—a relationship which would continue until his death and which would draw Robinson ever closer to the British. In any case he was slowly becoming an Anglophile. Yet this love of the British did not soften his views on the world-debt issue. Much to the consternation of delegates from other countries, he delivered a speech upholding the American position that Allied war debts and reparations were separate problems. The United States, he asserted, would work out "amiable" reimbursement schedules from its former allies independently of German compensation. After a few weeks of rest and relaxation he returned to Arkansas and then to Washington where he would soon be formally elected minority leader.[24]

Almost immediately after his return in December 1923, Robinson faced his first test—the scandals of the Harding administration; in August 1923, the president had died, just as the aroma of corruption began to waft through Washington. Over the next year as the stench tainted many officeholders, Robinson took a partisan position in helping lead the attack against the Republicans. While close friend Thomas J. Walsh of Montana orchestrated the investigative committee and fellow Arkansan

Thaddeus Caraway flailed cabinet members incessantly, Robinson kept the issue alive on the floor of the Senate. By using his outstanding skills as a parliamentarian, he helped secure a coalition of Democrats and progressive Republicans to scrutinize the executive branch. He also forced through numerous resolutions which were damaging to the conservative administration of Pres. Calvin Coolidge. On February 1, 1924, he introduced a resolution urging the president to fire Secretary of the Navy Edwin Denby; it passed forty-seven to thirty-four several days later.[25]

But that was just the beginning. Robinson soon took an even more partisan tone in his attacks while at the same time criticizing the Republicans for injecting politics into the investigation. He assailed the Harding administration for "prostituting its authority" by transferring the strategic oil reserves from the Navy Department to Interior. He roared against Denby for his "negligence or incompetence." He juxtaposed Wilson's concern for the future of the country's defense against Interior secretary Albert Fall's attention to the moneyed interests of Harry Sinclair and Edward Doheny. He castigated Coolidge for supporting Denby and Atty. Gen. Harry Daugherty when the Congress, if not the whole nation, had lost faith in their abilities and even their integrity. Robinson then berated Daugherty for continuing in office while the investigation was ongoing. This would, he asserted, taint the probe, making its conclusions suspect. While the harangue was vituperative, no Republican senator defended the attorney general; instead William Borah (Idaho) joined the demand for the resignation. In fact the only important Republican who fought for Daugherty was national committee chairman John T. Adams, who labeled the entire inquest as "cowardly . . . political terrorism" put forward by "a few political blackguards and scandalmongers"; Robinson simply lambasted him for playing a partisan game which would never work, since numerous Senate Republicans had also called for Daugherty to resign. At every opportunity Robinson tried to tie the scandal to the Republican party, especially the conservative leaders, in order to improve the Democrats' chances in the November presidential election; but he always couched his remarks in terms of trying to uncover the corruption in Washington—no matter who was to blame.[26]

The scandals, which were breaking daily, led many Democrats to believe that they could win the presidency in 1924, and therefore numerous men entered the fray. The front-runners were former Treasury secretary (and son-in-law of ex-president Wilson) William Gibbs McAdoo and New York governor Al Smith; however, both had liabilities which would preclude either man from winning the Democratic nomination. Although strong in the West and the South, McAdoo received a crushing blow on February 1, 1924, when Doheny revealed to a Senate committee that his company had retained the candidate as legal counsel for $250,000. While McAdoo was uninvolved in the Teapot Dome/Elk Hills scandals, his close, and profitable, association with Doheny would remove any advantage the Democrats might have had using corruption as an issue; therefore many party leaders urged him to withdraw, which he refused to do. McAdoo still had important support from prohibitionists and even from the Ku Klux Klan. On the other side, Smith, as a member of the New York City Tammany machine, alienated many reformers. While his urban credentials helped him in large cities, many rural voters were distrustful from the outset, especially by his denunciation of prohibition. In addition his Roman Catholicism frightened many Protestants who feared a papist takeover of the country if he won.[27]

Because of the increasingly acrimonious split between these two, numerous regional or "favorite-son" candidates emerged, including Robinson. The Arkansas delegation was instructed by the state Democratic convention to vote for Robinson and when the representatives arrived in New York City, they immediately held a caucus on June 23, 1924, to plan their strategy. The leader of the efforts was Sen. Thaddeus Caraway of Jonesboro. He led a group of one hundred "boomers" who had also traveled from Arkansas; each began scouring the convention hotels and restaurants for uncommitted delegates. To anyone who would listen they extolled the virtues of their hero. Then at a testimonial dinner in his honor the next night, Robinson outlined his platform: tax reduction, agricultural aid, business regulation (of monopolies), tariff reform, and railroad rate reductions. These proposals proved him to be a southern progressive. Numerous dignitaries attended, including thirteen senators. While they might not endorse Robinson, they could not ignore him, because of his growing power.[28]

The campaign appeared to many to be a last-minute effort, but in actuality Robinson had begun considering a race much earlier. In June

1923, Harvey Couch, president of the Arkansas Light and Power Company and perhaps the richest man in the state, wrote the senator encouraging him to enter the fray. He volunteered to contact his many associates across the nation, while also forwarding remarks from ex-ambassador James W. Gerard, who offered to obtain New York's support, after Al Smith had been eliminated from the contest. Robinson, however, declined to make a commitment to run, since his new post as minority leader required most of his attention.[29]

In March 1924 the campaign began to intensify. Robinson was not only running for president, he also was up for reelection to the Senate. He wanted to maximize his chances to lead the Democratic Party without risking his current post; such an opportunity came when his probable primary opponent, George W. Donaghey (the man he bested for the governorship in 1912), called a mass meeting for March 6, 1924, in Little Rock. Donaghey hoped to pledge the Arkansas delegation to William Jennings Bryan, thus robbing Robinson of the added prestige which a national race would have given him. The senator's supporters jammed the hall to overflowing, yelling for Robinson instead of Bryan. Then a letter from Bryan announced his intentions to forego a contest but recommending Robinson as a man in whom he had "every confidence." This ended Donaghey's political comeback and assured Robinson of an easy victory in his senatorial campaign. As W. T. Sitlington, editor of the *Arkansas Democrat*, said, "Donaghey made an ass of himself, and everybody is laughing about him being 'unable to control his own meeting.'" Of the three hundred in attendance, only twenty-two remained after the meeting to show they were "real Bryan supporters" as Donaghey had asked.[30]

The campaign strategy that Robinson had outlined months earlier was simple. Robinson knew that he could not win as a front-runner. Instead he decided to wait until the leading contenders had each proven their inability to capture the nomination; then he would make a move for the office. But to keep up this image, he wanted Arkansas's delegation to go to New York City officially unpledged. He urged his friends, therefore, to secure "loyal" delegates. If the opportunity appeared, he could then appeal to all sides since he would not have fought any of the major contenders.[31]

When the roll call of states reached Arkansas, early in the proceedings, former governor and close friend Charles H. Brough nominated Robinson for the presidency—in a disappointing address. Known as a great chautauqua speaker and perhaps the best orator from Arkansas, Brough bored most of the crowd, the only applause coming after a brief testament to Woodrow Wilson (which always brought approval from the delegates) and at the end of his speech. Robinson needed a tremendous, thundering opening to sway the undecided if he had any hope of gaining the nomination; instead Brough elicited only a whimper from the crowd. Surprisingly his speech was one of the shortest for any of the candidates, even briefer than some seconding speeches. And of the time taken, he wasted over a third on extraneous matter, while never giving any important, concrete accomplishments of Robinson nor any of his stands on the issues of the day—from the Ku Klux Klan to prohibition. The speech failed, apparently removing the Arkansan from serious consideration.[32]

In fact the contest was far from over; as many had predicted the convention hopelessly deadlocked between Smith and McAdoo. On Saturday, July 5, after six days of voting the delegates began demanding a decision; out of this groundswell came several proposals which culminated in a call for a "harmony conference" after the seventy-seventh ballot. The convention authorized chairman Thomas Walsh and Democratic National Committee chairman Cordell Hull to call a meeting of candidates' representatives to solve the impasse. As the deliberation continued over the weekend, hopes for rapidly choosing a nominee rose. Since obviously neither Smith nor McAdoo would allow the other to reach the two-thirds vote necessary for nomination, many urged them to withdraw and let the convention decide on a compromise choice. The McAdoo representatives refused, whereupon Senator Caraway, representing Robinson, proposed that all candidates release their pledged delegates, allowing the convention to settle on an alternate candidate more quickly. (Such a proposal would need a two-thirds approval of the convention.) Again McAdoo balked, sending instead a complicated proposal intended to gain him the nomination rather than end the stalemate. Representatives from every other candidate signed the agreement, but when the convention re-opened on Monday, it failed. Thus the much hailed "harmony conference" had been a dismal failure.[33]

One surprising outcome of the meetings, however, was the renewed opportunities it gave to the Robinson campaign. Throughout Saturday and Sunday rumors circulated that one of the dark horses would emerge from the meetings as the consensus candidate. Even though he had never had more than forty-six votes at any time, people said that Smith, McAdoo, and several other party leaders had settled on him. For instance, William Jennings Bryan, still a force in the party after nearly thirty years, announced that only McAdoo, Robinson, and former navy secretary Josephus Daniel could be nominated. Numerous news reports pointed out that as party leader in the Senate Robinson had many friends who were pledged to one of the front-runners, but who would be pleased to nominate the Arkansan. The *New York Times* declared that he had the "superior position as a compromise candidate." It further suggested that his selection was such a foregone conclusion that speculation in some circles had switched to who would be his choice for vice-president, rumored to be Sen. David I. Walsh of Massachusetts—a wet and a Catholic. Although he gained a few votes on Monday, the boom never materialized. Finally on the 103d ballot John W. Davis, a dark horse who had pursued a strategy similar to Robinson's, won the nomination and the ordeal in New York City ended.[34]

Just before the convention opened, however, Robinson's temper again made headlines, when he exploded in a fiery rage over a seemingly insignificant event. In late June at the Chevy Chase, Maryland, Country Club he physically attacked another patron during a golf game. Apparently at the eleventh hole Senators Thomas J. Walsh and John B. Kendrick (Wyoming) lost their golf balls. A threesome following them asked, as allowed by course rules, to play through. Irritated by the interruption, the senators had to agree. After quickly finding the ball, both groups arrived at the twelfth tee at the same time. While the accounts vary, according to some Robinson loudly complained that Dr. James F. Mitchell had been "insolent all the way around" at the previous hole. He then growled: "Go on and play before I hit you.

Mitchell smugly replied that golf was a gentleman's game and then "pushing his face forward said: 'You are going to hit me, are you? You wouldn't hit anybody.'" Challenging Robinson was the wrong response; immediately he struck Mitchell so hard it knocked him over a bench. Robinson followed him over, where they had to be separated by the other senators and players. Shortly thereafter the club suspended him from the course, although he was given an opportunity to appeal the ruling. Instead he never went to the club again. Once more his temper had embarrassed him not only in front of a few friends but throughout the nation as numerous newspapers retold the story, thus contributing to his choleric reputation.[35]

For the rest of the year, Robinson campaigned vigorously for the Democratic Party—with little success. Since his own reelection was already assured, he traversed the country speaking for the national ticket. Having castigated Coolidge from the Capitol on many occasions, he now just reiterated his charges that the president, having served in Harding's cabinet as an ex-officio member, was at least partially responsible for the corruption that abounded—especially Teapot Dome. But he urged voters not only to elect Davis but also to send a Democratic majority Congress—especially to the Senate. In the end, however, his efforts went unrewarded; the Republicans retained both the White House and the Congress. As before the November contest, he was the leader of the minority.[36]

Throughout the rest of 1924 and the first months of 1925, Robinson continued to pursue progressive legislation—sometimes fighting to change the status quo when it hurt the common man and other times striving to save reform measures which the Republican-dominated Congress was threatening. For instance, he supported a nepotism clause for the Tariff Commission after a member—whose wife owned a sugar processing plant—advocated a high tariff on foreign sugar. He also fought against reducing expenditures for the Federal Trade Commission, which was conducting investigations into questionable business practices. At the same time he favored full disclosure of all campaign contributions as a way to "penalize" any party or candidate accepting money from "questionable sources." And as usual, Robinson attacked the railroads for gouging the public, this time through what was known as a Pullman surcharge which added a fee to anyone using a Pullman car; he therefore urged that the rate be eliminated by law.[37]

As he had done several times in his career, Robinson once again argued, throughout 1924, for a constitutional amendment outlawing child labor. He scoffed at senators who accused supporters of the proposal of being "sinister . . . Bolshevists, socialists, or anarchists"; instead he labeled them as "patriotic" and "whose devotion to the public interest" was above question. He opposed every attempt to weaken the proposal, often breaking with other southern Democrats who feared the intrusion of government into business. In the closest vote, on regulating only those under age sixteen instead of under eighteen, Robinson joined his colleagues in defeating the amendment (by only three votes); southern Democrats and friends such as Thaddeus Caraway of Arkansas, Tom Heflin of Alabama, Pat Harrison of Mississippi, Furnifold Simmons of North Carolina, Walter George of Georgia, and Carter Glass of Virginia all wanted to weaken the proposal, perhaps to please the southern textile industry. Nevertheless, Robinson maintained his long-held opposition to child labor.[38]

The soldiers' bonus was one of the most talked about issues during the 1920s, and on this subject Robinson usually sided with the veterans. On numerous occasions in 1924 he argued that the men who had fought in World War I should receive some form of compensation. Yet he opposed cash disbursements, instead favoring an insurance plan by which soldiers or their heirs would be paid after twenty years. He asserted, however, that veterans should be allowed to borrow against that insurance policy, thereby putting cash into their pockets. When President Coolidge vetoed the measure, Robinson joined fifty-eight other senators and the House of Representatives in overriding his objections.[39]

One of the most interesting spectacles of the Sixty-eighth Congress was Robinson's disciplining of two fellow Democrats for party disloyalty —seen by the minority leader as a terrible character flaw; Robinson always viewed loyalty as an absolute necessity in life. First he castigated William Bruce of Maryland for defending Secretaries Denby and Fall during the Teapot Dome investigations. Then Robinson assailed him for denigrating the 1924 Democratic platform; and finally he attacked him for supporting Republican senator Albert Cummins of Iowa for chairman of the Interstate Commerce Committee over Democrat E. D. Smith of South Carolina. Robinson excoriated him in the Senate for his lack of allegiance in deserting his party. But that attack was only a warm-up; Robinson had far worse to say about Nathaniel Dial of South Carolina, who had delivered a Senate speech attacking the 1924 Democratic platform. Robinson accused him of equivocation, of offering a "pitiable" excuse and a "half-hearted apology for an offense which he has neither the courage to justify or the intelligence to withdraw." When other senators followed this lead, labeling him "virtually a traitor," Dial cratered to the relentless pressure orchestrated by Robinson and asked that the entire speech be stricken from the record. As always Robinson had defended his beloved party.[40]

Whenever time allowed between sessions of Congress, Robinson and his wife, Billie, would travel extensively, from Alaska to Panama, from Latin America to Europe, and even throughout Asia. Especially enjoyable to Robinson were the trips without official duties, such as one to Europe in the fall of 1925, when he could enjoy the life of an outdoorsman. Robinson was never far removed from his youth when he had been an outstanding hunter and fisherman. He bragged of shooting prowess until some Scottish hosts took him on a grouse hunt, where he set a new record for the manor. He also hunted wild game in Czechoslovakia and went fishing in Ireland. He even made money on his vacation by writing several articles about Ireland for the *New York Times*. When he returned from Europe, he was refreshed and ready for another tough session of Congress.[41]

During the closing years of the Coolidge administration Robinson fought several more battles which typified his southern progressivism and internationalist outlook; most of these, however, he lost to the opposition. For instance, in January 1926, when the Senate once again considered membership in the World Court, Robinson helped lead the unsuccessful fight. In June 1927, he also urged that the United States join with France in adopting the Kellogg-Briand Pact, which specifically outlawed war. After corrupt elections in Pennsylvania and Illinois, he proposed more stringent campaign rules in 1927, which were quickly buried in committee. Because of a long strike in the anthracite coal fields, in 1926 he proposed, without success, that the president or Congress be empowered to appoint a Board of Industrial Adjustments to investigate problems between management and labor whenever a "national emergency" occurred; the board could then investigate and provide the public with unbiased information, perhaps leading to binding arbitration. He also favored having an independent agency oversee radio transmissions rather than an executive department, which might be influenced by politics. And once more, in 1926, he called for an investigation of the Tariff Commission, since it urged increases rather than decreases in impost fees.[42]

Robinson continually hoped to improve, through legislation, the dismal state of American agriculture. When the McNary-Haugen bill to raise farm prices on basic commodities (cotton, wheat, corn, rice, and hogs) came before the Senate in 1927, he predicted a veto, and proposed an amendment dropping the controversial equalization fee. When this attempt to placate Coolidge failed to pass the Senate, he fully endorsed the measure. Then after Coolidge disapproved the subsidy plan, Robinson urged his fellow Democrats to join progressive Republicans in overriding the president. As earlier, he sided with the Farm Bloc; this time he lost.[43]

On the issue of prohibition, one of the major concerns of the 1920s, Robinson was a dry—at least officially. A lifelong member of the Concord Methodist Church (near his hometown of Lonoke and situated on the old family homestead), he supported their doctrine against liquor; yet he never signed "the pledge" forswearing alcohol forever. When in Arkansas, he neither drank in front of constituents nor kept alcohol at his home. Yet he was not "bone dry." He enjoyed whiskey with his friends in Washington, partaking with future Speaker of the House and Vice-President John Nance Garner of Texas. Nor did he have qualms about drinking when abroad on his many travels. Like many southerners, he was dry politically, not personally. In fact, only his close friends knew that he ever drank, since to do otherwise could hurt his reelection chances.[44]

Throughout the 1920s Robinson practiced law, thereby augmenting his Senate salary. Until 1925 he was a partner in a firm with Charles Coleman, Joe W. House, and Joe W. House Jr. (Coleman, Robinson, and House). The firm provided him an office and secretarial support whenever he visited Little Rock. Even though a partner, he only received compensation for cases on which he worked, often only three or four each year during recesses; for instance in 1923 he earned only $3,365.77. Yet his name on the firm added prestige and attracted clients.[45]

For some reason, perhaps a disagreement over money (the information is murky), the firm dissolved toward the end of 1925, and Robinson joined a new firm—Robinson, House, and Moses—which not only helped him financially but also politically. Again his work was light compared to the other members of the partnership; he received money only for the cases he actually tried. Perhaps more importantly, however, he received campaign aid. Partner Hamilton Moses was well known as the protégé of ex-governor Charles H. Brough, whom he had served as secretary. In addition he was the primary lawyer for Arkansas Power and Light, the utility company owned by Robinson's friend Harvey Couch. Moses now helped run Robinson's political organization within the state whenever Grady Miller was absent.[46]

Without question this partnership proved to be the most profitable of his career, because of the case of *Coats v. Barton*. T. H. Barton, one of the pioneers in the Arkansas petroleum business, had amassed a fortune through drilling in southern Arkansas. Two former partners, W. M. Coats and J. B. Sowell, sued him, each asking for a third of his profits from a company they had left. Robinson successfully defended Barton against the suit in federal court; Coats and Sowell then appealed the ruling and Robinson presented the case before the Circuit Court of Appeals, where he again won in 1927. The firm received $60,000 for their efforts with Robinson pocketing $25,000 for his fee.[47]

The money relieved Robinson of an awkward situation. For many years his mother-in-law and brother-in-law had shared a house with him in Little Rock. Since Grady Miller had now started a family of his own, the large home had become cramped; tempers occasionally flared between the close family members as both Miller and Robinson claimed to own the house. While the argument never became public knowledge, strife became commonplace at home—something to which he was unaccustomed. To end the conflict, he took the proceeds of the trial and bought one of the showplace homes of Little Rock, the Foster House on Broadway. He then left the disputed home for Grady Miller and his growing family; the dispute never caused any further problems between the men and Miller continued as his closest confidant.[48]

The Foster House was indeed magnificent for Little Rock. The brick structure had a large front porch accented by a high gable. Numerous peaks in the roof made it one of the architectural landmarks of the burgeoning silk-stocking district. Copper mantels on the fireplaces, numerous chandeliers, and a large formal dining room highlighted the interior. Beautiful etched-glass doors separated several rooms such as the library, music room, and parlor from the immense, formal living room. Built on a corner lot, it had a large yard with a carriage house as well as a commanding view of Broadway—the main thoroughfare of the district and the most distinguished address in Little Rock. The house matched his growing prestige.

By the time candidates began jockeying for position in the 1928 presidential campaign, Robinson could look back with pride at his rapid advancement. He had parlayed his chairmanship of the 1920 Democratic convention and his staunch support of Wilson into the leadership of the Senate Democrats. He had also gained prestige from his role at the 1924 convention when he was mentioned seriously as a compromise presidential candidate. And he had pushed several progressive Democratic measures to the forefront of national political debate. Yet his greatest accomplishments were still in front of him.

James and Matilda Robinson

Robinson home in Lonoke, before the family moved to Little Rock in 1913

An early portrait of Robinson, perhaps
in his congressional years

Jeff Davis

George W. Donaghey

Robinson is presented a gavel at the 1920 Democratic National Convention where he served as chairman.

Left to right: Joe T. Robinson, Mississippi senator Pat Harrison (temporary chair of the 1924 Democratic National Convention in which Robinson was a "favorite son" candidate), and Utah senator William H. King, secretary of the Democratic National Committee, talking on the steps of the Capitol before the 1924 convention in New York City

Senator Robinson and his family

Senator and Mrs. Robinson,
happy over his nomination

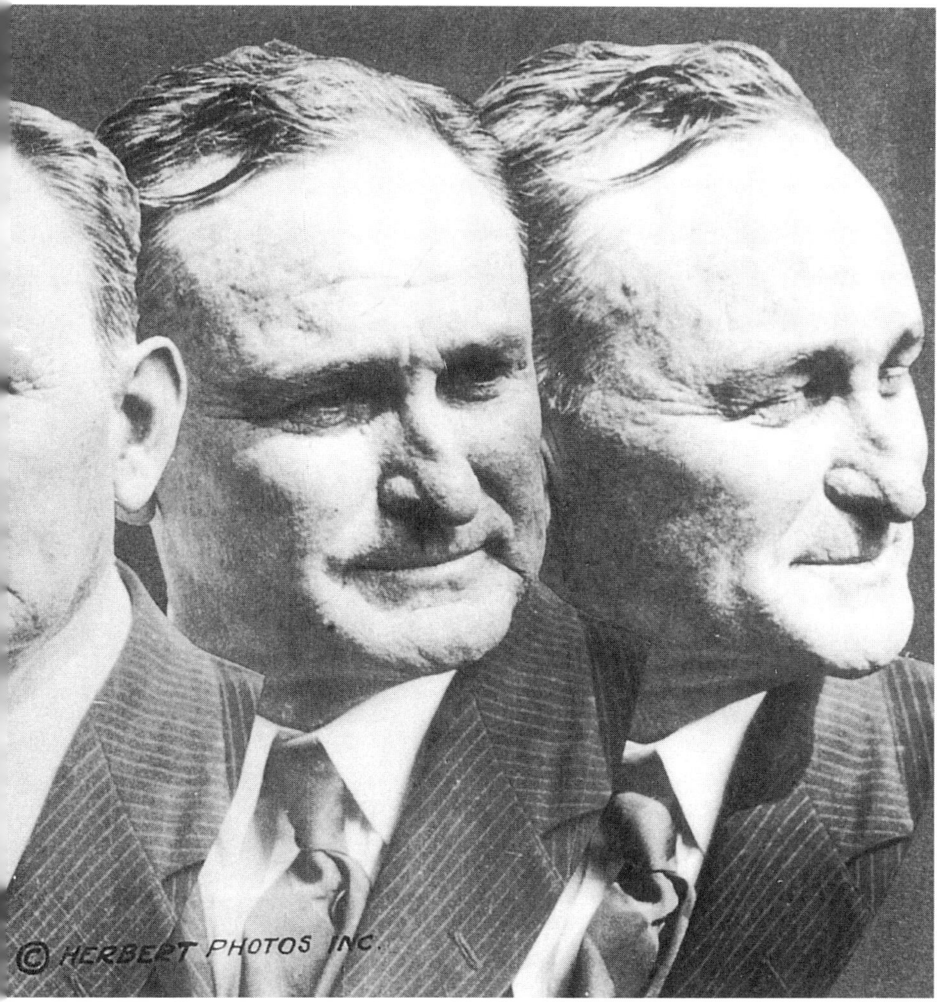

A five-angle campaign photo of 1928 Democratic vice-presidential candidate Joseph Taylor Robinson

Robinson home on Broadway in Little Rock, after 1928.
This is the home that FDR visited in 1936.

This photo from the *Wichita Eagle* shows
Robinson in knickers playing golf.

Delegates to the London Naval Conference with Pres. Herbert Hoover, 1930

Republican senator David Reed (Pennsylvania) and Robinson, 1930, as delegates to the London Naval Conference

Robinson and FDR confer at Warm Springs,
Georgia, before FDR's inauguration.

Robinson with FDR and Eleanor Roosevelt in Little Rock in 1936

Joe T. Robinson and FDR on the back of a train in Little Rock with two unidentified men. This was the first time a sitting president visited Arkansas.

Robinson as chairman of the 1936 Democratic National Convention

Joe T. Robinson with 1936 Democratic ticket at the 1936 Democratic National Convention

Robinson with Key Pittman as they prepare to leave for the Jefferson Island Club in 1937

Robinson with nephew Grady Miller Jr. at the Jefferson Island Club, 1937

Mrs. Robinson and brother Grady Miller after memorial service for Joe T. Robinson in the Senate, July 1937

Vice-President John Nance Garner, Mrs. Robinson, and Arkansas senator Hattie Caraway

Joseph Taylor Robinson

9 VICE-PRESIDENTIAL CANDIDATE

In 1928 the United States seemed to be more prosperous than ever before. With people leaving the farm for industrial occupations, the cities were growing at astonishing rates. Manufacturers expanded with almost reckless speed. Americans now found both the automobile and the radio necessities not luxuries. And the stock market was beginning its bull run as countless Americans invested in Wall Street offerings.

But more important to Robinson and many other Democrats than the booming economy, 1928 was a presidential election year; perhaps they could regain control of the government and end an eight-year drought in Washington. For the first time since 1916 the upcoming convention promised to have a friendly atmosphere rather than a warlike attitude. Most observers believed that Gov. Al Smith of New York would win the nomination handily after being denied it twice before. And unlike 1924 the incumbent Republican was not seeking reelection, possibly allowing Democrats to take the White House and the Congress.

Two problems seemed to blur the picture, however, making the Democratic resurgence uncertain. First, Smith was a Roman Catholic, and no one of his faith had ever become president. In fact many people opposed him simply because of his beliefs, most notably Ku Klux Klan members. In addition Smith was a "wet" on prohibition. Although assuring the public that he would enforce the ban on alcohol, even promising to curb substantially the corruption and crime of the past decade, he also urged that the Eighteenth Amendment be modified or repealed. To many Protestants, especially southern evangelicals and fundamentalists, Smith was a dangerous heretic for this "sinful" belief. Numerous regional leaders urged their friends to bolt the Democratic Party if Smith were nominated and to support Republican Herbert Hoover.[1]

In the Senate Tom Heflin (D-Alabama) led this movement. Throughout 1927 and the first part of 1928 he had made what he called his "Catholic" speech on numerous occasions. Each time he castigated the Pope for trying to take over the United States through the election of Al Smith. He hinted darkly that American priests were involved in a conspiracy, based in Rome, which would eventually force America to become a Catholic country. Each time he gave the speech, it became a bit more vitriolic, a bit more flamboyant.[2]

Early in January, however, this situation became more volatile. The Hearst papers printed charges that the Mexican government was bribing several senators, including Heflin. Immediately the Senate ordered an investigation (which later proved the charges to be groundless sensationalism), but Heflin saw a sinister plot by Catholic authorities in Mexico to embarrass and ruin their most outspoken foe. He, therefore, spewed forth a venomous attack on all Catholic priests, nuns, and bishops, reserving his most critical remarks for the Pope who, he claimed, was trying to involve the United States in a war with Mexico and Nicaragua. He also included an assault on Smith, arguing that Democrats should "bow their heads in shame" at the mere mention of his name.[3]

For months Heflin's attacks had gone unchallenged, but on January 18, 1928, Robinson furiously rebutted. Red in the face and pointing at the Alabaman, he raged that Heflin did not speak for the Democratic Party, that his views were "contrary to the teachings of the Master and to the spirit of this government," and that when someone "lights the torch or sounds the cry of religious intolerance and persecution," he "does his country no service." As always, his best speeches were unplanned and extemporaneous, carried out in the heat of anger; and without question this address became famous.[4]

The debate on the Senate floor quickly intensified and became even more personal. Heflin argued that Robinson no longer represented the majority of their party and should be removed. And then with an angry smirk, he countered that the Democratic leader would never dare make that speech in Arkansas for fear of ending his political career. Robinson, before packed galleries of shocked listeners, replied that not only would he continue attacking religious bigotry in his home state but in "Alabama, too" (which Heflin said would lead to "tar and feathers"). In disgust Robinson shook his head and muttered, "This shows how a good man can go wrong and how far wrong he can go and what a fool he can make of himself."[5]

The confrontation ended behind closed doors the next day. Robinson called a conference of all Democratic senators, whereupon he resigned his position as leader. Immediately he was reelected with only one dissenting vote. Yet Heflin refrained from further anti-Catholic outbursts on the Senate floor.[6]

The reaction toward Robinson was immediate and favorable. Editorial writers praised him. Colleagues spoke of his courage. Countless letters and telegrams of support (many from Alabama) flooded his Senate office—including one from the mayor of Montgomery. The bishop of Little Rock thanked him for his efforts. And with only a few exceptions (such as S. E. Tull, the pastor of the First Baptist Church of Pine Bluff) the people of Arkansas rallied proudly behind their leader. (Several years later when Robinson was in Rome, he had an audience with the pope, who gave him a cane in appreciation for his stand against bigotry; Robinson later gave the cane to his good friend the bishop of Little Rock.)[7]

Perhaps in a more public and surprising way than ever before, Robinson had once more defended religious tolerance in America—a belief which was a basic part of his character. He would continue to attack religious bigotry in speeches across the South and the West in 1928, even when the Ku Klux Klan and many fundamentalist ministers attacked him and threatened his future political career. And in just a few years he would be defending German Jews in speeches aimed at Adolf Hitler and his prejudiced rhetoric. According to a former Robinson staff member, in an "official German rumor" Hitler announced that the senator's real name was "Robinsonowski," which explained his "pro-Jewish" rhetoric.[8]

This dramatic exchange on the Senate floor lifted Robinson to a new position in the Democratic Party. He became an anti-Klan hero to many. Newspapers around the country applauded his efforts, even mentioning him as a compromise candidate if the national convention again deadlocked. For instance, Massachusetts delegates announced that he was their second choice behind Smith. Many southerners then tried to get him to run as a favorite son for the nomination, including Will

Rogers of Oklahoma. Yet he turned down the opportunity to run and urged that the Arkansas delegation remain uncommitted (which it did).[9]

As the convention neared, Smith seemed to have the nomination secured. So, unlike the 1920 and 1924 gatherings, the focus switched to the convention officers, the platform, and the possible vice-presidential candidate. Robinson figured prominently in these discussions. Because of his surging popularity, many people mentioned him as a potential convention chairman, replaying his role of 1920. Since he was from the South, a dry, and a Protestant, many newspapers considered him a natural counterbalance to Smith. In addition he was known as a fiery orator who could, and would, attack the Republicans vigorously in his opening address. Thus when the Democratic National Committee met to finalize plans for the meeting, it followed the candidate's suggestions and named Robinson chairman.[10]

Then early in June, with speculation over a vice-presidential nominee increasing, Robinson once more dominated the discussions for obvious reasons. He would add balance to the ticket both regionally and philosophically. His prohibitionist stand might tone down the attacks on Smith's liquor beliefs. And, as a Protestant, he could confront charges of popery and a Catholic takeover. Representing a rural, agricultural state and being known as a proponent of the McNary-Haugen plan, he might reassure many farmers who had suffered under the Coolidge administration but did not trust a New York City, Tammany Hall politician. Finally, while the "solid South" had voted Democratic since the end of Reconstruction, many people speculated that the region might bolt to the Republicans, if Smith were elected; therefore, Robinson might help shore up Democratic support in his home area, as he would be the first southerner on a ticket since the Civil War.[11]

Although most of this maneuvering occurred out of public scrutiny, Senate colleagues ardently championed his nomination. For instance on June 18, 1928, Key Pittman (D-Nevada), a longtime friend and leader of the Smith forces in the West, wrote to Belle Moskowitz, a key advisor to the New York governor, and urged Robinson for the position. Robinson was the only possible candidate, Pittman stated, who was "stronger than Smith" in his home state and might be "stronger in Tennessee, Kentucky, Oklahoma, and Missouri," all questionable states. In addition, he was "presidential timber," fit to take over the post if called on. Nor would he ever "interfere with or injure" Smith's chances. And he would work well with Smith since he was "liberal at heart . . . tolerant, unselfish, and fearless."[12]

As the conventioneers began assembling, it became apparent that Smith had decided on Robinson. He had sent an advisor to Little Rock before the senator left for Houston. At the same time Robinson urged his fellow Democrats to unite harmoniously behind whomever the party selected. Simultaneously, however, word spread that the Arkansas delegation, perhaps at Robinson's instruction, would support Smith on the first ballot. Then prior to the convention the United Commercial Travelers held a Houston banquet in his honor at which many people expressed their support for Robinson. And on June 25, Mayor Frank Hague of Jersey City, a close confidant of Smith and vice-chair of the Democratic National Committee, announced that he had "128 votes for Robinson for Vice-President"; most now knew he would be Smith's choice.[13]

The new convention center, Sam Houston Hall, which had been constructed in a few short weeks, was indeed spectacular. In February 1928, promising to pay off the 1924 campaign debt if Houston hosted the convention, Texan and Democratic National Committee finance director Jesse Jones had pleaded to hold the meeting, the first southern location since the Civil War, guaranteeing a facility which could handle twenty-five thousand people. Since the city did not, as yet, have such a building, he employed a local architect to design the equivalent of an art deco armory. After forty-six days, the structure was completed, an amazing accomplishment since the city did not even own all of the land on which the building was to be erected when parts of the foundation were laid. Constructed of native Texas pine, the frame building covered more than a block. Around the perimeter twenty large flags flew from poles held in place on the roof by giant, spread-winged eagles; lavish, intricate woodwork decorated the entrance.[14]

The structure looked even larger on the inside. In order not to detract from the view of the delegates, the roof was barrel shaped, without trusses, reminding visitors of an enormous cavern. On the floor eleven hundred delegates and eleven hundred alternates could sit in chairs facing the high, bunting-encased, three-tiered platform. Thousands more could watch from the sides and back of the hall in raised seats (which were separated from voting delegates and alternates by a solid wall); at the rear of the building, a viewing mezzanine was designed to handle two thousand visitors per hour, who wanted only a glimpse of the proceedings. Over five thousand American flags decorated the inside of the building.[15]

After temporary chairman Claude Bowers opened the convention, had delegate credentials approved, and announced the convention officers, Robinson assumed leadership as permanent chairman. Using the hand-carved gavel made from a hickory tree from the Andrew Jackson estate, he called the convention to order. His first, and perhaps most important duty, was to deliver a stirring address—and he did! He praised all of the party leaders since Jefferson and Jackson, with a prolonged eulogy of Wilson. He attacked the corruption within the Republican administration and lauded the integrity of the Democratic Party. He even endorsed prohibition on behalf of the South. But he brought the delegates to their feet with comments, not found in his printed text, defending religious liberty. In a clear, crisp voice he reminded the delegates that Jefferson had "gloried in the Virginia statute of religious freedom," that he had "rejoiced in the provision of the Constitution that declares no religious test shall ever be required" to hold office. Before he finished this extemporaneous statement, delegates began rising from their chairs and applauding. A wild display began—and soon disorder. Delegates from Mississippi grabbed their banner and marched, skipped, and danced down the aisles. Soon other delegations joined them. While bands were playing, crowds swarming, and reporters busily writing stories, a fight inevitably erupted when several delegates tried to pull down the banners of anti-Smith southern states which were seated at the front of the hall to join the parade, especially the poles of Alabama and North Carolina. After the Houston police resorted to night sticks, the fight ended; meanwhile, the demonstration continued unabated around the hall. After some time Robinson restored order and quickly finished his speech.[16]

That night several southern delegates announced that Robinson could never receive the vice-presidential nomination, because his speech had betrayed the South with a call for religious tolerance; they then proposed to support Sen. Alben Barkley of Kentucky. Yet in the end Robinson was unstoppable. After Smith won the nomination on June 28, 1928, his lieutenants quickly lined up votes for vice-president, and

Robinson was selected the next day on the first ballot with 1,035 ⅙ votes out of 1,099 cast. The dump Robinson movement had died swiftly.[17]

But in Arkansas the anti-Smith movement began immediately to take shape, even with Robinson on the ticket. Most of its leaders were clergymen. Some argued that Smith's wet position was the issue. For instance, Hubert Knickerbocker, minister of the First Methodist Church of Little Rock, where Robinson attended when in the state capital, berated the ticket from the pulpit. Nor did he back down when sixty-four of the sixty-seven members of the boards of trustees and of stewards formally apologized to the senator. (He would be transferred at the next Methodist conference.) Others did not even couch their religious bigotry in prohibitionist terms. S. E. Tull, pastor of one of the largest congregations in the area, the First Baptist Church of Pine Bluff, opposed the Catholic faith and therefore led a rally of nearly ten thousand against the ticket. In a letter to Robinson earlier in the year he had vehemently denounced all Catholics, since the church was not a religion but a "vast, intriguing, murderous POLITICAL power."[18]

Yet clerics were not the only opponents; the Ku Klux Klan also fought Robinson in Arkansas, just as Heflin had predicted. The Grand Dragon for the Realm of Arkansas, James A. Comer, addressed a scathing letter to all candidates for statewide and local office. Characteristically he attacked the pontiff for wielding enormous influence "through Al Smith and Joe T. Robinson, Tammany Hall and the Democratic party." In pointing to Smith's unfitness for office, he called the governor a "wet in the extreme . . . [who] does not object to night clubs running full blast . . . where white girls and black men dance together." Comer thereby tried to combine religious and racial prejudice to defeat Smith.[19]

Since the first job of any vice-presidential nominee is to carry his home state, Robinson immediately began shoring up support for the Democratic ticket. In July and August he criss-crossed the state numerous times, speaking at such places as Conway, Little Rock, Pine Bluff, and Hot Springs. State party bigwigs, all friends of Robinson, threatened to block anyone from voting in the August Democratic primary who opposed the Smith-Robinson ticket. In addition, they refused to place on the ballot anyone who did not support the duo. And leaders of the state party announced that they would not appoint any anti-Smith people to the Democratic State Central Committee.[20]

At the end of July, some of the most prominent state politicos* formed the Democratic Victory Legion to run the campaign in Arkansas and to ensure the success of the ticket. They chose a chairman for each county to build and run a campaign organization. In fact, volunteers prepared to contact Democrats in each township to have them sign a party-loyalty pledge card. The county chairmen were also responsible for sending large delegations to the upcoming ceremony in Hot Springs where Robinson would be officially notified of his selection as the vice-presidential nominee.[21]

After Robinson wired the national committee that Arkansas was safely in the Democratic column, planning turned to the traditional notification ceremony—one of the biggest political events in Arkansas history. Gov. Harvey Parnell declared it a state holiday so that more people could attend. Crowds converged on Hot Springs to the large Arlington Hotel which served as the official Robinson election headquarters. Between twelve and fifteen thousand rain-soaked supporters braved the deluge to applaud the first native son ever nominated on a presidential ticket. Countless thousands listened to the speech over a fifty-station, nationwide radio hookup. Smith's daughter, Mrs. Emily Warner, and John J. Raskob, Democratic national chairman, represented the top candidate and the party. Just as the rain ended, party historian and orator Claude Bowers officially offered the position. And when Robinson moved forward to accept the post, the moon broke through the clouds and the cheering began. In his speech Robinson outlined his campaign themes: aid to farmers, Republican corruption, and Smith's prohibition views, especially pledging to enforce the laws honestly.[22]

The event was a spectacle unlike any ever seen before in Arkansas. The enormous crowd, said to be the "greatest multitude" ever gathered in the state for a political rally, filled the park while thousands more packed Central Avenue as far as could be seen; hundreds more hung out

---

*Some of those at the meeting were Sen. Thaddeus Caraway of Jonesboro and H. L. Ponder of Walnut Ridge in northeast Arkansas; national committeeman Vint Miles of Fort Smith and Dave Partain of Van Buren in west-central Arkansas; state central committee chairman J. S. Utley of Little Rock, Thomas C. Trimble Jr. of Lonoke, and R. N. Robbins of Conway in central Arkansas; national committeewoman Alice Cordell and Joe Mahoney of El Dorado in south Arkansas; Congressman Heartsill Ragon of Clarksville and Sam Rorex of Russellville from the Arkansas River Valley; as well as numerous other politicians from across Arkansas.

of the windows of businesses along the street for at least one-half mile. Listening over numerous amplifiers placed around the park and down the street, Arkansans roared their approval, with the noise welling up like a tidal wave from the back of the crowd before crashing against the speakers' stand. Immediately following the speech, the 153d Field Artillery Band gave a concert as the regiment passed in review before the dais. Then from nearby East Mountain a twenty-one-gun salute reverberated through the town to mark his acceptance. Robinson moved through the crowd "shaking a thousand outstretched hands" as the crowd, content from the demonstration, quietly dispersed.[23]

After the notification ceremonies Robinson campaigned nationally, thereby initiating a strenuous personal effort. Between September 3, 1928, and November 3, 1928, he traveled over twenty-five thousand miles by train, the national committee coordinating his itinerary with local Democrats. He made sixty major speeches and over one hundred and fifty platform appearances and talks from the rear of his railroad car, even though his staff consisted only of a personal secretary and one advance man, Harry Robinson (not a relative but an employee of the *Southwest American*, a newspaper in Fort Smith, Arkansas). Nor did he have a speech writer or a research assistant; he depended on his own knowledge of the issues and whatever information his brother-in-law Grady Miller could gather in Little Rock. Often his speech highlights were extemporaneous remarks; in each city he asked the local party leaders what the important issues were and he would then tailor his remarks to the crowd and their concerns. Without exception he added something about religious tolerance or a defense of Smith's views on prohibition.[24]

At each stop Robinson also served as an intelligence gatherer for the national headquarters. He relayed needs to New York, usually pleading for money to help the state organizations. He also asked for campaign literature for the southern and western states, especially when none had been sent for distribution. He continually battled a prejudice within the campaign for the Northeast, in funds, speakers, literature, and information. In a letter to his close friend Bernard Baruch, he asserted that the national headquarters was inept and "too slow." Yet, as a loyal Democrat he did not complain publicly.[25]

Robinson divided his efforts into two trips across the country. In each area he had a specific purpose. For instance, his first tour took him across the South where he intended to reinvigorate the party and strengthen suspected weaknesses in the "solid South." Beginning in Dallas on Labor Day, he spoke in numerous cities such as Nashville and Chattanooga, Tennessee; Richmond, Virginia; Raleigh and Charlotte, North Carolina; Columbia, South Carolina; Savannah, Georgia; Jacksonville, Florida; and Owensboro, Paducah, and Mayfield, Kentucky. His railroad car also stopped for many more rear-of-the-train appearances. Often, at the insistence of local party leaders, he added sections to his speech attacking religious bigotry.[26]

In Florida, however, Robinson had to react quickly when a hurricane came ashore and wrecked the planned itinerary. After speaking in Jacksonville on September 15, he traveled to Miami for a rally. But two days later a hurricane struck; the meetings had to be canceled; and the campaign train suddenly became a relief effort as it moved northward carrying doctors, nurses, and food. The campaign train, although soon out of supplies, fed more than one hundred people. Robinson immediately wired the national headquarters, suggesting that some prominent Democrat head up an emergency relief effort. After missing scheduled appearances in Atlanta, Georgia, and Bowling Green, Kentucky, because of washouts under the road beds, he resumed the campaign at Owensboro, Kentucky, on September 20.[27]

Crowds, as large as ten or fifteen thousand (far more than expected), greeted Robinson at each stop; yet he realized that the ticket was in danger of losing in November. He wrote to national chairman Raskob begging for money for the southern states and urging the national committee to establish a southern headquarters to solidify his appearances. The national leaders found it hard to imagine the South voting Republican and ignored his requests. Robinson met with numerous local leaders in planning strategy in the states where Democratic officeholders, such as Sen. Furnifold Simmons of North Carolina, were leading the anti-Smith forces. On September 22, 1928, upon returning to Little Rock, he publicly announced that the Democrats would once more carry the South, even though the religious issue was being demagogued throughout the region. Yet privately his letters did not show this same optimism.[28]

After a four-day respite Robinson began the western trip, his purpose that of appealing to the region's concerns. To sway the farm vote away from Republican Herbert Hoover, he attacked the inaction of the Harding and Coolidge administrations as well as Hoover's disdain for the

McNary-Haugen farm-relief proposal. In Nevada and California he announced support for the Boulder Dam project and other water power/conservation efforts. During this trip he realized how disenchanted the farmers were and sent Smith a proposal demonstrating a way for the Democrats to win the West; Smith should announce that, when elected, he would call a special session of Congress immediately after his inauguration to address the crisis in the heartland. Yet Smith still ignored the farm crisis, as he had throughout the campaign. And the campaign leaders ignored this proposal. Then, late in October, just a few days later, Hoover announced that, if elected, he would call Congress back to Washington to aid the farmers. Robinson's idea worked well for Hoover and helped bolster any waning agrarian support.[29]

The campaign reached its most tiring—as well as frustrating—point for Robinson on this western swing. He spoke in Missouri, Oklahoma, Kansas, Texas, New Mexico, and Arizona before October 9, 1928. Then he went to Los Angeles, San Francisco, and Reno, before heading north for engagements in Oregon, Washington, Idaho, and Utah. From there Robinson moved into the wheat belt of the Great Plains where once more he mercilessly attacked the Republican record of inaction in agriculture. Yet Robinson was at a disadvantage because Smith never endorsed the McNary-Haugen program. Even though drawing large crowds in Nebraska, Iowa, South Dakota, North Dakota, and Minnesota, he could not gauge the results. And once more lack of support from national headquarters plagued him; in fact, many western states had received no literature which would "educate" the voters about Smith.[30]

Late in October Robinson had to fight a vile Republican story which was circulated among blacks in northern cities. It continued the opposition policy of portraying Robinson as a racist in order to lessen the number of African-American votes for the Democratic ticket. In fact, the rumor went so far as to say that one morning, upon awakening ill, he "killed a couple of negroes before breakfast" to feel better. Robinson, incensed at the accusation and fearing the damage to the already besieged Democratic campaign, countered this outrageous tale. He had several prominent Arkansas blacks write testimonials which stated he had always "enjoy[ed] the respect and confidence of the colored voters" of Arkansas. By the time he reached East St. Louis for a speech on October 30, the problem had disappeared.[31]

Although originally scheduled to return home at the end of October, the national campaign added several stops to take advantage of Robinson's growing popularity and strong speeches. From October 30 through November 3 he delivered four major speeches in Illinois, three in Indiana, and two in Ohio, ending his peripatetic travels in Clarksburg, West Virginia. At the end of the campaign he optimistically predicted a Democratic victory in the farm belt, just as he had earlier prophesied for the South. He feared, however, that religion and prohibition could change the outcome.[32]

After this exhausting effort Robinson returned to Little Rock on Monday, November 5, to an immense reception. Governor Parnell and five former state governors welcomed him at the train station. On the state capitol grounds later that evening he spoke to thousands of supporters as well as countless others over a twenty-three-station regional radio hookup. With his usual verve he excited the crowd upon saying: "We must not imprison human thought . . . [or] build dungeons of despair for hope." Instead, he fervently announced, let "men worship as they will," for to do otherwise would let "terror and dread . . . rule the world." Just as he had started the year, he ended it, with an appeal for religious tolerance.[33]

On election day November 6, 1928, the Democrats suffered an overwhelming defeat. Hoover received over twenty-one million votes (nearly 59 percent) while Smith and Robinson received just over fifteen million votes. In the electoral college, Hoover won 444 votes to 87 for the Democrats. And for the first time since the end of Reconstruction the Republicans split the "Solid South," taking Texas, Tennessee, Virginia, North Carolina, and Florida as well as the border states.

Without question Robinson, in reflecting on the campaign, believed that the dominant issue was Catholicism. In the South and West such Protestant groups as the Methodists and Baptists tied religion closely to prohibition, waging war on liquor and anyone against prohibition—specifically Al Smith. To Robinson religious bigotry overshadowed all other issues, making a campaign based on policies impossible. It split the Democratic Party in the South and obscured agricultural reform. Americans were not ready to elect their first Catholic president.[34]

Even so Robinson furthered his career and raised his prestige noticeably during 1928. For instance, his continued stand against religious bigotry had made him a hero to many people who would have otherwise dismissed him as another southern klan sympathizer. At the national level he had proven himself an outstanding stump speaker who had thrilled crowds across the South, West, and Midwest. He had led the ticket to a 60 percent victory in Arkansas and had received acclaim from virtually all of the political leaders of the state. In two years he would have to run for reelection; consequently, the 1928 effort had proven his strength at home, virtually assuring him of an uncontested primary. And within the Senate he had strengthened his hold on the loyalties of many colleagues by his nonstop, cross-country campaign. At the same time he had become acquainted with important people in many states, some of whom would later serve with him in Congress. Thus his position as leader was more firmly held after 1928 than before.

Yet Robinson was not finished with government service. The campaign had been but a brief interlude in his Washington stay. The next nine years would be more fruitful.

10 DIPLOMAT AND OPPOSITION LEADER

As Robinson recovered from the 1928 vice-presidential defeat, neither he nor anyone else could foresee the severe shift that the economy would take over the next several years; at present the nation was booming. The stock market was flourishing, industry increasing. Prosperity seemed guaranteed, growth limitless. The Republican expansion appeared destined to last indefinitely.

Yet, in agriculture, many were already suffering from years of depression in the heartland. Newly inaugurated Pres. Herbert Hoover therefore decided to attack the problem directly. In April 1929, he fulfilled a campaign pledge to Sen. William E. Borah (R-Idaho) by summoning a special session of Congress to rejuvenate the farm economy. Hoover urged Congress to raise the tariff rates on agricultural products in order to boost commodity prices. In addition, he asked for the authority to increase or lower import fees upon the recommendation of the Tariff Commission, since referring each change in the tax structure normally brought acrimonious debate and political maneuvering. According to Hoover, whenever Congress became involved, higher rates were destined to occur. And he asked Congress to create the Federal Farm Board to loan money to cooperatives and to stabilize prices.[1]

Immediately, however, Hoover faced opposition in the Senate, especially by Robinson. When the president announced that the special session would only consider tariff and farm measures, the senator attacked him, arguing that the executive office did not have the constitutional authority to limit the topics addressed in a session. In fact, he announced that flood control legislation, amendments to the Federal Reserve Act, and even the census and reapportionment should be considered. Also disheartening to him was the vagueness of the administration's plan; therefore, he doubted its benefits. Even worse, a tariff change at that time would be inadvisable because it would likely include a general revision upward which would hurt most farmers because of higher prices. According to Robinson, "there is a real danger that the benefits from any farm relief bill . . . will be offset by increased burdens growing out of the revision."[2]

But Robinson's comments merely initiated the congressional battle. The concentrated fight centered around Democrats and progressive Republicans who wanted to add an export-debenture plan onto the Agricultural Marketing Act. (They believed this proposal would increase farm income by paying growers a bounty for excess crops which were sold overseas, while guaranteeing a higher domestic price.) Although Hoover strongly opposed the idea, Robinson allied with progressive (or insurgent) senators Borah and George Norris (I-Nebraska) to gather votes for the proposal. Then on April 24 Robinson chaired the Democratic caucus, determining that the vast majority of his colleagues favored the export fund. While no senators were bound by the vote of the group, the Democrats apparently united under Robinson's leadership. When the vote was taken, only two Democrats from the Northeast opposed the plan.[3]

After this strategy session, Robinson moved the battle to the Senate floor where a rancorous, partisan debate ensued. He attacked Oregon Republican Charles McNary, who had earlier co-sponsored the McNary-Haugen plan for agricultural price supports, for abandoning the farmer for political reasons. In much the same vein he castigated Majority Leader James Watson (R-Indiana), who had supported the twice-vetoed McNary-Haugen bill but was now ready to do the bidding of Hoover in killing the proposal. According to Robinson, "something mysterious" had happened to Watson, who apparently "wants to perpetuate" the farm problem so that it can remain in the "politics of the country." After several weeks of such belligerency, the Senate passed the debenture plan fifty-four to thirty-three, with thirty-four Democrats being joined by twenty insurgent Republicans.[4]

At this point the tariff measure went back to the House for approval, where passage appeared unlikely. Speaker Nicholas Longworth (R-Ohio) supported Hoover, who denounced the debenture plan. In fact, several Republican congressmen argued that the Senate did not have the constitutional authority to add the debenture plan onto the Agricultural Marketing Act, since all tax bills had to originate in the House. (Robinson called such accusations a mere "subterfuge" and "cowardly.") A stalemate then developed in the conference committee until mid-June when the Senate finally dropped the debenture plan rather than bear the criticism for blocking a farm-aid package.[5]

At this point, when the tariff became the central issue, Robinson had greater success. While the traditional "logrolling"—that of tying increases on farm products to those of industrial goods—continued and while realizing that the Smoot-Hawley Tariff could not be defeated, Robinson was able to slow it down. By opposing the plan to give the president the authority to change the import fees according to the Tariff Commission recommendations, he stalled the entire process for nearly a year; the Senate changed the measure so much that it languished in the conference committee. Not until June 1930 did the measure finally become law.[6]

Even as the debate over the tax schedule was being planned the nation's economy collapsed. On October 24, 1929, the value of stocks began to fall precipitously only to recover later in the day. On several occasions the ticker lagged behind for more than an hour. Then on October 29 the crash occurred—a record sixteen million shares traded hands, mostly downward. By mid-November, industrials on the *New York Times* list had fallen by more than one-half. And, in the aftermath of the crash, business in general began to contract, if not fail, causing a continuous panic.[7]

Before Americans realized the depth of the depression, however, Robinson embarked on a new mission as a Hoover-appointed delegate to the London Naval Conference. Because of continual international discussions which had begun with the Washington conference of 1921–22 and because of an earlier meeting between Hoover and British prime minister Ramsey MacDonald, the conference appeared likely to produce an agreement to reduce armaments. Many hoped that the meeting would end escalations in naval expenditures and ship building, thereby making war less likely. And in the wake of the recently approved Kellogg-Briand Treaty to outlaw war, the talks appeared to be the next practical step to implement that visionary peace accord. In particular, American delegates would propose or support the limit on small cruisers and destroyers (which had been ignored in the Washington talks), the abandonment of submarines, and the equality of the American and British navies.[8]

Yet, from the outset, the participating nations had conflicting goals. England and the United States agreed to approximately equal tonnage in ships, but disagreed on how it could be used. The Japanese wanted to increase their naval ratio from 60 percent to 70 percent of the United States and England. Italy wanted a navy equal to that of France, while the French demanded a larger fleet, since they had to defend shores both on the Atlantic and the Mediterranean. Such differences had stymied all efforts at naval reduction since the Washington conference.[9]

On January 9, 1930, with great fanfare and pomp, a distinguished American diplomatic delegation left for London on board the passenger liner the *George Washington*, used over a decade earlier to transport Wilson and his retinue to the Paris Peace Conference. Secretary of State Henry Stimson chaired the group and acted as the official spokesman for President Hoover. Secretary of the Navy Charles Francis Adams, of the famous Massachusetts family which claimed two past American presidents, represented the navy. Three ambassadors (two already in Europe) increased the prestige of the group, Dwight Morrow envoy to Mexico, former vice-president and emissary to the Court of St. James (the United Kingdom) Charles G. Dawes, and ambassador to Belgium Hugh Gibson, who had represented the United States at the failed Geneva Conference in 1927. Rounding out the official party were Republican senator David Reed, chairman of the Committee on Military Affairs, and Robinson, the Democratic leader in the Senate and a member of the Foreign Relations Committee. These two men, in particular, were added to make the Senate passage of any agreement easier; Hoover did not want to follow the example set by Woodrow Wilson of snubbing the Senate or the opposition party, thereby dooming his proposal.[10]

From the very beginning Robinson stressed the nonpartisan nature of the meeting and the teamwork to be exercised by the negotiators. In a letter to former Arkansas governor Charles Brough, he explained that the delegation was "united in purpose" and that it would be inconsistent with "patriotic motives to inject partisan politics into international questions." Yet he did not suggest that an agreement was so necessary that a poor treaty would be hailed as an accomplishment, just to have a signed piece of paper. Instead, from the deck of the *George Washington*, he announced that "failure" would be better than an "arrangement consummated through intrigue or based upon discrimination against any signatories."[11]

After arriving in London on January 17, 1930, Robinson participated in an impressive spectacle. To open the conference, King George V walked into St. James Palace, escorted by the Lord Chamberlain and Prime Minister Ramsey MacDonald, and delivered a warm welcoming speech. After George V left, the delegates assembled around tables arranged in a "U" shape with the British delegation at the head, the French and American delegations on the right, and the Italian and Japanese on the left. Staffers and stenographers occupied the center. By an agreement made the night before the opening, MacDonald served as chairman. He therefore delivered the first speech, followed by the head of each delegation.[12]

Soon the conference settled into a sometimes tedious and tiresome routine. Each morning the delegations conferred on any proposal made the day before and debated propositions to be put forward. According to Ambassador Dawes, Robinson was "in a powerful position on our delegation, . . . [and] a constructive statesman." In a "clear, straightforward way," he helped formulate proposals which the American delegation used to bargain with the British. In fact, Dawes credited much of the success at the conference to Robinson, pointing out his "real usefulness" in negotiations, "a willingness to work for the substance of things quietly and effectively" while not seeking "concurrent credit and publicity." At times, however, Robinson impatiently complained that the meeting was "proceeding slowly," although admitting that the participants were probably making "as much progress . . . as one could reasonably anticipate." Only rarely did all of the delegates meet in the plenary sessions such as on the opening day. Instead the real work occurred in committees that met between the large assemblies and even more so in small informal gatherings. Robinson attended several of these smaller assemblies. Meanwhile, the delegates had to pacify the press with news releases and occasional speeches. Robinson and Reed, however, had an additional job, that of communicating with an anxious Senate.[13]

Robinson took these tasks seriously, fulfilling them whenever possible. He urged his fellow senators in Washington to ignore the rumors reported in the press and to reserve judgment until the treaty was completed and submitted for ratification. He even confronted his own party members, such as Sen. Kenneth McKellar (D-Tennessee), who attacked the proposal before anything had been agreed upon. Then to further assuage concerned Americans, Robinson addressed the entire nation through a radio hookup on February 19. In a speech approved by Stimson and given to the Association of American Correspondents, he asserted that the United States wanted definite limits on cruisers and submarines which, he believed, would then lead to a reduction in the larger, deadlier battleships. He surprised many people by renouncing any plan that would force the United States into a defensive alliance with any European power—even though that might destroy any chance of completing a treaty. (Less than a week later President Hoover endorsed this idea.)[14]

Perhaps Robinson's greatest contribution to the conference was a contingency clause (Part III, Article 21), which guaranteed the safety of all signatory nations. Unlike a similar section from the Washington conference, this proposal, written by Robinson, allowed a nation to begin or increase its shipbuilding if a nonsignatory nation threatened its safety—without first convening a conference to gain approval of the other nations. This section had been one of the reasons Robinson had opposed the Washington treaty. While requiring a country to notify other nations of a building program, it did not give others a veto over such action. The British endorsed the concept quickly, and eventually the Japanese also agreed to it. This proposal made the treaty more palatable to Robinson and increased the chances of ratification by the Senate—one of Robinson's major goals.[15]

All was not work for Robinson and his wife, Billie, however. They settled into a somewhat exciting social life while staying at the luxurious Ritz Hotel in London. The most enthralling event to them was a reception that King George hosted at Buckingham Palace. Later they attended a resplendent dinner at Guildhall over which the Lord Mayor of London presided. On several occasions they dined with their longtime friends the Churchills. And, early in February, Prime Minister MacDonald took the American delegates and their wives to the country estate Chequers, which was reserved for the head of the government. At other times Lady Astor entertained them both in London and at her country estate, where Robinson relaxed by playing golf. He also returned to Scotland to defend his reputation as an outstanding marksman and superb grouse hunter. And at a formal luncheon he became better acquainted with former British prime minister David Lloyd George. He entertained the gathering with a comical story about the Ozarks. In turn, Lloyd George responded with a joke about his native Wales. Afterward both sought out each other to recount other amusing yarns.[16]

By mid-April 1930, the conference closed with only partial success, according to Robinson. Then in a radio address delivered from London on April 20, he outlined the successes and shortcomings of the treaty. On the positive side, all five nations agreed to limit submarine warfare to the same rules followed by surface ships; that is, the safety of passengers and crew members on merchant ships must be provided for before a ship could be sunk. In addition, the countries continued to sanction a battleship-building "holiday"—no new juggernauts until 1936. But here any further agreements ended because of the bickering between France and Italy over naval parity. The United States, Great Britain, and Japan limited all other shipbuilding at a ratio of equality between Americans and English, while the Japanese could construct vessels at approximately 65 percent of that level. The one exception occurred in submarines where all three nations were allowed the same rate. While conceding that the treaty was imperfect, Robinson urged ratification by the Senate because it had been negotiated "in a spirit of nonpartisanship."[17]

In May, shortly after the return of the delegation, President Hoover submitted the treaty to the Senate where Robinson's strong support signaled an easy victory for the administration. From the beginning, Robinson defended Stimson and the treaty during hearings held by the Senate Foreign Relations and Naval Affairs committees. For instance, when several admirals opposed the treaty, he launched a blistering and "acrimonious" cross-examination, brutally questioning the propriety of naval officers to determine when a treaty should be negotiated.[18]

When Hoover called the special session of Congress for July 7, 1930, Robinson moved to the fore, successfully defending the treaty against all opponents—Republican or Democrat. When some complained that the difference in the caliber of guns left the United States at a disadvantage, he characterized their fears as trivial, since the gun size had been weighed against ship maneuverability. He also ridiculed those who feared "mysterious messages" and were asking the president to release all secret cables from the conference. And when a formal resolution was presented, demanding the release of the documents, Robinson emasculated it through amendment, requiring the president to turn the documents over only if he deemed it "in the best interest" of the nation. Thus on July 21, after two weeks of vigorous debate, the Senate ratified the treaty by a fifty-eight to nine vote; Robinson had succeeded in swinging Democrats to the president's side; only two voted nay. But in the long run, the treaty had limited impact, other than to strengthen Anglo-American goodwill. As the world changed, especially in Japan, during the 1930s, the treaty and the hopes it represented died.[19]

Even while in London, Robinson had tended to the home front; political gadfly Tom Campbell of Randolph County (north-central Arkansas) announced for the Senate in the August 1930 primary. None of the leading politicos could fathom his reasons for entering. Campbell was not a promising candidate, since he had never won a major race. In addition, few people publicly supported him. In fact, two men rumored to head his campaign, Frank Pace and Wallace Davis (from the old Jeff Davis machine), were, at least in public, strong supporters of Robinson. Some suggested that the Ku Klux Klan was financing Campbell with as much as one hundred thousand dollars. Others claimed that a former Robinson legal client was bankrolling the campaign out of anger over an unjust fee. Still others believed that some state railway labor leaders were opposed to Robinson because of several votes throughout his career, although most union members supported the senator. Yet despite such speculation, organized statewide support never materialized.[20]

Campbell caused some worries, however, because of his reputation as a "dirty" campaigner who was unencumbered by the truth; this election was no different. He condemned Robinson because his law firm—Robinson, House, and Moses—represented several of the largest corporations in the state, such as Arkansas Power and Light, the state's main utility. Similarly, he supported George Norris's plans for public power and cheap fertilizer from the Muscle Shoals Dam in Alabama, intimating that Robinson opposed the plan. He also charged that the senator had not been friendly to agriculture by opposing the McNary-Haugen farm bill. In actuality, all of these charges were incorrect. For instance, Campbell did not mention that Robinson received fees only from the cases that he personally tried and never from the utility companies which had been clients of partner Hamilton Moses even before the firm was formed. In addition, Robinson had supported public power at Muscle Shoals as well as the McNary-Haugen plan. After the campaign Campbell admitted that the charges were untrue but that he had been "willing to use any method to get elected."[21]

With little effort but supremely confident, Robinson campaigned successfully for reelection in 1930. From May to early July he stayed in Washington to fight for the London Naval Treaty. But during the last week of July he returned to Arkansas for a few speeches. In general he followed the advice of his brother-in-law and political organizer Grady Miller and ignored his opponent. On August 12, 1930, Robinson received the largest primary victory in state history, garnering 183,627 votes out of 246,649 cast (nearly 75 percent). He was thus assured of reelection because the Democratic nomination in Arkansas was tantamount to victory.[22]

In November 1930, Democrats won majorities in both the House and Senate as the Great Depression soured voters. With a political split between the executive and legislative branches, Robinson, along with seven other congressional Democratic leaders, announced that he would cooperate with Hoover in battling the depression—a decision which would occasionally haunt him. Many people hailed his efforts at first, but soon grumblings began in his own party. In order to pass an unemployment and drought-relief bill, something Hoover had previously opposed, Robinson introduced a sixty-million-dollar compromise proposal which he believed to be better than nothing. Once into the session, however, most Democrats, realizing that, with the progressive Republicans, they held a majority, argued for a larger appropriation of up to one hundred and fifty million dollars. Robinson, however, refused to renege on his agreement with Hoover, thereby causing both consternation and criticism by some of his colleagues. Much of the same reaction happened over direct government "doles" of food. Robinson suggested—and his cohorts agreed to—an amendment for an additional twenty-five million, even though Hoover threatened a veto and another session of Congress to enact relief legislation. Perhaps because Arkansas had been devastated by a severe drought, Robinson quickly compromised with Hoover and supported a twenty-million-dollar proposal.

Many senators, such as Burton Wheeler (D-Montana), argued that eventually they could have forced the greater expenditures, but Robinson stuck by his deal with Hoover, thus alienating fellow Democrats.[23]

Soon thereafter, however, Robinson began to strengthen his relations within the Democratic Party by criticizing the president and by proposing unemployment relief measures. Throughout 1931 and 1932 he never missed an opportunity to assail Hoover's inaction. He ridiculed the White House staff when it tried to "humanize" the president by showing his concern for helpless people, even when he opposed legislation to better their existence. In general he belittled the efforts of the Republicans, taking a more partisan approach, thereby mollifying those who believed he had become "too friendly" with the "enemy." Then in May, he further enhanced his reputation with the progressive wing when he introduced a $2.3-billion public works program which would put people back to work.[24]

But in January 1932, Robinson decided to cooperate with Hoover once again, this time delivering enough Democratic votes to ensure passage of the Reconstruction Finance Corporation (RFC). While disappointed that the measure did not apply directly to farmers or provide money for the most needy, Robinson still believed that it would help alleviate some of the worst aspects of the depression and might avert a catastrophic collapse of many banks. He worked with Speaker of the House John Nance Garner (D-Texas), thereby providing the majority needed to pass the billion-dollar loan agency. As a reward for his support Hoover appointed Arkansas's most famous industrialist and longtime Robinson friend, Harvey Couch, to the seven-member board that would administer the RFC. (Couch had been one of Robinson's chief supporters during his unsuccessful presidential bid in 1924; they remained close friends and "hunting buddies" for the remainder of their lives.)[25]

During this session Robinson also became increasingly irritated by Sen. Huey Long (D-Louisiana) and his flamboyant tirades, especially his personalized attacks against the Democratic leadership. On April 29, 1930, for instance, Long criticized Robinson and other party leaders for working with Hoover (even attending meetings at the White House) instead of passing his "Share-the-Wealth" proposals. He asserted that, if the Democrats should nominate someone as conservative as Robinson for president in 1932, he would "vote for a Farmer-Laborite" or even a

Republican. Waltzing up and down the aisle, mopping his brow with a pink handkerchief, Long dramatically resigned from all Senate committees, since Robinson had appointed him to the posts—he would not be obligated to the Arkansan. Finally he announced that the Democrats in the next few years needed new, more "radical" leadership, different from the "reactionary," nearly Republican Robinson. "We cannot sit here and tell the people that they can swap the devil for a witch."[26]

Robinson, red faced and visibly angry, exploded in reply. He castigated Long for his "comic opera performance" which did "not do justice to the dramatic talents and powers of the great actor from Louisiana." He even sarcastically offered to give the job of minority leader to Long, if his fellow Democrats wanted him to. But most consistently he violently attacked the "Share-the-Wealth" concept as confiscatory, a large leap beyond mere taxation.[27]

On May 3, Long renewed the attack, embarrassing Robinson deeply. He read into the *Congressional Record* a list of corporate clients represented by the law firm of Robinson, House, and Moses, including Arkansas Power and Light, Louisiana Power and Light, and Mississippi Power and Light—the same charges raised by Campbell in the 1930 election. Once more a dismayed Robinson explained he received little money from the firm, and then only for cases he personally tried. But chagrined by the charges, Robinson resigned from the law firm.[28]

The battle between the two continued later in the summer. Long came into Arkansas and directed Hattie Caraway's reelection bid in order to threaten Robinson's strength in the state. (The widow of former senator Thaddeus Caraway, she had been left destitute by the stock market crash, even having her home foreclosed on. The governor had appointed her to fill the position under the assumption that she would not run at the next election.) Long decided to help "the brave little lady"—and help he did! He brought his Louisiana campaign, sound trucks, handbills, band, and all, into Arkansas for a whirlwind, week-long campaign just before the August primary. He stumped the state nonstop, addressing large crowds at each stop—twenty thousand in Pine Bluff and thirty thousand in Little Rock. Surprisingly Caraway defeated six well-known opponents, causing speculation that Long would use this machine to harass and humiliate Robinson in the Senate and to defeat his reelection in 1936.[29]

The election did have some fallout, although not major. Surprisingly,

Robinson was not upset at Caraway's victory, having been a friend of Thaddeus Caraway and having even quietly urged some of his relatives to volunteer in her effort. Because of the large number of candidates who had originally entered the contest, he had not endorsed anyone in the election. His views toward the Louisianan, however, hardened. Until Long's death in 1935, the two would continually tangle in the Senate. Long was also a possible threat to Robinson's reelection in 1936. And in the Senate he would remain the primary obstacle to the Democratic leadership.[30]

As the 1932 presidential election came closer, Robinson became involved in the campaign, although not as actively as in past national efforts. Before the race even began, he surprised many people by withdrawing from presidential consideration. Then at the national convention in Chicago, he refused to endorse a candidate. Yet after the national gathering, he forcefully endorsed Gov. Franklin Delano Roosevelt of New York and even traveled to Hyde Park to confer with him. And although delivering some speeches in behalf of the Democratic ticket, he allowed others to carry the burden of campaigning.[31]

Yet as soon as Roosevelt won the election, Robinson began preparing for the most important and most successful legislative efforts of his career.

11 MAJORITY LEADER

After Franklin Delano Roosevelt's landslide election in November 1932, Democrats began pouring into Washington in hopes of securing presidential appointments. Some came because they had labored in the campaign and expected federal jobs as a reward. Others had served in the Wilson administration and desired to work in government again. Still others, left unemployed by the deepening depression, had little or nothing else to recommend them except their traditional loyalty to the Democratic Party. Trained professionals, such as lawyers, economists, and agriculturalists, descended to accept jobs held by Republicans for the previous twelve years. Even once powerful elected officials were pleading for places in the government.

Cabinet posts were the most important positions, with speculation over who would fill them pervading the capital. In fact, Robinson received serious consideration for secretary of state because of his impeccable qualifications. As one of the highest ranking Democrats on the Foreign Relations Committee, he was a popular choice in the Senate. In addition, he was well known in diplomatic circles. Internationalists and supporters of Wilson would also be pleased; he had fought valiantly for the Versailles treaty as well as for membership in the World Court. And he was popular with many wings of the Democratic Party because of his herculean efforts as the 1928 vice-presidential nominee. But, in the final analysis, the president needed his acumen for passing legislation rather than for negotiating treaties. Roosevelt appointed Sen. Cordell Hull of Tennessee instead.[1]

At the same time, however, it was rumored that the Senate Democrats might replace Robinson as leader. Newly elected William

Gibbs McAdoo (D-California) told Thomas Walsh (D-Montana) that Robinson should be replaced by a more progressive or liberal senator. Others, like Huey Long (D-Louisiana), believed that he would impede rather than speed up New Deal legislation. Capitol gossip even mentioned such possible successors as James Byrnes (D-South Carolina) and Pat Harrison (D-Mississippi).[2]

But the revolt dissipated just as rapidly as it formed. Walsh calmed McAdoo, writing that, "while Joe is by no means quite so progressive as you or I would like . . . he is not a reactionary and goes along with the majority" even when unable to accept "whole-heartedly" their views. Shortly thereafter Byrnes issued a statement to the press (sending a copy to Robinson) that he "was not and would never be a candidate for Robinson's position." Then Harrison, in a speech to the Democratic Club in Washington, "unqualifiedly" endorsed Robinson. Before the caucus voted, Robinson was confident of his reelection. And afterward, he observed that there had "never been any substantial opposition" to him, merely a couple of reporters, who were searching for "something unusual and sensational" even if the story was "untruthful and unreliable."[3]

Once elected Senate majority leader, Robinson personally organized his Democratic colleagues. He received authorization to appoint all committees and their chairmen—a powerful responsibility. Of course, returning members traditionally took their places according to seniority, but Robinson decided what positions the newly elected senators received. And now that the Democratic Party was in the majority, thereby receiving additional assignments, Robinson determined whether a veteran legislator could fill a prized vacancy; many sought such a committee seat (Appropriations, Banking and Currency, Finance, Foreign Relations, and Judiciary). Robinson also served the Democratic caucus as chairman both of the Steering and the Policy committees. When appointing these positions, he "stacked" them with personal supporters, such as Harrison, Byrnes, Henry F. Ashurst (D-Arizona), and Alben Barkley (D-Kentucky), while not overlooking those who had opposed him in the previous session, such as Burton K. Wheeler (D-Montana). To ensure the swift passage of administration measures, Robinson imposed a rule on his Democratic colleagues, over the protests of Huey Long and Edward Costigan (D-Colorado), which bound all members to support any measure that a majority of the caucus endorsed. Previously the caucus only used this rule when a bill received a two-thirds approval. Then, perhaps to guarantee support for Roosevelt's program, or to soothe old hostilities, or even to consolidate his position, Robinson surprised many observers on March 8 by appointing as committee chairmen several members who had followed Long instead of the Democratic leadership less than a month earlier.[4]

While Congress was organizing, President Roosevelt rapidly attacked the banking crisis. On March 9, 1933, with many institutions already closed or teetering on the verge of insolvency, he called a special session of Congress to deal with the emergency as swiftly as possible. Surprising many Congressional leaders with a conservative plan, he proposed speedy action to restore public confidence in the old private-ownership system. Rather than nationalizing the financial institutions as some progressives desired, the administration's bill, if passed, would set the framework for rapidly reopening sound banks, for quickly issuing new Federal Reserve notes, and for immediately ending gold transactions and hoarding. Roosevelt thus confidently believed that Congress would enact his measure promptly, especially after Robinson promised that "the bill will be passed . . . tomorrow."[5]

On March 9, less than an hour after its introduction, the emergency banking bill sailed unanimously through the House. Then came the first test of strength in the Senate where free, open, and sometimes long-winded debates might retard the process. But such was not the case; Robinson saw to that. Shortly after noon, when the Senate convened, he asked for a recess until 1:30 P.M. so that members would have time to receive a copy of the proposed bill (S. 1). When they gathered again, Duncan Fletcher (D-Florida) read S. 1 before sending it to his Banking and Currency Committee. Biding time for several hours until the "hearings" were finished, Robinson, single-minded to the point of being arbitrary, announced that no other legislation would be considered in order to avoid any possible slowdown. (He allowed one exception, however, permitting George Norris [I-Nebraska] to introduce a measure for government operation of the dam at Muscle Shoals, Alabama, for public power production—the forerunner of the Tennessee Valley Authority.) When the banking bill came back to the floor that same afternoon, the only serious opposition came from Huey Long, who demanded that state banks be included as members of the Federal Reserve. At first Robinson tried to defuse this amendment by explaining that state banks could apply for inclusion in the Federal Reserve, if they so desired and were financially sound. But when Long continued to press the issue, Robinson accused him of trying "to pinprick a great measure" with unnecessary additions. He then called for the vote, decisively defeating the amendment. Shortly thereafter the emergency banking bill passed seventy-three to seven without any changes—and in less than eight hours.[6]

Continuing this rapid pace for Congress, Roosevelt presented an austere measure "to Maintain the Credit of the United States" (S. 233) on March 10, which was designed to cut $500 million from the budget. Robinson, after introducing the measure for the president, once again escorted New Deal legislation quickly through the Senate. Sending the spending-cut bill to Harrison's Finance Committee, Robinson ensured that the measure would be brought to the floor rapidly and without substantive changes, especially since the chairman planned to hear opponents of the measure "only briefly." Two days later, on March 13, the economy bill reached the Senate floor. As in the past, spokesmen for the veterans railed against the "slaughter of the disabled servicemen," but with no success. Because of their failure, American Legion spokesmen offered to accept an across-the-board 25 percent cut in benefits. But Robinson, realizing that a compromise was unnecessary, informed the president that he had "enough votes" to push through the original proposal. At a little past 9:00 P.M. on March 15, the Senate approved the measure by a vote of sixty-two to thirteen.[7]

While the Economy Act was still under consideration, Robinson won several small skirmishes which resulted in another victory for the administration. On March 14 he introduced a bill (S. 320) which would allow state-chartered financial institutions to borrow money from the Federal Reserve banks if state banking commissioners certified them as "sound." He quickly voted down an all-inclusive amendment, which would enable any state bank, even without proof of solvency, to receive Federal Reserve loans. Then within fifteen minutes he passed the so-called "Robinson bill."[8]

The fight continued after the House passed a much different measure (H.R. 3757). Robinson thus had to stifle new amendments when the Senate reconsidered the bill on March 22. For instance, Huey Long proposed that a bank, which borrowed from the RFC, must receive money equal to 90 percent of the collateral used to back the loan—even if the bank did not ask for that much. Alva Adams (D-Colorado) also tried to remove the provision of the original bill that required a thorough examination of banks applying for loans. After Robinson nixed both efforts, the Senate ratified the measure. The House quickly approved the amendments, and Roosevelt signed the bill into law.[9]

At the same time, Roosevelt sent Congress a proposal to relieve unemployment. On March 21 Robinson and Robert Wagner (D-New York) introduced a bill establishing the Civilian Conservation Corps (CCC), an army-like public works organization for unemployed young men. On March 27, after "extensive hearings" (at least for legislation during Roosevelt's first one-hundred days), David Walsh (D-Massachusetts) reported the Robinson-Wagner bill out of the Education and Labor Committee with several substantive, but nonbinding, changes. The committee members dropped a thirty-dollars-per-month maximum wage as well as an involuntary salary allotment to dependents because of objections by organized labor. They also deleted provisions concerning the reforestation of any land not in the public domain. And they eliminated provisions dealing with military organization and regimentation. But, after removing such guidelines, the committee gave the president broad discretionary powers to reinstate any of the previous regulations.[10]

Even with Senator Walsh directing the floor fight, Robinson rebutted criticisms, answered questions, and defended the program. In order to finance the CCC, Roosevelt proposed transferring $140 million from already appropriated public works projects, which were still in the planning stages; therefore, many senators feared that, once the money was given to the CCC, then river and harbor improvements as well as other local projects would not be funded again. Robinson assured his colleagues that, by summer, the president would reappropriate all the money previously allocated. James M. Couzens (R-Michigan) then suggested that the government should house 88,000 young men in army camps without any work projects for the much more reasonable cost of $14–15 million. Robinson decried this proposal, arguing that the CCC might be the most beneficial legislation of the session, since it took unemployed young men, the most obvious targets of "subversives" (communists and fascists) and put them to work, giving them self-worth and pride. Because of his forceful direction, the Senate passed the measure on March 28; the House then passed the Robinson-Wagner bill the next day with several minor amendments. And on March 30 the Senate also approved such changes and sent the legislation to the president.[11]

Perhaps the greatest challenge for Robinson was pushing through the president's farm policy. Roosevelt had called agrarian leaders to Washington to decide the method to pursue. From this meeting came the basis for the Agricultural Adjustment Act (H.R. 3835)—a complicated and experimental omnibus farm bill—which he proposed on March 16, 1933. In Title I the government first agreed to lease prime land, perhaps as much as fifty or sixty million acres, and then to take it out of production. The plan also promised to pay much higher prices to those participating in the program. To provide compensation for the rented land and higher prices, the secretary of agriculture would collect a tax on commodity processors by issuing licenses to those engaged in interstate or foreign commerce with agricultural products; anyone operating without a permit could be fined up to one thousand dollars a day. The measure even allowed the secretary to make necessary regulations "with the force and effect of law," without congressional approval as well as employ any necessary personnel "without regard to the civil service law."[12]

In addition, Title II of the legislation, having been introduced earlier as the Emergency Farm Mortgage Act (S. 1110) by Robinson and Wagner and then incorporated into the Agricultural Adjustment Act, addressed the problems of farm mortgages. First it allowed the federal land banks to issue up to $2 billion in bonds to make new mortgages or refinance old ones—at lower interest rates not to exceed 4½ percent. Borrowers would not be required to pay installments on mortgage principals for five years and government-financed, five-year extensions were authorized for both old and new "deserving" borrowers. The measure also provided for the gradual liquidation of joint-stock land banks, most of which were nearly insolvent or already bankrupt. Through RFC loans the act allocated $100 million at a relatively low 4 percent interest rate to the struggling banks. But these institutions, before receiving the money, had to agree to reduce all mortgage rates to a maximum 5 percent and not to foreclose on any mortgages for two years "except in unavoidable circumstances." The bill permitted farmers to borrow $200 million directly from the federal land banks in amounts of $5,000 or less. Finally, the measure allowed the RFC to lend up to $50 million to districts for irrigation, drainage, and levee projects or to refinance their debts.[13]

On April 5, 1933, after nearly two weeks in committee, the Agricultural Adjustment Act reached the floor of the Senate. Robinson decided to direct the floor fight, since Agriculture and Forestry Committee chairman E. D. "Cotton Ed" Smith opposed many of the administration proposals. On April 7 he defended each provision of the bill. He railed against economists, who urged Congress to let the marketplace make any necessary readjustments, as "do-nothings . . . hopelessly impractical theorists posing as hardheaded, practical men." Instead, he loudly admonished fellow senators to abide by the "mandate" of the people and pass the measure in order to "jar the nation loose from the iron grip" of the depression. Robinson, while admitting that the bill might "not prove effective," argued that some action must be taken to save American agriculture. He explained that falling agricultural prices, combined with the relative inflexibility of industrial prices, acted as a "double-barrelled shotgun" with the "load from both barrels . . . lodge[d] in the farmer." In other words, agricultural prices fell much faster than industrial ones; therefore, the farmer received much less for his goods, yet paid substantially the same for such necessary items as fertilizer, clothing, shoes, automobiles, and gasoline. And finally Robinson reassured fellow senators representing urban areas that higher prices would be "reached step by step" in order to prepare the consumer for higher food prices.[14]

For the next three weeks the Senate vehemently debated the agriculture bill, sometimes five to seven hours a day, with Robinson struggling to push Roosevelt's proposal to passage. Senator Norris opposed the administration in the first skirmish, endorsing a committee amendment which allowed Secretary of Agriculture Henry Wallace to guarantee farmers their "cost of production." Robinson retorted that the radical Norris-Farmers' Union proposal would be too difficult to administer and that expenses would be too hard to determine. Even a fervent Wallace letter, denouncing the cost of production amendment, could not defeat it. The administration and Robinson lost forty-seven to forty-one. (But the conference committee, as Robinson quietly predicted, later deleted the guaranteed cost of production clause.) He then defeated several other amendments meant to weaken the bill, even when it meant opposing Agriculture and Forestry Committee chair Smith.[15]

After some initial losses, Robinson eventually won the next combat over which commodities would be declared "essential" and thereby guaranteed price supports. Carter Glass (D-Virginia) and Josiah Bailey (D-North Carolina) urged the inclusion of peanuts—even though both men opposed the bill and eventually voted against it. Robinson became enraged at the "inconsistency" of senators fighting this measure at every turn and at the same time trying to help their home states by including products native to their region. He suffered a temporary defeat when both peanuts and, shortly thereafter, sugar were added. But he regained control when the Senate defeated a motion by Senator Wheeler to add flax (32–48). Robinson then carefully orchestrated the removal of the two earlier provisions, showing both his legislative power and political prowess. Sen. James B. Frazier (D-North Dakota) moved to reconsider the vote on peanuts. Glass objected, stating that Frazier had voted against the measure and could not, under the rules of the Senate, make that motion. Robinson, however, by quickly using a parliamentary sidestep, insisted that, since no recorded vote had been taken, anyone could move to reconsider the amendment. Augustine Lonergan (D-Connecticut), the presiding officer at that time, upheld him. Glass then moved to table Frazier's motion. When the roll call was taken, the vote was a thirty-eight to thirty-eight tie. William Gibbs McAdoo (D-California) then tried to change his vote and side with Glass. But Vice-President John Nance Garner called him out of order and ruled that the motion had failed. A few moments later the Senate voted to remove peanuts from the essential commodities list by a close forty-one to thirty-nine vote.[16]

Even with the majority leader again firmly in control, the senators assailed the Emergency Farm Mortgage Act (Title II of the Agricultural Adjustment Act) from both the right and the left. But Robinson won every skirmish. First, the venerable author of the Federal Reserve Act, Carter Glass, attacked a proposal to force reserve banks to accept devalued federal land-bank bonds as collateral on fifteen-day loans. Fearing that it would undermine the stability of the reserve system, he pleaded with his colleagues to defeat the motion. He soon realized, however, that the votes were not going to change, then was overheard to mutter that he had been "so much disposed to yield to the Senator from Arkansas that I sometimes begin to think that I have not any mind of my own left." Once again Robinson's proposal was approved. Then from the left, Farmer-Laborite Henrick Shipstead of Minnesota suggested that any profit that the joint-stock land banks made during the liquidation period should be split pro rata among its borrowers. But Robinson opposed this amendment, arguing that it would force some of the banks into receivership and would cause courts to foreclose on farmers whose mortgages were held by the joint-stock land banks. After a heated debate, he defeated the Shipstead amendment without even a roll call vote. On April 14, 1933, the Senate approved the Emergency Farm Mortgage Act (Title II).[17]

But a new and larger battle soon erupted, this time over inflation. As late as the morning of April 17, 1933, Roosevelt still believed that a massive expansion of the currency was avoidable, especially since such a proposal had garnered only eighteen votes the previous January. Yet that afternoon Sen. Burton Wheeler (D-Montana) almost passed an amendment for the free coinage of silver at a ratio of sixteen to one. The measure garnered thirty-three votes, only sixteen shy of the number needed for ratification. And, according to assistant secretary of state and presidential advisor Raymond Moley, several senators—more than enough to give the inflationists a majority—had told him that they would support some type of expansionist legislation before the bill was completed. Robinson only temporarily put down the insurrection by informing silverite William E. Borah (R-Idaho) the president would veto the entire agriculture bill if the silver plan were adopted. Borah and several others therefore voted against the Wheeler amendment.[18]

Because of the strength and determination of the inflationists, Roosevelt decided two days later to support a less objectionable proposal authored by Sen. Elmer Thomas (D-Oklahoma), which would be added to the AAA—the Farm Relief and Inflation bill. And no wonder! The president would receive vast and unheralded power over the fiscal policies of the country. He would have authority to persuade the Federal Reserve banks to buy Treasury bills and other government obligations in an amount not to exceed $3 billion. He could then issue up to $3 billion in greenbacks in order to retire government obligations. Or, if necessary, he could reduce the gold content of the dollar up to 50 percent. And he could accept up to $100 million in silver as payment from foreign debtors (with silver not to exceed fifty cents per ounce). The president, however, had discretionary, rather than mandatory, powers.[19]

Once inflation became an issue on April 17, Republicans and

conservative Democrats in the Senate worked desperately to delay the entire agricultural bill as long as possible; but Robinson foiled every attempt. On several occasions he tried to limit debate through a unanimous-consent vote, but someone always objected, thereby causing up to an hour delay while he was urging a recalcitrant senator to withdraw his resistance. By April 21 enough rumors of a slowdown pervaded the cloakrooms that Robinson doggedly declared that no filibuster would be tolerated, since the president wanted action taken "as soon as practicable." But the majority leader did not convince opponents to end their dilatory tactics until April 26 after he threatened to hold late-night and early-morning sessions unless the debate was limited.[20]

On April 27, Robinson decisively defeated one last Fabian attempt to derail the agricultural proposal, when Arthur Robinson (R-Indiana) introduced an amendment to pay the veterans' bonus as a part of the inflation package. (The Indianan did not really favor paying ex-soldiers but, instead, was trying to make the AAA as unpalatable as possible in hopes of beating the bill.) Late in the day the majority leader took the floor in a heated response to all those who favored the bonus—even if it meant the defeat of the agriculture bill. He castigated the veterans for their heavy-handed lobbying. Then he attacked some of his colleagues who were threatening other senators with political defeat if they did not vote for the package. He also announced that since Roosevelt "strongly opposed" the plan, if it were enacted in its proposed discretionary form, the president would not distribute it. While at this fever pitch, Robinson even attacked Huey Long, who had been lamenting the poor state of veterans. Reminding his colleagues (though really speaking to the galleries) that the "Kingfish" often quoted scripture in his harangues, he announced, with a smirk, that he had finally found a verse appropriate for the Louisianan: "How long shall the words of thy mouth be like a strong wind." (The crowds roared with laughter.)[21]

A few moments later Robinson's arduous efforts came to a successful climax. First the senators defeated the bonus proposal by a sixty to twenty-eight vote. A little later in the day they passed—by an even wider margin (64–21)—the Thomas amendment, thereby giving the president the option of inflating the currency. Finally that afternoon the completed bill passed sixty-four to twenty, with only four Democrats voting against it.[22]

Robinson shepherded other administration measures through the Senate. In most instances he allowed the appropriate committee chairmen to direct the floor battles, but when a measure appeared on the brink of defeat, Robinson would lead the fight. For instance, early in April when Hugo Black (D-Alabama) pushed a thirty-hour-work-week bill through the Senate, Robinson proposed raising the hours to thirty-six. When that ploy failed, he tied the measure up in the Senate, keeping it there for "reconsideration," until mid-April when the House passed the National Industrial Recovery Act instead. And hence, on May 2, he confidently announced that the thirty-hour-work-week bill was no longer "in the picture." Again, later in May he had to save the administration's Truth-in-Securities bill. The Senate had passed an early version, which the White House "dumped" while it was being considered in the House, adopting instead a more strenuous version written by House Interstate and Foreign Commerce chairman Sam Rayburn (D-Texas). Yet many senators favored the original proposal and did not desire a change. "With a remarkable exercise of parliamentary skill," Raymond Moley observed, Robinson and James Byrnes appeased their colleagues while accomplishing the president's agenda. When the House approved its version and sent the Truth-in-Securities legislation to a conference committee, the Rayburn bill was adopted and then approved by the entire Senate, just as Robinson had quietly predicted during the floor fight.[23]

Even when not playing a major role in passing New Deal legislation, Robinson always supported the president—once more underscoring his deep loyalty to the Democratic Party. In the Senate he introduced measures that became the Federal Emergency Relief Act, the Home Owners Loan Act, the Work Relief Act (Title II of the National Industrial Recovery Act, which created the Public Works Administration), and the Railroad Coordination Act. He also endorsed the Tennessee Valley Authority Act, the Glass-Steagall Banking Act, and the Farm Credit Act. He voted with the administration more consistently than any other senator.[24]

Throughout the first one hundred days of the Roosevelt administration, Robinson deftly directed the president's program through the Senate labyrinth, his efforts definitely leading to the success of the New Deal. When speed was necessary, he pushed relentlessly, as in the case of the Emergency Banking Act, which was passed in seven and one-half hours. When colleagues worried that previous work might be undone by the proposals as in the CCC, Robinson reassured them, thereby winning their votes. But when the president needed more time to draft alternative legislation, Robinson slowed down or, if necessary, scuttled measures, such as the Black thirty-hour-work-week bill. If subtlety was required to appease the feelings of his colleagues, he used parliamentary maneuvers, especially in the passage of the Truth-in-Securities Act. And, on occasion, he even opposed fellow Democrats, whom he felt were slowing down needed reforms, and took over the floor leadership when committee chairmen were lukewarm, as in the battle for the AAA.

After the session Robinson returned to Arkansas then left for an extended trip to Europe in order to rest and recuperate. Near exhaustion from his nonstop exertion on behalf of the president, he apparently wanted to escape the glare of the press as well as the concern by his family. In mid-August 1933, he wrote to Roosevelt, stating that he had canceled plans to make an "elaborate campaign" for the NRA and that "upon advice of physicians [would] refrain from making any speeches in the immediate future." He and Billie then left the United States for Europe. Except for a letter (dated September 11, 1933) from Sen. Bronson Cutting (R-New Mexico) no mention about the trip occurred. But Robinson, according to Cutting, had suffered "a complete nervous breakdown and looks old and rather ghastly." His sister-in-law, Mrs. Grady Miller, years later remembered that he had been greatly fatigued, but she never heard about a collapse. She speculated, however, that if Robinson had experienced a dramatic decline, both he and Billie would have kept it a secret, even from the family. No other family members had ever heard about any physical trouble; however, they were not surprised, because he had been so tired during and after the session. In any case, upon returning from Europe in the fall 1933, he was refreshed as well as rejuvenated and was prepared for more legislative challenges. And those challenges would surely come.[25]

12 LEGISLATIVE LEADER

Throughout the rest of Roosevelt's first term, Robinson consistently supported New Deal legislation. But after the first one hundred days, he allowed his committee chairmen to lead the floor battles, usually barreling into the middle of a fight only when a bill seemed destined for defeat. In addition, he often spoke for the administration, attacking opponents across the political spectrum. When Huey Long or Father Charles Coughlin of Detroit raised the ire of workers, Robinson would take to the radio waves. Or when Al Smith attacked Roosevelt for espousing "communist" doctrines, Robinson responded. Yet, except for a few important instances, he stayed out of the limelight.

One of Robinson's most heroic fights, however, was for the United States to join the World Court, an independent body established in 1922 by the League of Nations to promote peaceful arbitration between nations. The World Court included more than forty nations—but not the United States. By January 1935, however, many Americans favored joining the organization. Presidents Warren Harding, Calvin Coolidge, Herbert Hoover, and Franklin Roosevelt had urged the United States to participate. In 1932 Republican and Democratic party platforms had recommended entering the tribunal. Many religious organizations, including the American Unitarian Association, the General Convention of the Protestant Episcopal Church, the Reorganized Church of Jesus Christ of Latter Day Saints, and the Southern Baptist Convention, had endorsed it. And such varied civic, business, and professional organizations as the National League of Women Voters, the U.S. Chamber of Commerce, and the American Bar Association had also espoused membership.[1]

Roosevelt, although having long advocated joining the World Court, did not press the issue until late in 1934. On December 28 he instructed Secretary of State Cordell Hull to prepare the basic legislation. The president then tried unsuccessfully to persuade Foreign Relations Committee chairman Key Pittman (D-Nevada) to lead the battle. (Pittman had been ambivalent about the treaty for several years.) Roosevelt next turned to Robinson, who readily accepted the task.[2]

At a strategy conference on January 5, 1935, Robinson advised the president of the bill's probability for passage. He had already contacted Minority Leader Charles McNary (R-Oregon) to determine the extent of opposition; only eight to ten Republicans appeared ready to fight the proposal. His own poll showed that only seven or eight Democrats disapproved of the treaty. Still, many were undecided, waiting "to see," Robinson quaintly asserted, "which way the cat was going to jump." As a consequence, opponents had not yet mustered the necessary one-third vote to block passage. With this encouraging information, the president instructed the Foreign Relations Committee chairman to report out the proposal. Surprising to no one, the committee passed it fourteen to seven.[3]

On January 15, 1935, Robinson opened the Senate debate, suggesting that "probably no subject has been so clouded" by its opponents. Some argued that, upon joining the World Court, the United States would be forced to send troops to different areas of the world in order to buttress failing empires. Others complained that, without prior Senate approval, the tribunal would rule on issues affecting the nation, causing a loss of American sovereignty in foreign affairs. Still others carped that the court was little more than a subterfuge by which the United States would join the League of Nations.[4]

Robinson methodically rebutted these arguments. He pointed out that the United States was powerless to stop the World Court from rendering decisions and issuing opinions that dealt with American interests, until it joined. While admitting that some advocates overstated the advantages that could reasonably be expected, Robinson castigated opponents who had "conjured up in their imagination disastrous results" that could never come, such as sending troops around the world without congressional support. The "sole specific obligation" to be incurred by the United States, he assured his fellow senators, was partial payment of the court's expenses, but only with the consent of Congress. At one point in the debate he called the opposition "sponges" who preferred that the nation use the organization without joining it. Indeed, he asked, did any senator want the nation to be a "parasitical dependent?" Members would be "surprised," he asserted, "at the thoughtfulness, the tolerance, and the impartiality" embodied in the World Court statutes—if they bothered to read them; for no one had yet devised a better plan for the "advancement of . . . peace."[5]

The opposition quickly retorted, using a shotgun approach—attacking widely, in the hope that one or more of their reasons might do serious damage. First, long-time isolationist Hiram Johnson (R-California) spewed forth a venomous attack on the proposal. Joining the court would lead the United States to "meddle and muddle" in European affairs. "Easy is the descent into hell," he argued, since membership in the World Court would be the "first step" toward the League of Nations. In addition, why should the United States allow "mooching" countries to dominate it? By not paying their obligations, they had defaulted their right to judge others. Huey Long (D-Louisiana) agreed wholeheartedly, insisting that the World Court was merely a "branch office" of the League. And as such, it could entangle the nation in another, distant war. Even more disturbing, according to Long, was that joining the court could abrogate the Monroe Doctrine. What would stop the tribunal from invalidating American treaties? In fact, Long asserted, the court was just a political body, reflecting the foreign policy desires of each nation and, therefore, unable to make a "fair ruling" in behalf of the United States.[6]

In the midst of this heated rhetoric, Robinson struggled, finally successfully, to end the debate. Opposition senators often put forth arguments which were spurious or "sheer nonsense," but any excuse was significant enough to prolong the controversy. Sensing the slowdown, Robinson pressed for a vote, since both sides had already discussed the topic thoroughly. Yet each time he proposed to limit the discussion, Johnson would object. Finally, after two days of negotiations, Robinson won, convincing the opposition to limit debate on Monday, January 28.[7]

As the vote approached, the opposition senators changed their tactics; instead of fighting to defeat the measure, they tried to emasculate it through amendments. If even one substantive change was made, then the United States's membership would have to be reapproved by every member of the World Court—an uncertain prospect at best. Each of these reservations was, therefore, potentially damaging. For instance,

Arthur Vandenberg (R-Michigan) proposed guaranteeing that the United States should not become involved in internal or political questions of foreign countries. His amendment pledged the nation to a vaguely worded "traditional policy," without relinquishing any authority over American issues. Assistant Secretary of State John Dickey sent Robinson a confidential memorandum outlining ten objections to the Vandenberg reservation. He maintained that the president did not want to follow such "traditional policies" as "dollar diplomacy" and "intervention." More importantly, he argued, the inclusion of this reservation might cause one of the Latin American countries to object to the treaty, thus dooming it. Yet, on January 24, Robinson finally had to accept this amendment, as the only method of gaining needed votes.[8]

Several other senators also offered amendments to weaken the original measure, but Robinson spearheaded the fight to defeat each of them. First, George Norris (I-Nebraska) proposed that the tribunal submit any dispute involving the United States to the Senate, which, in turn, would have to approve by a two-thirds vote. Robinson condemned this amendment, deeming it "subversive" to the purpose of joining the court. The majority leader won, but by a closer margin than expected, forty-seven to thirty-seven—a number of votes short of the necessary two-thirds majority. Next, Huey Long submitted a reservation which withdrew World Court jurisdiction over anything involving the Monroe Doctrine. Once again Robinson urged his colleagues to vote down the amendment, stating that it would condemn the treaty to failure in Latin America. By another close vote, forty-six to thirty-five, he prevailed.[9]

When Congress adjourned for the weekend of January 25–27, 1935, many political pundits still predicted that the treaty would be ratified early the next week. The opposition outside of Congress, however, used this time well to make one last, herculean effort to defeat the bill. The Hearst newspapers had daily lambasted joining the tribunal as another method of unnecessarily involving the country in European affairs. Humorist Will Rogers had also ridiculed the measure as worthless. Both now redoubled their efforts. And Father Charles E. Coughlin made an impassioned plea in his weekly radio address. In a Sunday sermon on January 27, entitled "The Menace of the World Court," he assailed the treaty for entangling the United States in Europe's conflicts. He therefore urged all of his listeners to telegram their senators immediately and voice their objections to the bill. Within hours messages deluged the desks of senators. Various estimates on the number of negative letters and telegrams sent to Washington over the weekend ranged from 50,000 to over 200,000.[10]

When Congress reconvened on January 28, 1935, the senators bowed to concerted public pressure. Although the majority followed Robinson's lead on several amendments, either accepting or rejecting them as he instructed, the votes were close. Then the next day, the Senate refused to approve the World Court by the necessary two-thirds approval. Even though Robinson had a plurality of sixteen, fifty-two to thirty-six, he fell seven votes short. Less than a week earlier most people believed the measure would pass, although with some difficulty. Although disappointed and perhaps a little stunned, Robinson pointed out that at no time had he received enough pledges to ensure passage of the bill. In the final vote most of the undecided senators voted against the measure.[11]

Robinson agonized over the defeat. After the final vote he stayed in the Senate chamber, head down on his desk, until the cleaning lady entered the room and asked if he was ill. Slowly he gathered his papers and left. Nearly twenty years of arduous efforts for internationalism had still been unsuccessful in bringing the United States into any global organizations. In addition, he had lost his first important battle as majority leader.[12]

Over the next week Robinson received a myriad of letters and telegrams thanking him for his efforts. Secretary of State Cordell Hull expressed his appreciation. Assistant Secretary of State Dickey, who worked most closely with Robinson on the measure, also commended his leadership, calling him "a general who is an army unto himself." The most meaningful statement, however, came from the president, who asked Robinson to thank all who had voted for the measure. And then concerning the thirty-six who had opposed joining the World Court, Roosevelt wrote: "I am inclined to think that if they ever get to Heaven they will be doing a great deal of apologizing for a very long time—that is if God is against war—and I think he is."[13]

After the World Court battle, Congress drifted, waiting for Roosevelt to chart new initiatives. The president did not present any important reform measures, however, until near the end of the session, after the

Supreme Court declared the NIRA unconstitutional on May 27, 1935. He then unleashed some of the most visionary reforms of the New Deal. For instance, the president drove bills through Congress establishing social security, the Rural Electrification Administration, and the Resettlement Administration (to move farmers from unproductive soil to better locations). In addition he pushed through the Wealth Tax Act (with estate and gift taxes, a higher surtax on large incomes, and an excess profits tax for business), the Wheeler-Rayburn Act (to liquidate superfluous utility holding companies), and the Wagner Act (to create the National Labor Relations Board).[14]

Throughout this "second" one hundred days in 1935 Robinson loyally supported the president, often speaking for New Deal proposals before Congress, over the radio, and to the press. Yet unlike much of the legislation of 1933 and the World Court fray, he allowed his lieutenants to lead the fight, content to control the flow of legislation to the Senate floor. Whenever a problem erupted, Robinson resolved it with relative ease. In general, however, he rarely had to take control, since the Democrats held an enormous majority and most progressive Republicans joined them in fighting for reforms. Robinson, although occasionally having to deal with a recalcitrant southern Democrat, had a much easier time during this session than in the 1933 Congress.[15]

When the Supreme Court declared the NIRA unconstitutional on May 27, 1935, immediately invalidating all NRA codes, many people in Washington began scrambling to restore some of the overturned government regulations. One of the most successful in these efforts was H. B. Teegarden, general counsel of the United States Wholesale Grocers' Association. Even before the court decision, he had prepared a bill to re-enact protections for small retailers. His proposal would amend section two of the Clayton Act in order to end price discrimination. He had also been making contacts with legislators who, he believed, would aid small businessmen. Early in June 1935, therefore, he persuaded Representative Wright Patman (D-Texas) to introduce the bill (H.R. 8442) in the House. And fifteen days later, on June 26, Robinson submitted it (S. 3154) to the Senate.[16]

The Robinson-Patman bill proposed several means of lessening the unfair advantages used by chain stores against independents. First, it outlawed price discrimination among "purchasers of commodities of like grade and quality" if that preference "substantially . . . lessen[ed] competition or tend[ed] to create a monopoly." It allowed the Federal Trade Commission to present a *prima facie* case, thus requiring manufacturers and retailers to prove their innocence if more than one price was used for an item. It also prohibited giving any buyer "brokerage fees" unless that retailer performed commensurate services such as warehousing. And it outlawed special allowances to (usually large) retailers for advertising and other sales-promotional services, especially since chain stores often used such "rebates" to lower their prices instead of publicizing the manufacturer's product. Since the bill banned retailers from "induc[ing] or receiv[ing] a discrimination in price," buyers were now liable along with sellers.[17]

The Robinson-Patman bill became sidetracked by the second hundred days push in 1935, because Roosevelt concentrated on other legislation. But the battle would continue during the second session of the Seventy-fourth Congress in January 1936. While the House panel held extensive, often acrimonious, hearings on the proposal, the Senate, under Robinson's prodding, sped the legislation through. On February 3, 1936, citing the wealth of information produced by the House investigation and the Federal Trade Commission Report of 1934, the Senate subcommittee quickly reported the bill out—without even holding any formal examinations. Aware that the full Judiciary Committee would not grant them a forum, many businessmen bitterly criticized the senators for "railroading" the measure. Even Robinson's close friend and former law partner Hamilton Moses of Little Rock telegraphed him, complaining about the rapid pace at which the bill was progressing. But Robinson was determined to pass it quickly, replying that "there will be no undue delay if I can help it." The Judiciary Committee then approved S. 3154 on March 9.[18]

Chain store operators then began a counteroffensive. They realized that some measure designed to end price discrimination would pass, but a less stringent Senate version, the Borah-Van Nuys bill, was more acceptable. Introduced by Senators William E. Borah (R-Idaho) and Frederick Van Nuys (D-Indiana), it levied punitive damages—a fine not to exceed five thousand dollars and a jail term of not more than one year—for price discrimination. But because of vague wording, enforcement would be difficult. The Senate Judiciary Committee hearings on the legislative draft turned into a forum against the Robinson-Patman bill, giving many businessmen the opportunity to voice their objections. At the same time the Institute of Distribution waged a campaign to defeat it. Labeling both bills a "devious and thoroughly camouflaged effort to favor a small group," the institute asserted that the Robinson-Patman measure not only weakened the Clayton Act but was "anti-consumer, anti-farmer, anti-labor." In another pamphlet—"The 28 Questions . . . And Their Answers!"—the institute asked extreme absurdities such as: "If a grocer gives a stick of candy to a customer's child . . . is he subject to damages if he does not give . . . candy to every child who comes in his store?" Apparently no ploy was too ridiculous to be used in fighting the measure.[19]

Soon thereafter the drama moved to the Senate floor, where Robinson deftly directed the participants. On Thursday, April 30, in order to speed up debate, he offered fellow senators a rare Friday-to-Monday recess if they passed the bill immediately. Then, as they submitted amendments one by one, if Robinson approved, he added them to the bill. Arthur Vandenberg (R-Michigan) offered a change exempting goods to be used in further manufacture. At first Robinson rejected the amendment. But seeing the potential danger of a filibuster or other dilatory tactics, he allowed it, predicting that conference committee members would remove it. To stymie any further opposition, Robinson allowed the entire Borah-Van Nuys measure to be attached as a final section to his proposal, which then passed on a voice vote.[20]

After the House approved H.R. 8442 on May 28, 1936, a conference committee assimilated the differences in the two measures, cutting out all of the unwanted amendments just as Robinson had predicted. The victory was at hand. The House passed the measure on June 15, when the conference committee presented its report. Three days later the bill sailed through the Senate, and, on June 19, president Roosevelt signed the legislation over the objections of some businessmen and congressmen led by Rep. Emanuel Celler (D-New York).[21]

Robinson was proud of the finished measure, envisioning it as a great help to small businesses. He thought the law was enough "anti-Monopoly . . . to give protection to independent dealers against unjust methods." And since he believed that small businesses and widespread competition were basic to a healthy nation, he argued that both should be preserved—by the government if necessary. Immediately after the legislation passed, Robinson summed up his reasons for sponsoring it: "I have long been a believer in the philosophy that the chief function of government is to protect the weak against the strong." And, he confidently predicted, the Robinson-Patman Act would do just that.[22]

Throughout this time Robinson continued to defend the New Deal from left- and right-wing attacks. For instance, he assailed both Huey Long's Share Our Wealth Plan and Dr. Francis Townsend's "Old Age Pension Bill" for their radical schemes. In a speech entitled "Gilded Gateways to Economic Paradise," he belittled both programs as irresponsible and irrational. New Dealers reprinted and widely distributed his speech as an answer to the radicals. Later he also became one of the chief spokesmen against Liberty League members who labeled Roosevelt a "socialist." For instance, he sarcastically ridiculed former Democratic National Executive Committee chairman Jouett Shouse, comparing him to the "wealthy du Pont brothers." In a mocking tone Robinson admitted that what he thought were humane relief measures must, instead, be "undermining the moral fiber of children," as Shouse suggested. Still, he could not see the harm caused by "repairing damaged shoes" when it was "ten degrees below zero." And later when Liberty Leaguers attacked the president's budget, he responded that if Roosevelt had recited the Ten Commandments they would have "accused him of plagiarism and . . . found some ulterior motive for his quoting the Decalogue."[23]

Robinson saved his angriest criticisms, however, for former Democratic presidential candidate Al Smith, who on January 23, 1936, castigated Roosevelt as a Socialist during a speech to the Liberty League; and he could be particularly effective since he had been Smith's running mate in 1928. Over a nationwide radio hookup later that week, Robinson responded for the administration, attacking Smith for betraying the principles for which he stood when running for president. In fact, he answered Smith by quoting from previous speeches of the former New York governor in 1928. In conclusion he bemoaned Smith's newly found, haughty, pretentious attitude, signified by exchanging his "brown derby for a top hat." (Because of the success of the speech, the White House sent out innumerable copies over the next several months.)[24]

Robinson also focused on an especially large problem in the cotton plantations of northeast Arkansas, that of farm tenancy. In 1936 violence erupted in Crittenden, Cross, and St. Francis counties (near Memphis) between the landless farmers and the plantation owners. The Southern Tenant Farmers' Union (STFU) was organizing the underpaid, overworked, and abused day laborers in order to double the daily wage from 75 cents per twelve-to-fourteen-hour day to $1.50 per ten-hour workday. The owners, supposedly just eking out a living in tough times, refused, resorting to violence to win the argument. Nightriders—unknown or masked men who intimidated through threats and violence—frightened the uneducated farmhands, while bullies brutalized any "agitators" with "floggings," beatings, and threats of lynchings. In addition, peaceful meetings and marches were broken up and the basic civil rights of the tenant farmers denied. In fact, this intimidation and violence had been going on for over a year.[25]

Norman Thomas of New York, the Socialist Party presidential candidate in 1928 and 1932, wrote to the president, outlining these grievances. Then at FDR's request, a special agent from the Justice Department investigated and came up with mixed conclusions about the incidents. He researched the complaints of kidnapping, mail fraud, and peonage, then concluded that no federal laws had been violated, although state laws concerning assault and false imprisonment obviously had been broken—even by elected officials. In general, however, he found few problems (besides the low wages and harsh conditions existing throughout the South) among tenants in Arkansas, except in the three counties where the STFU was strongest and where the landowners were fiercely fighting the union.[26]

In response to an inquiry from Mrs. Roosevelt, Robinson found himself in the unpleasant—indeed impossible—position of rationalizing the "mean things happening" in Arkansas. In a seven-page letter, he delineated the problem and feebly, even spuriously, defended the landlords. He asserted that most of the trouble was orchestrated by "outside agitators"; yet the organizer, H. L. Mitchell, who was originally from western Tennessee and had lived in Arkansas for several years, could hardly be classified an "outsider." He then charged that the union often bilked the poor out of large amounts of money, a false charge. In a moment of supreme understatement, he argued that only a small amount of violence had occurred, but that the events had been exaggerated by the press. He further stated that observers from "New York" (such as Thomas) who did not know the people or the problems were wasting their time in Arkansas when many problems still needed to be settled in their native state.[27]

Although portrayed by the STFU as "Greasy Joe" and its "nemesis," Robinson stated that he was not indifferent to the plight of sharecroppers and tenant farmers. He had grown up on a farm and sympathized with their hardships. He proudly pointed out that he had supported the Bankhead-Jones Farm Tenancy Act, which, if passed in the next session of Congress, would set aside $500 million to enable sharecroppers and tenants to buy their own farms. Even the next year he was still so upset by a proposed story in *Fortune* stating that he opposed the sharecroppers, that he castigated author Archibald MacLeish for not mentioning his role in the Bankhead bill.[28]

Shortly thereafter the farm tenancy issue waned in importance. After the passage of the Bankhead bill in 1937, tenant farming became less of a national problem because some sharecroppers and tenants borrowed money from the federal government to buy their own land, while others were resettled on better farms or found work in urban areas. Rural violence also decreased, and the issue retreated from the headlines. In any case other events, such as the reorganization of the Supreme Court, moved to the forefront, removing the issue from the spotlight.[29]

During the spring of 1936 Robinson experienced one of the highlights of his life. Roosevelt traveled to Little Rock and ate lunch at the Robinson home on Broadway. To ease the president's stay, the Robinsons constructed a ramp up the front porch for FDR's wheelchair. In addition, they added a first-floor restroom. One of their biggest concerns, however, was how to feed the entire presidential party (including the press), which they assumed would number less than thirty. In normal Arkansas fashion they borrowed china and glassware from their family and friends for the guests, many of whom eventually ate in the yard. Another issue was liquor. Billie could not decide whether to serve any, since the senator was officially dry, as were most of his constituents. As one niece put it, "he never drank—in Arkansas." Finally, Billie decided to exclude alcohol, arguing that lunch was too early in the day to serve it.[30]

Arriving to celebrate the state's centennial, Roosevelt—the first president to visit Arkansas while in office—spoke at the capitol in the morning. But unforeseen problems soon occurred. Because of the huge crowds, the schedule ran late all day. More perplexing to Mrs. Robinson, however, was that the traveling contingent numbered more than sixty—twice her estimate. Quickly she had to find more dishes and glasses and silverware for lunch. Then, as the presidential motorcade turned onto Broadway, the entire street filled with onlookers who hoped to meet Roosevelt. After slowly driving through the throng, he finally reached the porch where he spoke a few words endorsing his "good friend" Robinson. Immediately he rolled into the house and back to the library, where with a sly grin he said: "Joe, I need a drink." Billie quickly sent relatives scurrying to neighbors searching for whiskey. And once the president inhaled his portion, others expected a similar offering, especially several journalists and Postmaster General Jim Farley. Later in the afternoon Roosevelt left for Hot Springs to Harvey Couch's home, ending perhaps the most memorable day in Little Rock's first century.[31]

The Roosevelt visit helped reinforce Robinson's supremacy among state politicos, underscoring his invincibility. In the primary during the summer of 1936, he had no serious opposition. With the assassination of Huey Long (September 7, 1935), who had threatened to campaign against Robinson in Arkansas, a primary win was assured. Yet Robinson had been preparing for the campaign for two years; even before Long's death he believed he would easily triumph. And in the general election in November he received the highest percentage ever given a statewide candidate.[32]

At the Democratic National Convention in 1936, Robinson was, for the third time, selected as permanent chairman—for several reasons. Roosevelt saw the Robinson selection as a way to thank him for the recent defense of the New Deal as well as the best way to "endorse" him prior to the Arkansas primary. The post was also a recognition of the many legislative accomplishments of the past four years which had been affected, in large part, because of Robinson's efforts. In addition, Robinson was popular with many members of the Democratic National Committee, especially those wanting a southern chairman. And, finally, he was an exciting orator whose main job at the Philadelphia meeting was to deliver a speech which could be used throughout the campaign.[33]

The general election of 1936 was a huge Democratic success. Roosevelt won a landslide victory, carrying all but two states. Consequently, the Democrats achieved an even greater majority in the Senate, thereby assuring Robinson the largest body of Democrats with which he had ever worked.

In 1936 Robinson was at the pinnacle of his personal prestige. He had entertained the president in his home. He had won reelection by the largest majority in state history. He had chaired the Democratic National Convention. He had successfully traveled throughout the Midwest for his party, speaking in numerous states. And he had pushed the Robinson-Patman Act, the only legislation bearing his name, through the Senate—and without White House aid. The year 1937 would possibly bring even greater accomplishments.

13 THE FINAL ACT

Perhaps nothing better summed up the height to which Robinson had risen during his tenure in the Senate than the 1937 inauguration. On January 20 he rode in the lead car from the White House to the Capitol with Roosevelt. Then, as the ceremonies began, he escorted the president to the platform. And for the first time in American history, the vice-president also took the oath of office as part of the official rites; Robinson, at John Nance Garner's request, administered the oath of office. As one of his nephews remembered, it was "impressive that someone from Lonoke was so important."[1]

Yet, despite his enormous victory in 1936, Roosevelt faced a perplexing problem. During the previous two years the Supreme Court had invalidated much New Deal legislation, including the Agricultural Adjustment Act, the National Industrial Recovery Act, the Guffey Coal Act, and the Railroad Retirement Plan. The president, interpreting his overwhelming victory as a mandate for his programs, prepared to confront the "nine old men" of the Supreme Court. On February 5, 1937, he announced his plan to reorganize the federal judiciary. In order to stifle the power of the conservative majority, the president had developed, in complete secrecy, a plan to appoint six new justices. These men could thereby ensure that no more New Deal legislation would be declared unconstitutional.[2]

The proposal immediately divided Congress. Chairman of the House Judiciary Committee Hatton Sumners (D-Texas) resolved to kill the measure. By mid-February he had already persuaded a majority of his committee. To circumvent Sumners, however, House Speaker William Bankhead (D-Alabama) and Majority Leader Sam Rayburn

(D-Texas) convinced Roosevelt to open debate in the Senate. Indeed, forcing the bill through the lower chamber would entail a bitter, costly fight, antagonizing many congressmen.[3]

Rather than risk possible defeat, the administration moved the bill to the Senate on February 8 and placed it under the supervision of the ever-loyal Robinson. He soon faced stiff opposition in his attempt to direct the bill. In fact, on February 19 he could count, at most, only fifty-four or fifty-five votes favoring or leaning toward the measure, and greater than forty votes definitely against it. What hurt Robinson more, perhaps, was that the principal adversaries of the bill were fellow Democrats. Instead of facing Republican senators such as Charles McNary of Oregon and Arthur Vandenberg of Michigan, he had to combat Burton K. Wheeler (D-Montana), Tom Connally (D-Texas), and his old friend Carter Glass (D-Virginia).[4]

Moreover, Robinson also had to battle the well-financed and hostile opposition press. In February, powerful New York newspaper publisher Frank Gannett, leader of the assault by founding the National Committee to Uphold Constitutional Government, immediately began a nationwide mass-mail campaign against the proposal, raising more than $190,000 to defeat the measure. With the help of the American Bar Association, which also opposed the bill, he sent out blank petitions in "protest against the President's . . . power to remake the Supreme Court and to pack it with men to interpret the Constitution as he wishes." Gannett even appealed to the nation on a CBS radio hook-up on February 21. He thus flooded Robinson's office, as well as other congressional offices, with numerous signed petitions.[5]

Meanwhile the fight shifted to the Judiciary Committee, where Robinson intensified the attack. On the evening of March 30 he spoke nationwide over a CBS radio hookup in which he assailed the adversaries of the bill, as well as their arguments. Asserting that nothing was "sacred" about the "number nine," he declared that the president had the constitutional right to enlarge the court. He then verbally harassed colleagues William Borah (R-Idaho) and Carter Glass for wanting to put supporters of their economic views on the court seven years earlier, while condemning the president for making such a proposal in 1937. Robinson then closed with a snipe at Associate Justice James McReynolds, one of the court's most conservative members. The justice had complained about Roosevelt's "lack of sportsmanship" in proposing the "Court-Packing" plan after the administration had lost several cases before the tribunal. Robinson pointed out that, when the court voted against McReynolds's views, the justice often launched vitriolic attacks on his colleagues.[6]

Despite such arguments, Robinson quickly lost control of the battle. Because Roosevelt and his staff were directing the effort from the White House, Robinson was unable to make any deals that would expedite passage of the bill. On April 12 apprehension increased when the Supreme Court reversed itself on the National Labor Relations Act (Wagner Act) by a five-to-four decision, thereby upholding the measure. The court decision deprived the "packing" bill's proponents of their strong argument, that the "nine old men" were thwarting the will of the people. With the Court apparently no longer opposing the New Deal, Robinson realized that some lukewarm reorganization backers might now switch sides.[7]

At this point Robinson argued, albeit unsuccessfully, for a compromise. As he explained to White House liaison Joe Keenan: "This bill's raising hell in the Senate. . . . [B]ut if the president wants to compromise I can get him a couple of extra justices tomorrow." Roosevelt, however, had no intention of making concessions and, in fact, feared that Robinson might do so without consulting him. And no wonder, since Vice-President John Nance Garner, an opponent of the bill from its inception, was also a close friend of Robinson and could perhaps use this relationship to harm the bill's chances. Nevertheless, when the president determined to fight for the bill, Robinson, as usual, stood steadfastly by his chief.[8]

Two unexpected events, however, jolted the bill's supporters on May 18. The Senate Judiciary Committee, by a ten-to-eight vote, recommended the defeat of the bill, forcing Robinson to oppose the largely Democratic committee that he had appointed less than six months earlier. Then, and far more important to him, anti-Roosevelt justice Willis Van Devanter resigned, potentially increasing the slim five-four New Deal majority to six-three, thus further lessening the urgency of the measure.[9]

With the Van Devanter resignation Robinson hoped to realize his most cherished personal dream—that of serving on the Supreme Court. Around Washington, politicos knew that Roosevelt had promised him the first opening on the bench as a reward for his dedicated, unshakable service to the administration. Moreover, before being elected to Congress, he had been a successful criminal lawyer; the court appointment would cap his legal career. And he had a further reason for coveting the position: he hated the ordeal of running for public office, especially after Huey Long had embarrassed him in 1932.[10]

The timing of the Van Devanter resignation, coupled with Roosevelt's earlier pledge to appoint Robinson, caused consternation at the White House. While the proposal had been promoted as a way of getting new, young blood on the court, Robinson could only be considered an "elder politician." And although he had been Senate floor leader for much of the New Deal legislation, many liberals viewed him as a southern conservative who would side against Roosevelt's programs once he donned the august robes of the Supreme Court. Finally, and perhaps even more significantly, appointing Robinson might look like a political payoff.[11]

Even so, fellow senators made a powerful case for Robinson. When Van Devanter's resignation was announced, many gathered around his desk congratulating him and addressing him as "Mr. Justice." Both friends and foes of the bill joined together in "booming" the majority leader for the position. Even court bill opponents, such as Glass and Borah, wrote Roosevelt, urging that their comrade be appointed. Anticipation of Robinson's elevation to the high court swept away much of the earlier animosity fostered by the court bill. Many observers, thus, believed that if the president did not appoint him to the bench, an open revolt would occur in the Senate.[12]

Yet Roosevelt did not announce any appointment to the court. He instead left Robinson wondering whether or not he would receive the position. Such inaction nearly doomed the plan. Robinson, insulted by this treatment, would not consult with the president; he waited for him to make the first move. Had Roosevelt appointed Robinson to the Supreme Court without delay, a compromise plan for two additional justices might have been easy to negotiate. Now, Robinson and his friends were furious, costing the president precious support.[13]

Roosevelt therefore decided that appeasement was crucial. In order to smooth "ruffled feathers," he asked Postmaster General Jim Farley to phone the majority leader to assure him of the appointment. Robinson, upon receiving the call, delightedly told friends Senators Pat Harrison

(D-Mississippi) and James Byrnes (D-South Carolina), who were standing in his office. Yet he had still not been personally approached by Roosevelt, who, therefore, sent his son James to offer a White House invitation for a conference on June 3. Robinson, although protesting that it would appear that he was begging for the Supreme Court appointment, agreed to the meeting, prompting Roosevelt to phone him shortly thereafter.[14]

Thus reassured, Robinson went to the White House to discuss the court fight. During the two-hour meeting, he asserted that the six-judge bill was dead. Moreover, any measure to add new justices to the bench would face major obstacles, unless he was given complete freedom to work out the best possible settlement. Roosevelt agreed. Then, regarding the Supreme Court vacancy, he told Robinson: "If there was to be a bride [Robinson as a justice], there must also be bridesmaids—at least four of them." In other words, if he appointed Robinson to the bench, he would have to appoint at least four other justices. Robinson left the meeting thinking that he would be nominated and convinced that he could forge a compromise.[15]

Over the next month Robinson worked with his lieutenants on new proposals. For instance, Sen. Charles Andrews (D-Florida) suggested a total of eleven judges—a chief justice appointed at-large and one associate justice from each of the ten judicial districts. Robinson rejected the measure after receiving a confidential memo from Roosevelt, who opposed it.[16]

Robinson then decided on a proposal by Sen. Carl Hatch (D-New Mexico), which would meet the president's requirements and still allow his own appointment. The president would be authorized to appoint one new justice, or "coadjutor," a year for each member on the bench over the age of seventy-five. This plan would allow the president to appoint three justices by January 1938, plus the fourth "bridesmaid" by 1941.[17]

In hopes of ensuring passage of the bill, Robinson decided to make an appeal to party unity before introducing it. On the last weekend in June 1937, he invited the president and all Senate Democrats to the Jefferson Island Club in Chesapeake Bay. With joviality and camaraderie, he tried to end all animosity among his colleagues. Many opponents of the reorganization left the meeting with unchanged minds, but with less enmity toward fellow Democrats. Two weeks later Robinson noted that the predicted bitterness and acrimony over the bill had not yet arisen.[18]

Back in Congress early in July, Robinson opened the debate in behalf of the measure, but success eluded him. In a rousing speech, his thick, bull voice resounding throughout the chamber, he announced that the measure was going to pass. He threatened vengeance against the opposition, insisting that any attempted filibuster would not be tolerated. After this opening salvo, however, his colleagues continually harassed him with numerous interruptions. Following a series of questions from Sen. Edward Burke (D-Nebraska), Robinson turned red in the face, gasped for air, and hurriedly left the chamber, obviously not well. "No more questions today," he muttered. "Reserve them until next week."[19]

When he returned on July 8, Robinson relied upon his parliamentary skill and congressional friendships to advance the battle. In an aggressive parliamentary move, he caught opponents unprepared by announcing that the rules of Senate debate would be strictly enforced—something that had not occurred in two decades. As a result, no one could interrupt a senator without his consent and then only for a question. Nor could anyone conduct any other business except by unanimous consent. And no senator could speak more than twice on the same subject in one "legislative" day. Robinson also decreed that the Senate would not adjourn at night but instead would recess each evening, thereby keeping the same "legislative" day until voting on the measure. Several senators, trying to challenge this parliamentary rigidity, objected; but president Pro Tempore of the Senate Key Pittman (D-Nevada) upheld his old friend, helping to end the chances of a successful filibuster. Verbal attacks followed; yet Robinson still kept fighting for his life's ambition—a place on the court. Arguing, asking, even pleading for support, he was determined to win.[20]

A few days later, however, all such controversy ended. On Monday, July 12, he sparred verbally with opponents until late in the afternoon. Tired and ill, he left the sweltering, non-air-conditioned Senate chamber for the relative comfort of a porch rocker. Then he sent for several of his lieutenants and told them that he was leaving for the day; an ominous chest pain was too great for him to bear. The next day he did not make it to the floor of the Senate, resting at his apartment instead. Then on the morning of July 14, a maid found his body sprawled, pajama-clad on the floor with a copy of the previous day's *Congressional Record* by his right hand, his life cut short by a heart attack.[21]

The chances of passing the reorganization bill ended with his death. In his quest for a Supreme Court seat, Robinson had secured many personal pledges—rather than for the bill—from those who opposed the measure but did not want to deny their old friend and colleague a seat on the Court. They were now at liberty to oppose the bill. Angry at the way Robinson had been treated many supporters blamed Roosevelt and the court proposal for his untimely death. Still others realized that, with an upcoming battle for the majority leader position, no one was yet powerful enough to force the measure on recalcitrant senators. Opposition leader Wheeler even went so far as to say that God had shown his displeasure with the bill through Robinson's death.[22]

Thus, as the Robinson funeral train departed for Little Rock, the president's forces were leaderless and in disarray. Consequently, the opposition increased the pressure on the few undecided votes as well as many of the supporters that Robinson had secured. Complicating the issue was the contest for majority leader. Two staunch administration supporters, Alben Barkley (D-Kentucky) and Pat Harrison (D-Mississippi), battled each other rather than the opponents of the proposal. When the cortege returned to Washington, Vice-President Garner informed the president that the bill was already dead, with no hope of reviving it.[23]

If Robinson had not died, would the court reorganization plan have passed the Senate? Probably. The vote would have been close, with a tie possible. In that case many contemporaries believed that Vice-President Garner would cast the deciding vote against the bill, since he had been opposed to the measure from the outset. In June he had shown his displeasure with the bill by leaving for his home in Uvalde—the first time he had departed Washington while Congress was in session. In a June 28 letter to Robinson, however, he said that only two people could entice him to return to Washington: "one of them is you, and the other is the 'Chief' [Roosevelt]." And if the fight had become close enough that his one vote was needed, he was prepared to do his "duty." Clearly while disapproving of the plan itself, Garner would not allow his friend to be deprived of a position on the court. With the combined pressure of Robinson, Roosevelt, and Garner, the bill would probably have passed.[24]

Without question Robinson thought that the battle was won. In a letter to Garner written on July 2, he was confident—in fact, certain—that a prolonged filibuster was preventable. And he had "enough votes pledged to pass it." Sen. Hiram Johnson of California, who actively fought the bill, wrote on July 7, "they have the votes at present to put it over." Robinson said that if it were not for Wheeler, "the opposition could be pretty well pacified." That Robinson left in his papers no list of committed senators is not proof that he did not have the necessary votes. One of his traits was to write very little information down; instead, he kept the lists in his head since some of the senators' votes were "confidential and not to be revealed even to the White House." It seems plausible, therefore, that if Robinson had lived, then the measure could have passed. But with his death, the tenuous Senate coalition that he had built crumbled—dooming the "court-packing" proposal.[25]

In retrospect, Robinson's life can be viewed in several ways. In Arkansas, he was the most important political figure of the first half of the twentieth century. He, and his friends and supporters, dominated the executive committee of the state Democratic Party for nearly a quarter century. He had outlasted the foes of his early career and no one of the next generation had successfully challenged him. For nearly twenty years he had controlled political patronage, doling out federal judgeships, postmasterships, and marshalls' badges to his supporters, thus ensuring a strong machine at each reelection. But to most Arkansans he was not a master politician, but, instead, simply "Joe T."—a man they had known, respected, and trusted for over thirty years. After his burial at Roselawn Cemetery, several friends proposed building a bell tower as a memorial, but in depression Arkansas money was scarce and the plans faded. Later, the city auditorium in Little Rock, an army camp nearby, and a U.S. Navy ship were named for him—all fitting tributes.

Nationally, he was a lifelong progressive, always fighting for the "common man." As Labor Secretary Frances Perkins remembered, he had a "humanitarian impulse" which pervaded his politics. For instance, he had fought for restraints on child labor when many southerners objected to such government interference. He had also supported railroad regulation since his days in the Arkansas General Assembly. He had even advocated a form of social security as early as 1911. And he had culminated his legislative career by supporting the numerous and far-reaching reforms of the New Deal. Robinson did not formulate the New Deal policy, but rather, he paved the legislative road which allowed for the passage of Roosevelt's legislation. He was the senatorial tactician who found ways to pass bills which many people believed were destined to defeat.[26]

His vision of a better world was not, however, restricted to the United States. He had long worked for international cooperation. In fact, the greatest defeats he ever suffered were over internationalist principles. In 1920 he had stood by Woodrow Wilson until the end, fighting for the Versailles treaty and the League of Nations. On many occasions he had represented the United States at the International Parliamentary Union, making contacts with other statesmen from around the globe. In addition, he had represented the nation in the delegation to the London Naval Conference in 1930. And during Roosevelt's first term he had waged a fierce, yet unsuccessful, battle to join the World Court.

But of all of Robinson's many qualities, perhaps the most notable was his loyalty—especially to the Democratic Party. Starting in the 1890s when, as a young man, he ran against the Populists, he had never faltered in his devotion to "the party of Jefferson." And although he often worked with Republicans in passing legislation and counted many as his friends, if a battle became partisan, then he would always side with his party. Clearly, he realized that without the Democratic Party he would never have moved from the small county courthouse of Lonoke to the halls of Congress and the corridors of the White House. His loyalty and hard work had been well rewarded. He had served three terms as chairman of the Democratic National Convention, in 1920, 1928, and 1936. In addition he had been the vice-presidential nominee in 1928 and the leader of his party in the Senate from 1923 until his death in 1937. In each instance, at every juncture, and through each debate, he was always a loyal Democrat.

NOTES

1 ANCESTRY AND YOUTH

1. Ray Allen Billington, *The Far Western Frontier, 1830–1860* (New York: Harper and Row, 1962), pp. 90–91, 116–24, 134–36, 143–67; William Ransom Hogan, *The Texas Republic: A Social and Economic History* (Austin: University of Texas Press, 1969), pp. 3–24.

2. E. R. Robinson, "Dr. James Madison Robinson—1816–1892," n.d., pp. 1–2, manuscript in the possession of Mrs. Lloyd Willmon, Lonoke, Arkansas (hereafter cited as Robinson, "Robinson, 1816–1892"); E. R. Robinson, "Brief History and Character Sketch of Dr. James Robinson," n.d., p. 1, manuscript in the possession of W. T. Robinson, England, Arkansas (hereafter cited as Robinson, "Character Sketch"); untitled biographical sketch, n.d., manuscript Joseph Taylor Robinson Papers, David Mullins Library, University of Arkansas, Fayetteville (hereafter cited as RP); Nevin Emil Neal, "A Biography of Joseph Taylor Robinson," Ph.D. dissertation, University of Oklahoma, Norman, Oklahoma, 1958, pp. 4–5; Gene Newsom and Karl Kastner, *"Our Joe": An Illustrated, Biographical Sketch of Arkansas' Super-Senator, Joseph Taylor Robinson* (North Little Rock, Arkansas: Times Printing Company, n.d.), pp. 3–4; interview with W. T. Robinson by author, February 12, 1988, England, Arkansas, in the possession of the author.

3. Robinson, "Robinson, 1816–1892," p. 1; W. T. Robinson interview; Newsom and Kastner, *"Our Joe,"* p. 3; John Gould Fletcher, *Arkansas* (Chapel Hill: University of North Carolina Press, 1947), pp. 108–30.

4. "Lonoke County: Perhaps It Is Not the Garden Spot of the World, but It Is the Garden Spot of the Arkansas Prairies," *Lonoke (Arkansas) Democrat,* February 25, 1885, p. 2; "Lonoke County," ibid., April 6, 1898, p. 2; "Lonoke," ibid., April 9, 1903, p. 2; Gerald T. Hanson and Carl H. Moneyhon, *Historical Atlas of Arkansas* (Norman: University of Oklahoma Press, 1989), pp. 2–3.

5. Robinson, "Robinson, 1816–1892," pp. 1–2; Robinson, "Character Sketch," p. 1; W. T. Robinson interview; Neal, "Robinson Biography," pp. 4–5.

6. Interview with Maysell Walls Currie by author, February 12, 1988, Pine Bluff, Arkansas; Robinson, "Robinson, 1816–1892," p. 2; Neal, "Robinson Biography," pp. 4–7.

7. Interview with Mrs. Lloyd Willmon by author, February 11, 1988, Lonoke, Arkansas; W. T. Robinson interview; Robinson, "Character Sketch," p. 1; Robinson, "Robinson, 1816–1892," p. 1; Neal, "Robinson Biography," pp. 4–5; Newsom and Kaster, *"Our Joe,"* pp. 3–5.

8. Robinson, "Robinson, 1816–1892"; Robinson, "Character Sketch"; W. T. Robinson interview; "Speaker Eagle," *Lonoke Democrat*, February 5, 1885, p. 2; "Death Claims W. H. Eagle," ibid., March 15, 1906; W. G. Swaim, "Some information about the Swaim Family," n.d., manuscript in the possession of Mrs. Lloyd Willmon; Neal, "Robinson Biography," pp. 5–6.

9. W. T. Robinson interview; Robinson, "Character Sketch," pp. 6–7; Robinson, "Robinson, 1816–1892," p. 3; Neal, "Robinson Biography," p. 5.

10. Robinson, "Robinson, 1816–1892," p. 1; Robinson, "Character Sketch," pp. 1–2; Newsom and Kastner, *"Our Joe,"* pp. 4–5; Neal, "Robinson Biography," p. 6; tombstones, Concord Methodist Church cemetery, Lonoke County, Arkansas.

11. Robinson, "Robinson, 1816–1892," p. 2; Robinson, "Character Sketch," pp. 6–7; Joe T. Robinson Jr. interview; Newsom and Kastner, *"Our Joe,"* p. 3; [Archibald MacLeish], "The Senator from Arkansas: The Life and Opinions of Joseph Taylor Robinson, upon Whose Ability to Control the U.S. Senate Now Hangs the Political Destiny of President Franklin Delano Roosevelt," *Fortune*, January 1937, p. 90.

12. Newsom and Kastner, *"Our Joe,"* pp. 3–5; Currie interview; Robinson, "Character Sketch," pp. 2–4; Neal, "Robinson Biography," pp. 7–8.

13. Robinson, "Character Sketch," p. 5; W. T. Robinson interview; Newsom and Kastner, *"Our Joe,"* pp. 3–5; Currie interview; Neal, "Robinson Biography," pp. 7–8.

14. Robinson, "Robinson, 1816–1892," pp. 2–3; Robinson, "Character Sketch," p. 5; W. T. Robinson interview; Currie interview; Newsom and Kastner, *"Our Joe,"* pp. 3–5; Neal, "Robinson Biography," pp. 7–12.

15. Robinson, "Character Sketch," p. 3; Newsom and Kastner, *"Our Joe,"* pp. 4–5; Neal, "Robinson Biography," pp. 9–10.

16. Currie interview; W. T. Robinson interview; Newsom and Kastner, *"Our Joe,"* pp. 5, 9–10; Neal, "Robinson Biography," pp. 11–12; [MacLeish], "Senator from Arkansas," p. 90.

17. Currie interview; Neal, "Robinson Biography," pp. 13–14; "Vice Presidential Candidate, Who Is the Guest of Sioux City Today, Began Political Career at Age of 16 with Impromptu Platform Debate," *Sioux City [Iowa] Journal*, October 24, 1928, RP; Newsom and Kastner, *"Our Joe,"* p. 9; [MacLeish], "Senator from Arkansas," p. 90; Joseph Alsop Jr. and Turner Catledge, "Joe Robinson, The New Deal's Old Reliable," *Saturday Evening Post*, September 26, 1936, p. 6.

18. Newsom and Kastner, *"Our Joe,"* p. 8; Neal, "Robinson Biography," p. 1.

19. Currie interview; Teacher's License, November 14, 1891, RP; Neal, "Robinson Biography," pp. 14–15; Newsom and Kastner, *"Our Joe,"* pp. 9–10; [MacLeish], "Senator from Arkansas," p. 90.

20. Neal, "Robinson Biography," p. 16; Newsom and Kastner, *"Our Joe,"* pp. 6–7.

21. Neal, "Robinson Biography," p. 16; Newsom and Kastner, *"Our Joe,"* pp. 6–7; [MacLeish], "Senator from Arkansas," p. 90.

2 LAWYER OR POLITICIAN?

1. Untitled biographical sketch used in the 1912 gubernatorial race, RP; Neal, "Robinson Biography," pp. 15–17; W. T. Robinson interview.

2. Neal, "Robinson Biography," pp. 16–17; Newsom and Kastner, *"Our Joe,"* p. 7; W. T. Robinson interview; [MacLeish], "Senator from Arkansas," p. 90.

3. Untitled 1912 sketch; Neal, "Robinson Biography," p. 17; Newsom and Kastner, *"Our Joe,"* p. 7; [MacLeish], "Senator from Arkansas," p. 90.

4. Neal, "Robinson Biography," p. 22.

5. Untitled article, *Lonoke Democrat,* February 27, 1902, p. 2; Neal, "Robinson Biography," pp. 17–18.

6. Joe Tolbert Seagraves, "Arkansas Politics, 1874–1918," Ph.D. dissertation, University of Kentucky, Lexington, Kentucky, 1973, pp. 232–73; Fletcher, *Arkansas,* pp. 281–82; Newsom and Kastner, *"Our Joe,"* pp. 9–11; C. Armitage Harper, ed., *Historical Report of the Secretary of State (Arkansas)* (Little Rock, Arkansas: Pioneer, 1968), pp. 241, 359–61; Neal, "Robinson Biography," pp. 18–20. As a biography, this study tries to keep the focus on Robinson and does not try to decide all of the historiographical battles with the different political eras in Arkansas or the nation. Seagraves, "Arkansas Politics," offers a good overview of the birth and early years of the Populists in Arkansas, while Richard Niswonger, in *Arkansas Democratic Politics, 1896–1920* (Fayetteville: University of Arkansas Press, 1990), does a good job on the early years of populism and how the Populists were brought back into the Democratic Party. Also see James R. Green, *Grass-roots Socialism: Radical Movements in the Southwest, 1895–1943* (Baton Rouge: Louisiana State University Press, 1978). On a regional and national level many works deserve mention. John Hicks's original *The Populist Revolt* (1931) is still an outstanding chronicle of the period which sees the Populists as the first great reformers. Richard Hofstadter's *The Age of Reform: From Bryan to FDR* (1955) differs with Hicks by belittling the farmers and pointing out numerous negatives, from anti-semitism to nativism, even portraying them as bumbling bumpkins. He sees populism and progressivism as separate movements. Lawrence Goodwyn, in *Democratic Promise: The Populist Moment in America* (1976), argues that the entire argument has been miscast; the politics of the farmers was the final and last offshoot of their numerous cooperative efforts of trying to deal with an industrial nation which placed little value on the individual. Other overviews and syntheses include Robert C. McMath, *American Populism: A Social History* (1993) and Norman Pollack, *The Human Economy: Populism, Capitalism, and Democracy* (1990). For a southern viewpoint, see C. Vann Woodward, *Origins of the New South, 1877–1913* (1951), pp. 264–90; Steven Hahn, *The Roots of Southern Populism* (1983); and Edward L. Ayers, *The Promise of the New South* (1992). For a state view, see Sheldon Hackney, *Populism to Progressivism in Alabama* (1969) or Walter Nugent, *The Tolerant Populists: Kansas Populism and Nativism* (1963). For individual biographies, see C. Vann Woodward, *Tom Watson* (1963).

7. Newsom and Kastner, *"Our Joe,"* pp. 9–11. The *Lonoke Democrat,* the newspaper which circulated throughout the district in 1895–1896, can be found on

microfilm from several sources. Unfortunately, nothing from the time period of the campaign, nor his term in the General Assembly, is on these rolls. The election, as well as local reaction to Robinson's role in the legislature, is somewhat sketchy, with many details missing.

8. Ibid.; Neal, "Robinson Biography," pp. 18–20; Harper, ed., *Historical Report*, pp. 359–61.

9. "In Cluster," [Little Rock] *Arkansas Gazette*, January 9, 1895, p. 4; "Population of Arkansas," *Lonoke Democrat*, October 11, 1900, p. 1; Fletcher, *Arkansas*, pp. 66–75, 265–70; Seagraves, "Arkansas Politics," p. 135; George W. Donaghey, *Building a State Capitol* (Little Rock, Arkansas: Parke-Harper Company, 1937), pp. 3–11; Jerry Hinshaw, *Call the Roll: The First One Hundred Fifty Years of the Arkansas Legislature* (Little Rock, Arkansas: Rose Publishing Company, 1986), pp. 155, 209.

10. *Journal of the House of Representatives, State of Arkansas, Thirtieth Session* (Little Rock, Arkansas: Brown Printing Company, 1895), pp. 7–48 (hereafter cited as *House Journal*); "In Cluster," *Arkansas Gazette*, January 9, 1895, p. 1; "The Lawmakers," ibid., January 10, 1895, p. 1; "In Session," ibid., January 15, 1895, p. 1; "Colquitt Elected Speaker of the House on the Twenty-fourth Ballot," ibid., January 16, 1895, p. 1; Neal, "Robinson Biography," p. 20.

11. *House Journal*, pp. 239–45, 262, 562; "The Legislature: The House Committees Are Announced by the Speaker," *Arkansas Gazette*, January 20, 1895, p. 1; "Held a Caucus," ibid., February 12, 1895, p. 1; "The Legislature," ibid., February 15, 1895, p. 1; "Spirited Debate," ibid., February 22, 1895, p. 1; "Arkansas Legislature," *Fayetteville (Arkansas) Sentinel*, February 19, 1895, p. 2; "Arkansas Legislature," ibid., February 26, 1895, p. 2; Neal, "Robinson Biography," p. 21.

12. *House Journal*, pp. 431, 455, 556, 742–44; "Grinding Away," *Arkansas Gazette*, February 21, 1895, p. 1; "Voice of the Arkansas Press," *Memphis (Tennessee) Commercial Appeal*, March 19, 1895, p. 4; "Ghouls Get a Black Eye," ibid., March 22, 1895, p. 1; "Row over in Arkansas," ibid., March 23, 1895, p. 1; "Ghouls in High Glee," ibid., March 24, 1895, p. 1; untitled article, *Fort Smith (Arkansas) Elevator*, March 8, 1895; untitled article, *Sentinel*, March 5, 1895, p. 2; Richard L. Niswonger, *Arkansas Democratic Politics, 1896–1920* (Fayetteville: University of Arkansas Press, 1990), p. 107; Seagraves, "Arkansas Politics, 1874–1918," pp. 251–52; Neal, "Robinson Biography," pp. 20–21.

13. "Bribed by the Ghouls," *Commercial Appeal*, April 7, 1895, p. 1; "The Truth at Last," ibid., p. 4; "Spat on the Governor," ibid., April 8, 1895, p. 1; "The Last Straw," ibid., p. 4; "Gov. Clarke Set Right," ibid., April 9, 1895, p. 1; "Now Cox Is in for It," ibid., April 10, 1895, p. 1; "Rang down the Curtain," ibid., April 11, 1895, p. 1; "Gone," ibid., p. 4; "Bribery," *Arkansas Gazette*, April 7, 1895, p. 1; "Bribery Charges," ibid., April 9, 1895, p. 1; "The Lobby at Little Rock," *Springdale (Arkansas) News*, April 12, 1895, p. 2; "Legislative Matters," *Fort Smith Elevator*, April 12, 1895, p. 2; "The Legislature," ibid., April 19, 1895, p. 2; Seagraves, "Arkansas Politics, 1874–1918," pp. 251–52; Neal, "Robinson Biography," pp. 20–21.

14. "Bribery," *Arkansas Gazette*, April 7, 1895, p. 1; "Bribery Charges," ibid., April 19, 1895, p. 1; "The Lobby at Little Rock," *Springdale News*, April 12, 1895, p. 1; "Clarke Says," ibid., April 19, 1895, p. 1; "The Bribery Case," *Pine Bluff*

(Arkansas) Commercial, April 8, 1895, p. 2; untitled article, ibid., April 12, 1895, p. 2; Seagraves, "Arkansas Politics, 1874–1918," pp. 251–52.

15. "Bribery," *Arkansas Gazette*, April 7, 1895, p. 1; "Bribed by the Ghouls," *Commercial Appeal*, April 7, 1895, p. 1; "Now Cox Is in for It," ibid., April 10, 1895, p. 1; "Arkansas Legislature," *Sentinel*, April 17, 1895, p. 2; "The Bribery Case," *Commercial*, April 8, 1895, p. 2.

16. *House Journal*, pp. 1283–85; "Now Cox Is in for It," *Commercial Appeal*, April 10, 1895, p. 1; "Arkansas Legislature," *Sentinel*, April 17, 1895, p. 2; Seagraves, "Arkansas Politics, 1874–1918," pp. 252, 266–71; Neal, "Robinson Biography," p. 21; Harper, ed., *Historical Report*, p. 184.

17. Untitled article in special section on the Thirtieth General Assembly, *Arkansas Gazette*, April 14, 1895.

18. John Minor to Joe T. Robinson, May 29, 1895, RP; James P. Clarke to Robinson, August 22, 1895, RP; untitled 1912 campaign sketch, RP; Neal, "Robinson Biography," p. 16.

19. Untitled 1912 campaign sketch, RP; Newsom and Kastner, "*Our Joe*," p. 7; [MacLeish], "Senator from Arkansas," p. 90; Neal, "Robinson Biography," p. 17.

20. "Mrs. Joe T. Robinson," October 19, 1951, RP; P. Arthur Thibaut to Robinson, December 10, 1896, RP; Neal, "Robinson Biography," pp. 22–23.

21. Neal, "Robinson Biography," pp. 22–23.

22. "Marriage: Miller-Robinson," n.d., clipping in RP; "A Beautiful Wedding: Hon. Joe T. Robinson and Miss Willie Miller," *Lonoke Citizen*, supplement, December 16, 1896; Neal, "Robinson Biography," p. 23; Newsom and Kastner, "*Our Joe*," p. 23. Numerous copies of their wedding pictures were disseminated by the Democratic National Committee in 1928 in conjunction with the vice-presidential race. Many newspapers, such as the *Boston Globe*, and the *Sioux City Tribune* ran them. Clippings may be found in RP.

23. Neal, "Robinson Biography," pp. 28–32; Currie interview.

24. Neal, "Robinson Biography," pp. 33–34; Newsom and Kastner, "*Our Joe*," p. 7.

25. Neal, "Robinson Biography," pp. 33–35; Newsom and Kastner, "*Our Joe*," p. 7.

26. Neal, "Robinson Biography," pp. 33–35; Newsom and Kastner, "*Our Joe*," p. 7.

27. Neal, "Robinson Biography," pp. 33–35; Newsom and Kastner, "*Our Joe*," p. 7.

3 POLITICIAN

1. "A Young Elector," *Lonoke Democrat*, July 2, 1896, p. 2; "Democratic State Ticket," ibid.; untitled article, ibid., July 23, 1896, p. 2; Seagraves, "Arkansas Politics, 1874–1918," pp. 264–67; Neal, "Robinson Biography," p. 23.

2. "The Proper Test of a Political Party," speech given by Joseph Taylor Robinson during 1896 election, RP; "Read What Others Say of the Life and Public Services of Hon. Joe T. Robinson," pp. 5–7, RP (hereafter cited as "Read What Others Say"); Neal, "Robinson Biography," p. 23.

3. Untitled article, *Lonoke Democrat*, July 23, 1896, p. 2; another untitled article, ibid.; "Senatorial," ibid., February 17, 1898, p. 2.

4. "Texarkana, Aug. 20, 1896," speech given by Robinson to Southern Teachers Association, Texarkana, Arkansas, August 20, 1896, RP; "Masonis [sic] Address Clarendon June 23rd, 1899," speech given by Robinson, Clarendon, Arkansas, June 23, 1899, RP; "Read What Others Say," pp. 5–7; Neal, "Robinson Biography," pp. 23–26.

5. "County Convention," *Lonoke Democrat*, June 21, 1900, p. 2; "Democratic Convention," ibid., July 5, 1900, p. 1; "State Convention," ibid., p. 2; "Read What Others Say," p. 5; Neal, "Robinson Biography," p. 25.

6. "Democratic Speaking," *Lonoke Democrat*, October 11, 1900, p. 2; untitled article, ibid., October 18, 1900, p. 2; "Public Speaking," ibid.; "Democratic Speaking," ibid.; untitled article, ibid., October 23, 1900, p. 2; "The Debate of Monday," ibid.; "Read What Others Say," pp. 3–5; Neal, "Robinson Biography," p. 25.

7. John W. Crockett, *Arkansas: Biennial Report of the Secretary of State* (Little Rock, Arkansas: Tunnah and Pittard, 1903); "Sixth Congressional District," *Lonoke Democrat*, July 23, 1896, p. 2; Neal, "Robinson Biography," p. 57.

8. "Not a Colonel Sir," *Lonoke Democrat*, August 8, 1901, p. 2; "Read What Others Say," pp. 1–2, 8; Samuel Taylor, "To the Democratic Voters of Arkansas County," 1902, manuscript in RP; "Qualifications of Sam M. Taylor" [1902], manuscript in RP; "Sam M. Taylor, Campaign of 1902," manuscript in RP; Neal, "Robinson Biography," pp. 57–59.

9. Untitled article, *Lonoke Democrat*, September 12, 1901, p. 2; "As to Congress," ibid., February 13, 1902, p. 2; "Read What Others Say," pp. 1–2.

10. "A Few Suggestions to Active Supporters of Joe T. Robinson," 1902, manuscript in RP; Thomas Trimble to Robinson, January 17, 1902, RP; Thomas Trimble, untitled personal notes on the Sixth Congressional Steering Committee meeting, January 28, 1902, Rison, Arkansas, manuscript in RP (hereafter cited as Trimble, untitled notes); Joe T. Robinson, "My Views on Issues of National Importance," 1902, manuscript in RP (hereafter cited as Robinson, "My Views").

11. Currie interview; W. T. Robinson interview; Robinson to Sam Taylor, October 22, 1901, RP; Taylor to Robinson, February 4, 1902, RP; "Joe T. Robinson campaign of 1902 speaking engagements," manuscript in RP; Neal, "Robinson Biography," pp. 59–60.

12. Trimble, untitled notes; Trimble to Robinson, January 17, 1902, RP; W. T. Robinson interview; Joe T. Robinson Jr. interview; E. R. Robinson to Robinson, February 14, 1902, RP; R. F. Blair to Ewilda Robinson, March 26, 1902, RP; Ewilda Robinson to Robinson [1901–02], RP; Robinson to Ewilda Robinson, March 24, 1901, RP; Neal, "Robinson Biography," pp. 61–62.

13. Robinson, "My Views"; "Read What Others Say," pp. 6–8; "As to Congress," *Lonoke Democrat*, February 13, 1902, p. 2; Robinson campaign card, 1902 election, in RP; Neal, "Robinson Biography," pp. 60–61.

14. J. L. Spence to Robinson [1902], RP; Robinson to Harry Vaughn, March 5, 1902, RP; "Open letter by former Governor James P. Eagle," March 1, 1902, RP; William Wright Barnes, *The Southern Baptist Convention, 1845–1953* (Nashville, Tennessee: Broadman Press, 1954), pp. 308–9; Neal, "Robinson Biography," p. 60.

15. "Read What Others Say," pp. 2–7; "As to Congress," *Lonoke Democrat,* Feburary 13, 1902, p. 2; untitled article, ibid.; untitled article, ibid., February 27, 1902, p. 2.

16. "The Election: Judge H. T. Bradford, Hon. Joe T. Robinson, and Hon. W. P. Fletcher Were Elected," *Lonoke Democrat,* April 3, 1908, p. 2; untitled article, ibid., April 10, 1902, p. 2; Neal, "Robinson Biography," pp. 62–64.

17. Untitled article, *Lonoke Democrat,* April 10, 1902, p. 2; "Political Support of Robinson in Election of 1902," *Stuttgart Republican,* 1902, clipping in RP; Neal, "Robinson Biography," pp. 63–64.

4 CONGRESSMAN

1. Dewey W. Grantham, *Southern Progressivism: The Reconciliation of Progress and Tradition* (Knoxville: University of Tennessee Press, 1983), pp. xv–xxiii; Richard Hofstadter, *The Age of Reform: From Bryan to F.D.R.* (New York: Random House, 1955), pp. 174–214; George E. Mowry, *The Era of Theodore Roosevelt and the Birth of Modern America, 1900–1912,* New American Nation Series (New York: Harper and Row, 1958), pp. 59–84. For other, conflicting overviews of the era, see Robert H. Weibe, *The Search for Order, 1877–1920* (1967), which uses an organizational model in arguing that progressive reforms were supported by businessmen and the middle class; Gabriel Kolko, *The Triumph of Conservatism: A Reinterpretation of American History, 1900–1916* (1963), which concludes that the Progressives were really conservative businessmen who sought the end of growing competition in the economy; Alan Dawley, *Struggles for Justice: Social Responsibility and the Liberal State* (1992), which views the Progressive era positively; and Arthur S. Link and Richard L. McCormick, *Progressivism* (1983).

2. Mowry, *Era of Roosevelt,* pp. 123–42, 165–80, 197–225; Hofstadter, *Age of Reform,* pp. 132–33, 167, 238–39; Richard B. Morris, ed., *Encyclopedia of American History* (New York: Harper and Brothers, 1953), pp. 266–70.

3. Mowry, *Era of Roosevelt,* pp. 115–21; Neal, "Robinson Biography," pp. 82–83.

4. Constance McLaughlin Green, *Washington: Capitol City, 1879–1950* (Princeton, New Jersey: Princeton University Press, 1963), II, 132–46.

5. Ibid., pp. 147–70.

6. Ibid., pp. 187–206.

7. Robinson to King White, March 16, 1903, RP; W. N. Trulock to Robinson, September 29, 1903, RP; Robinson to S. M. Taylor, November 10, 1903, RP; "Pine Bluff Will Soon Have $75,000 Federal Building," newspaper clipping in RP; *Congressional Record,* 58th Cong., 2d sess., Appendix, pp. 75–76; ibid., 59th Cong., 1st sess., p. 49; ibid., 2d sess., p. 1378; ibid., 60th Cong., 1st sess., p. 4363; Neal,

"Robinson Biography," pp. 89–90; John E. Chiles, "The Early Public Career of Joseph Taylor Robinson," M.A. thesis, Vanderbilt University, Nashville, Tennessee, 1949, pp. 10–11.

8. Neal, "Robinson Biography," pp. 64, 67, 85–86, 89; *Congressional Record*, 58th Cong., 2d sess., p. 572; ibid., 61st Cong., 2d sess., p. 4310; ibid., 3d sess., pp. 337, 543, 1618, 1881; ibid., 62d Cong., 2d sess., p. 358. For a more detailed view of the beginning of rice cultivation in Arkansas and the farmers initially involved, see Henry C. Dethloff, *A History of the Rice Industry, 1685–1985* (College Station: Texas A and M University Press, 1988), pp. 81–94.

9. *Congressional Record*, 58th Cong., 2d sess., pp. 510, 588, 851, 1873, 3180, 3239, 4198, 4641; ibid., 59th Cong., 1st sess., pp. 115, 131, 568, 5524, 6471, 9007, 9085; ibid., 60th Cong., 1st sess., pp. 114, 222, 814, 1343; ibid., 61st Cong., 2d sess., pp. 91, 2651, 3587, 6650; ibid., 3d sess., pp. 231, 1210, 1461, 1966, 2743; ibid., 62d Cong., 1st sess., pp. 82, 270, 352, 625; ibid., 2d sess., pp. 286, 5985, 6779, 6931, 7268, 8683, 11140; "Boundary Reservation at Hot Springs, Ark.," House of Representatives Report No. 1683, 59th Cong., 1st sess.

10. Neal, "Robinson Biography," pp. 77, 90, 91; *Congressional Record*, 58th Cong., 3d sess., p. 115; ibid., 59th Cong., 1st sess., pp. 50, 309, 11793, 13308; ibid., 2d sess., pp. 2308–10; ibid., 60th Cong., 1st sess., pp. 602, 5145, 5567; ibid., 61st Cong., 2d sess., pp. 138, 653; Chiles, "Early Career of Robinson," pp. 27, 33–34.

11. "To Refund Cotton Tax," February 14, 1905, newspaper clipping in RP; *Congressional Record*, 59th Cong., 1st sess., p. 50; ibid., 60th Cong., 1st sess., pp. 15, 222; ibid., 61st Cong., 2d sess., p. 3835; ibid., 62d Cong., 1st sess., p. 593; Neal, "Robinson Biography," p. 67.

12. "Career of Robinson Had Start in Clash with Teddy Roosevelt over Congressional Release; As Senator He Was Wilson's Confidant during War," *Commercial Appeal*, August 28, 1934 [?], RP; Newsom and Kastner, *"Our Joe,"* pp. 11–12; Neal, "Robinson Biography," pp. 87–88.

13. "Career of Robinson," *Commercial Appeal*, August 28, 1934, RP; Newsom and Kastner, *"Our Joe,"* pp. 11–12; Neal, "Robinson Biography," pp. 87–88.

14. "Career of Robinson," *Commercial Appeal*, August 28, 1934, RP; Newsom and Kastner, *"Our Joe,"* pp. 11–12; Neal, "Robinson Biography," pp. 87–88.

15. *Congressional Record*, 58th Cong., 3d sess., pp. 3703–5; ibid., 60th Cong., 1st sess., p. 15; "Not in Harmony on Rate Issue," newspaper clipping in RP; Mowry, *Era of Roosevelt*, pp. 202–7; Neal, "Robinson Biography," pp. 71–73; Chiles, "Early Career of Robinson," pp. 31–32.

16. *Congressional Record*, 59th Cong., 1st sess., pp. 49, 5569–70; ibid., 60th Cong., 1st sess., p. 15; "Not in Harmony on Rate Issue," newspaper clipping in RP; Mowry, *Era of Roosevelt*, pp. 202–7; Neal, "Robinson Biography," pp. 71–73; Chiles, "Early Career of Robinson," pp. 31–32.

17. *Congressional Record*, 59th Cong., 1st sess., pp. 8971–78, 9075–76; Neal, "Robinson Biography," pp. 72–73; Mowry, *Era of Roosevelt*, pp. 207–8.

18. *Congressional Record*, 58th Cong., 2d sess., pp. 3067–69; Mowry, *Era of Roosevelt*, pp. 170–71; Chiles, "Early Career of Robinson," pp. 10–11.

19. *Congressional Record*, 59th Cong., 2d sess., pp. 1452–53, 3004; ibid., 60th

Cong., 1st sess., p. 24; Neal, "Robinson Biography," pp. 81–83; Chiles, "Early Career of Robinson," pp. 29–30.

20. *Congressional Record,* 61st Cong., 1st sess., pp. 1301, 4427–31, 4440; Neal, "Robinson Biography," pp. 77–79; Chiles, "Early Career of Robinson," pp. 13–15, 19–20.

21. *Congressional Record,* 62d Cong., 1st sess., pp. 1837–41; Chiles, "Early Career of Robinson," pp. 20–21.

22. *Congressional Record,* 62d Cong., 1st sess., pp. 220, 241–42, 2433; Neal, "Robinson Biography," p. 79; Chiles, "Early Career of Robinson," pp. 37–40.

23. *Congressional Record,* 60th Cong., 1st sess., pp. 4438, 6034; "Labor Day," speech given by Robinson at Corning, Arkansas, September 4, 1911, in RP; Neal, "Robinson Biography," pp. 84–85.

24. *Congressional Record,* 61st Cong., 1st sess., pp. 2000–2001; "Says Reciprocity Can Never Be," newspaper clipping in RP; Neal, "Robinson Biography," pp. 69–70, 85; Chiles, "Early Career of Robinson," pp. 40–41.

25. *Congressional Record,* 60th Cong., 1st sess., pp. 321, 427–28, 2962, 3149, 6908–9, 6923; Neal, "Robinson Biography," pp. 75–76; Chiles, "Early Career of Robinson," pp. 21–24.

26. *Congressional Record,* 61st Cong., 2d sess., pp. 5055–59; Neal, "Robinson Biography," pp. 75–76; Chiles, "Early Career of Robinson," pp. 21–24.

27. *Congressional Record,* 60th Cong., 1st sess., p. 6924; ibid., 61st Cong., 2d sess., pp. 5055–59; W. E. Humphrey to Robinson, June 1, 1911, RP; Neal, "Robinson Biography," pp. 75–76; Chiles, "Early Career of Robinson," pp. 21–24.

28. *Congressional Record,* 59th Cong., 1st sess., pp. 5568–69; ibid., 61st Cong., 1st sess., p. 1999; Chiles, "Early Career of Robinson," pp. 15–17.

29. *Congressional Record,* 61st cong., 1st sess., pp. 4020–21, 4025; H. C. Phillips to Robinson, February 18, 1904, in RP; Neal, "Robinson Biography," pp. 85–87; Chiles, "Early Career of Robinson," pp. 36–37.

30. Joe T. Robinson, "The Panama Canal as Seen by Congressman Joe T. Robinson," newspaper clipping in RP; Joe T. Robinson, "The Panama Canal," newspaper clipping in RP; Joe T. Robinson, "As to the Work Done and the Progress Now Being Made in the Construction of the Panama Canal," newspaper clipping in RP; *Congressional Record,* 59th Cong., 1st sess., p. 5569; Chiles, "Early Career of Robinson," pp. 28–29.

5 GOVERNOR AND BEYOND

1. V. O. Key, *Southern Politics in State and Nation* (New York: Alfred A. Knopf, 1949), pp. 183–204; Boyce Drummond "Arkansas Politics: A Study of a One Party System," Ph.D. dissertation, University of Chicago, Chicago, Illinois, 1949, pp. 227–31; Seagraves, "Arkansas Politics, 1878–1918," pp. 394–411; Niswonger, *Arkansas Democratic Politics, 1896–1920,* pp. 23–30.

2. Raymond Arsenault, *The Wild Ass of the Ozarks: Jeff Davis and the Social Bases of Southern Politics* (Philadelphia: Temple University Press, 1984), pp. 1–4, 13–18, 151–52; Fletcher, *Arkansas*, pp. 302–14; Seagraves, "Arkansas Politics, 1878–1918," pp. 277–78, 281, 283–86, 288–89; Niswonger, *Arkansas Democratic Politics, 1896–1920*, pp. 23–30.

3. Arsenault, *Wild Ass of the Ozarks*, pp. 137–41, 146–48, 154–57; Seagraves, "Arkansas Politics, 1878–1918," pp. 307–8; Niswonger, *Arkansas Democratic Politics, 1896–1920*, pp. 135–36.

4. "Ex-Gov. Eagle Declines to Give Resignation," *Arkansas Gazette*, April 4, 1902, p. 3; "Ex Gov. Jas. P. Eagle Declines to Resign," ibid., April 8, 1902, p. 3; Arsenault, *Wild Ass of the Ozarks*, pp. 158–60; Seagraves, "Arkansas Politics, 1878–1918," pp. 296–97; Niswonger, *Arkansas Democratic Politics, 1896–1920*, pp. 141–44.

5. Trimble to Robinson, March 10, 1904, Trimble and Trimble to Robinson, April 28, 1908, A. J. Walls to Robinson, April 30, 1908, Robinson to Walls, May 4, 1908, A. F. Milwee to Walter Hendricks, May 5, 1908, RP; Neal, "Robinson Biography," pp. 93–95; Arsenault, *Wild Ass of the Ozarks*, pp. 197, 229; Seagraves, "Arkansas Politics, 1878–1918," pp. 309–15; Niswonger, *Arkansas Democratic Politics, 1896–1920*, pp. 149, 154–56, 183–87.

6. Margaret Ross, "The New Madrid Earthquake," *Arkansas Historical Quarterly*, XXVII (summer 1968): 83–89; Lee A. Dew, "The J.L.C. and E.R.R. and the Opening of the 'Sunk Lands' in Northeast Arkansas," ibid., XXVII (spring 1968): 22–24; Niswonger, *Arkansas Democratic Politics, 1896–1920*, pp. 114, 191–94; Arsenault, *Wild Ass of the Ozarks*, pp. 238–39. For a description of the later use of this land, see Larry D. Ball and William M. Clements, "The Very Last Timber: Harvesting Chemical Wood in Northeastern Arkansas," *Forest and Conservation History*, 36 (April 1992): 73–81.

7. Niswonger, *Arkansas Democratic Politics, 1896–1920*, pp. 192–93; Arsenault, *Wild Ass of the Ozarks*, pp. 288–89.

8. Robinson to G. W. Hendricks, May 16, 1911, RP; Niswonger, "Arkansas Democratic Politics, 1896–1920," pp. 194–95, 198–99; Neal, "Robinson Biography," pp. 94–96; Stuart Towns, "Joseph Taylor Robinson and Arkansas Politics, 1912–1913," *Arkansas Historical Quarterly*, XXIV (winter 1965): 292–93. For more information on Donaghey, see Calvin R. Ledbetter Jr., *Carpenter from Conway: George Washington Donaghey as Governor of Arkansas, 1909–1913* (Fayetteville: University of Arkansas Press, 1993).

9. "Robinson Makes Opening Speech," *Arkansas Gazette*, July 5, 1911, RP; "Robinson Opens Gubernatorial Race," *Pope County Record* (Russellville), July 7, 1911, p. 1; Neal, "Robinson Biography," pp. 96–97; Towns, "Robinson and Arkansas Politics," pp. 291–92.

10. Towns, "Robinson and Arkansas Politics," pp. 292–93; Harper, ed., *Historical Report*, pp. 356–58, 366, 368–69; Arsenault, *Wild Ass of the Ozarks*, pp. 71, 235; Ledbetter, *Carpenter from Conway*, p. 120.

11. George W. Donaghey, "My Campaign for a Third Term," pp. 1–5, manuscript, Martha Louvenia Wallace Donaghey Papers, Arkansas Historical Commission, Little Rock, Arkansas; George W. Donaghey, *Autobiography of George*

W. Donaghey: Governor of Arkansas, 1909–1913 (Benton, Arkansas: L. H. White Printing Company, 1939), pp. 271–76; George W. Donaghey, *Building a State Capitol* (Little Rock, Arkansas: Parke-Harper Company, 1937), pp. 286–93; Towns, "Robinson and Arkansas Politics," pp. 295–96.

12. Donaghey, *Building a State Capitol*, pp. 288–89; Charles Jacobson to Robinson [September 1911?], Robinson to Jacobson, September 7, 1911, Jacobson to Robinson, October 12, 1911, RP; Donaghey, "My Campaign for a Third Term," pp. 1, 5; Ledbetter, *Carpenter from Conway*, pp. 119–20; "Governor Donaghey Announces for a Third Term," *Arkansas County Democrat* (De Witt), October 26, 1911, RP; Seagraves, "Arkansas Politics, 1878–1918," p. 341; Towns, "Robinson and Arkansas Politics," pp. 294–96.

13. "Governor Donaghey Announces for a Third Term," *Arkansas County Democrat*, October 12, 1911; Donaghey, *Autobiography*, pp. 272–75; Donaghey, "My Campaign for a Third Term," pp. 2–5; Ledbetter, *Carpenter from Conway*, pp. 121–22; Seagraves, "Arkansas Politics, 1878–1918," p. 341; Towns, "Robinson and Arkansas Politics," p. 295; Neal, "Robinson Biography," pp. 97–98.

14. Hal Norwood to Robinson, January 18, 1912, RP; Norwood to R. D. Bobo, January 16, 1912, RP; Norwood to J. M. Futrell, January 18, 1912, RP; Norwood to C. A. Bridewell, January 18, 1912, RP; Norwood to Isaac McClellan, January 18, 1912, RP; Norwood to J. V. Bourland, January 22, 1912, RP; W. L. Parker to Norwood, January 20, 1912, RP; Towns, "Robinson and Arkansas Politics," p. 300; Ledbetter, *Carpenter from Conway*, pp. 123–24; Niswonger, *Arkansas Democratic Politics, 1896–1920*, p. 199. Norwood would later serve as attorney general for three more terms, 1929–1934. Harper, ed., *Historical Report*, p. 253.

15. "Robinson Opposes New Revenue Law," *Commercial Appeal* [September 2, 1911?], RP; "Joe T. Robinson: An Interview and Review by an Observer," *Harrison Times*, October 7, 1911, p. 1; "Robinson Pleased Large Crowd Friday Night," *Fort Smith Times Record*, March 21, 1912; "Donaghey Announces for Third Term," *Arkansas County Democrat*, October 26, 1911; Donaghey, *Autobiography*, pp. 273–75; Donaghey, *Building a State Capitol*, p. 290; Niswonger, *Arkansas Democratic Politics, 1896–1920*, p. 201; Seagraves, "Arkansas Politics, 1878–1918," pp. 339–42; Neal, "Robinson Biography," pp. 97–98, 100; Towns, "Robinson and Arkansas Politics," pp. 296–98.

16. "Donaghey Announces for Third Term," *Arkansas County Democrat*, October 26, 1911; Donaghey, "My Campaign for a Third Term," p. 2; "Robinson Pleased Large Crowd Friday Night," *Fort Smith Times Record*, March 21, 1912, p. 1; Neal, "Robinson Biography," pp. 97–100; Niswonger, *Arkansas Democratic Politics, 1896–1920*, pp. 200–201; Seagraves, "Arkansas Politics, 1878–1918," p. 341; Ledbetter, *Carpenter from Conway*, pp. 123–26; Towns, "Robinson and Arkansas Politics," p. 299. Using the local option approach, prohibitionists had outlawed alcohol in seventy of the seventy-five Arkansas counties by 1912.

17. John A. Treon, "Politics and Concrete: The Building of the Arkansas State Capitol, 1899–1917," *Arkansas Historical Quarterly*, XXXI (summer 1972): 121–31; Donaghey, *Building a State Capitol*, pp. 198–283; Niswonger, *Arkansas Democratic Politics, 1896–1920*, p. 296; Donaghey, "My Campaign for a Third Term," pp. 2–4. For the opposing views of the capitol construction controversy, see George Donaghey,

Building a State Capitol, which lauds his accomplishments and ignores his mistakes; for a less favorable discussion of Donaghey's role, see John A. Treon, "Politics and Concrete: The Building of the Arkansas State Capitol, 1899–1907," *Arkansas Historical Quarterly*, XXXI (summer 1972): 99–149. Treon depends heavily upon a letter written by architect George Mann, whom Donaghey replaced near the end of construction. Mann's lengthy letter is printed as an appendix to the article. For a more recent view, see the appendix to Ledbetter, *Carpenter from Conway*, pp. 162–219.

18. Norwood to Robinson, January 18, 1912, RP; Niswonger, *Arkansas Democratic Politics, 1896–1920*, p. 199; Seagraves, "Arkansas Politics, 1878–1918," p. 342; Ledbetter, *Carpenter from Conway*, p. 123; Arsenault, *Wild Ass of the Ozarks*, pp. 241–42; Neal, "Robinson Biography," pp. 98–99, 103–4.

19. "The People's Battle for Good Government Is Won," *Pine Bluff Daily Commercial*, March 23, 1912, p. 7; "Hinemon Acrobat," ibid., March 23, 1912, p. 5; "A Letter to Judge Kirby Exposing Some Enemies of Square Deal Taxes and of Governor Donaghey," *Commercial Appeal*, March 14, 1912, p. 10; "Mr. Hinemon Is Our Best Little Explainer—Let him Explain This. And You, Mr. Robinson, Let Us Hear from You," ibid., March 27, 1912, p. 11; "To the People of Arkansas," ibid., March 27, 1912, p. 11; Ledbetter, *Carpenter from Conway*, p. 126.

20. "Speaker Champ Clark Approves the Record in Congress Made by Robinson," *Commercial Appeal*, March 20, 1912, p. 8; Neal, "Robinson Biography," p. 107.

21. "Donaghey the Tax Dodger," *Commercial Appeal*, March 8, 1912, p. 3; "Donaghey and Prohibition: No Faith in Donaghey's Sincerity," ibid., March 15, 1912, p. 8; "Heed Not the Howl of the Statehouse Ring," ibid., March 16, 1912, p. 8; "Donaghey's Campaign Manager No. 2," ibid., p. 9; "Answer This Gov. Donaghey," ibid., March 17, 1912, p. 15; "Donaghey Does Things," ibid., March 21, 1912, p. 10.

22. Donaghey, *Autobiography*, p. 276; Towns, "Robinson and Arkansas Politics," p. 301.

23. "Both Donaghey and Robinson Are Claiming Big Majority," *Pine Bluff Daily Commercial*, March 27, 1912, p. 1; "Night Letter Concerning the Evolution of Sentiment in Jefferson County—Arthur Murray, Prominent Editor Reviews the Situation in Pine Bluff Where the People Are Tumbling into the Donaghey Bandwagon," ibid., March 26, 1912, p. 11; "Donaghey's Nomination Absolutely Certain," *Commercial Appeal*, March 13, 1912, p. 9; "Distress Signals Out," ibid., March 17, 1912, p. 14; "Donaghey Has Won," ibid., March 21, 1912, p. 11; "Donaghey's Majorities," ibid., March 25, 1912, p. 9; Ledbetter, *Carpenter from Conway*, p. 126; Harry Lee Williams, *Forty Years behind the Scenes in Arkansas Politics* (Little Rock, Arkansas: Parkin Printing and Stationery Company, 1949), p. 11; Towns, "Robinson and Arkansas Politics," p. 302.

24. "Robinson Wins Governor's Race; Davis Has Defeated Brundige," *Pine Bluff Daily Commercial*, March 28, 1912, p. 1; "Geo. Donaghey Defeated for Third Term by 50,000," *Commercial Appeal*, March 28, 1912, p. 1; "Senator Jeff Davis' Victory Is Conceded," ibid., March 29, 1912, p. 1; Williams, *Behind the Scenes*, p. 11; Donaghey, *Autobiography*, pp. 278–80; Donaghey, "My Campaign for a Third Term," pp. 7–8; Seagraves, "Arkansas Politics, 1878–1918," pp. 343–46; Neal, "Robinson

Biography," p. 104; Towns, "Robinson and Arkansas Politics," p. 302; "Eight Delegates At Large to Baltimore Convention," *Pine Bluff Daily Commercial*, June 4, 1912, p. 1; "Speaker Clark Carries Arkansas," *Commercial Appeal*, April 7, 1912, p. 16; Hinshaw, *Call the Roll*, p. 79.

25. "Big Crowd to Little Rock," *Pine Bluff Daily Commercial*, June 4, 1912, p. 1; "Harmony for the Convention," ibid., June 4, 1912, p. 1; "Ark. Democrats in Convention," ibid., June 5, 1912, p. 1; "Eight Delegates At Large to Baltimore Convention," ibid., June 6, 1912, p. 1; "No Prohibition in Platform," ibid., June 7, 1912, p. 3; Neal, "Robinson Biography," pp. 105–8.

26. Robert Carl Scott, "William McCombs and the 1912 Democratic Presidential Nomination of Woodrow Wilson," *Arkansas Historical Quarterly*, XLIV (autumn 1985): 246–47, 259; Seagraves, "Arkansas Politics, 1878–1918," pp. 346–47; Niswonger, *Arkansas Democratic Politics, 1896–1920*, pp. 206–8.

27. Niswonger, *Arkansas Democratic Politics, 1896–1920*, pp. 207–8; Seagraves, "Arkansas Politics, 1878–1918," pp. 346–47; Harper, ed., *Historical Report*, pp. 354–62.

28. "Ark. Democrats in Convention," *Pine Bluff Daily Commercial*, June 5, 1912, p. 1; "Eight Delegates At Large to Baltimore Convention," ibid., June 6, 1912, p. 1; Seagraves, "Arkansas Politics, 1878–1918," pp. 346–47; Niswonger, *Arkansas Democratic Politics, 1896–1920*, p. 307; Neal, "Robinson Biography," pp. 106–7.

29. "No Nomination on the Second Ballot," *Pine Bluff Daily Commercial*, June 28, 1912, p. 1; "Woodrow Wilson Wins on 46th Ballot," ibid., July 2, 1912, p. 1; Donaghey, *Autobiography*, pp. 279–80; *Congressional Record*, 62d Cong., 3d sess., p. 909; Seagraves, "Arkansas Politics, 1878–1918," pp. 343–46; Niswonger, *Arkansas Democratic Politics, 1896–1920*, pp. 208–9; Towns, "Robinson and Arkansas Politics," p. 304; Neal, "Robinson Biography," pp. 108–13.

30. "Jeff Davis Died Suddenly at His Home Early This Morning," *Arkansas Democrat*, January 3, 1912, p. 1; "Sen. Jeff Davis Is Dead; Is Ill but Ten Minutes," *Arkansas Gazette*, January 3, 1913, p. 1; Arsenault, *Wild Ass of the Ozarks*, pp. 243–45; Seagraves, "Arkansas Politics, 1878–1918," pp. 348–50; Towns, "Robinson and Arkansas Politics," pp. 305–6; Neal, "Robinson Biography," pp. 114–15; "The Election of a Senator," *Arkansas Gazette*, January 4, 1913, p. 9.

31. "Unfettered Solons to Elect Senator," *Arkansas Gazette*, January 4, 1913, p. 1; "Brundige to Be Candidate," ibid., January 4, 1913, p. 1; "Four Giants in Race for Toga," ibid., January 5, 1913, p. 1; "Political Tangle Still Anraveled [sic]," ibid., January 6, 1913, p. 1; "Donaghey's Place in Race to Kirby," ibid., January 7, 1913, p. 1; "Jeff Davis Died Suddenly at Home Early This Morning," *Arkansas Democrat*, January 3, 1913, p. 1; "Davis' Funeral to Be Held at 3 P.M. Sunday," ibid., January 4, 1913, p. 1; "Four Looming Large in Race for the Senate," ibid., January 6, 1913, p. 1; "Politics Is Now Absorbing Topic in Capital City," ibid., January 7, 1913, p. 1; Hamp Williams to Robinson, January 11, 1913, RP.

32. "Unfettered Solons to Elect Senator," *Arkansas Gazette*, January 4, 1913, p. 1; "Brundige to be Candidate," ibid., January 4, 1913, p. 1; "Four Giants in Race for Toga," ibid., January 5, 1913, p. 1; "Political Tangle Still Anraveled [sic]," ibid., January 6, 1913, p. 1; "Donaghey's Place in Race to Kirby," ibid., January 7, 1913, p. 1; "Jeff Davis Died Suddenly at Home Early This Morning," *Arkansas Democrat*, January 3, 1913, p. 1; "Davis' Funeral to Be Held at 3 P.M. Sunday," ibid., January 4,

1913, p. 1; "Four Looming Large in Race for the Senate," ibid., January 6, 1913, p. 1; "Politics Is Now Absorbing Topic in Capital City," ibid., January 7, 1913, p. 1; Seagraves, "Arkansas Politics, 1878–1918," pp. 349–50; Neal, "Robinson Biography," pp. 114–15.

33. "Robinson in Race; Primary Proposed," *Arkansas Gazette*, January 9, 1913, p. 1; "Gov.-Elect Joe T. Robinson Enters Race for U.S. Senate," *Arkansas Democrat*, January 8, 1913, p. 1; Neal, "Robinson Biography," pp. 115–16.

34. John S. Yarnell to R. C. Love, January 13, 1913, and A. E. Moon to Love, January 8, 1913, sent to Robinson by Love, January 13, 1913, RP; W. D. Mauck to Robinson, January 11, 1913, RP; J. C. Clarry to H. S. Taylor, January 22, 1913, RP; "Robinson in Race; Primary Proposed," *Arkansas Gazette*, January 9, 1913, p. 1; "Brundige Wants Primary," ibid., January 9, 1913, p. 1; "Donaghey's Place in Race to Kirby," ibid., January 7, 1913, p. 1; "Kavanaugh Men in War Council," ibid., January 18, 1913, p. 1; "Norwood Agrees to Primary Plan for U.S. Senator," *Arkansas Democrat*, January 9, 1913, p. 1; Seagraves, "Arkansas Politics, 1878–1918," pp. 351–52; Niswonger, *Arkansas Democratic Politics, 1896–1920*, p. 202.

35. "Robinson Cohorts Claiming Victory," *Arkansas Gazette*, January 10, 1913, p. 1; "Hardage Is Chosen Speaker of the House," ibid., January 11, 1913, p. 1; "Brundige Again Urges Primary," ibid., January 12, 1913, p. 1; "Senatorial Test May Come Today," ibid., January 13, 1913, p. 1; "Conferences Chief Work in Politics," *Arkansas Democrat*, January 10, 1913, p. 1; "House Speaker and Chief Clerk Chosen in Caucus," ibid., January 11, 1913, p. 1; "First Blood in Clash between Opposing Factions in Senate," ibid., January 13, 1913, p. 1; "Senate's Filibustering Methods Are of Short Duration," ibid., January 14, 1913, p. 1; Neal, "Robinson Biography," p. 117.

36. "To Ask Committee to Call Primary?" *Arkansas Gazette*, January 16, 1913, p. 1; "Representative Patterson Wants Senatorial Primary," ibid., January 15, 1913, p. 1; "Vote on Primary Measure Delayed," ibid., January 17, 1913, p. 3; "Senatorial Situation Still Uppermost with Lawmakers," ibid., January 17, 1913, p. 1; "Senatorial Primary Gets Death Blow in State Senate," ibid., January 20, 1913, p. 1; "Kavanaugh Men in War Council," ibid., January 21, 1913, p. 1; "Robinson Forces Claim a Victory," ibid., January 21, 1913, p. 1; "Senate Primary Plan Is Beaten," ibid., January 21, 1913, p. 3.

37. "Politics in Arkansas Is Indeed Great Game," *Arkansas Gazette*, January 13, 1913, p. 6; "No Senatorial Fight Tomorrow," ibid., January 20, 1913, p. 1; "The Arkansas Senatorial Situation," *Arkansas Democrat*, January 20, 1913, p. 6.

38. "Robinson Forces Test Strength," *Arkansas Gazette*, January 24, 1913, p. 1; "Norwood Asserts He'll Win Fight," ibid., January 25, 1913, p. 1; "Tuesday to Bring Senatorial Contest," ibid., January 26, 1913, p. 1; "Senatorial Fight Begins Tomorrow," ibid., January 27, 1913, p. 1; "Senatorial Racers Reach Finish Tape," January 28, 1913, p. 1; "Senatorial Forces Still Contend for Vantage Point," *Arkansas Democrat*, January 21, 1913, p. 1; "United States Senatorial Squabble Still in Limelight," ibid., January 24, 1913, p. 1; "The Senatorial Fight Goes Merrily On," ibid., January 25, 1913, p. 1.

39. "Senatorial Fight Begins Tomorrow," *Arkansas Gazette*, January 27, 1913, p. 1; "Miss Robinson Laid to Rest," ibid., p. 2.

40. "Robinson Loses Test by 5 Votes," *Arkansas Gazette*, January 29, 1913, p. 1; "Robinson Has 16 in Senate," ibid., p. 3; "How the House Cast Vote," ibid., p. 3; "No Choices for Long Term Senator on the First Ballot," *Arkansas Democrat*, January 28, 1913, p. 1.

41. "Robinson Victor in the Senate Race," *Arkansas Gazette*, January 30, 1913, p. 1; "Brundige Meets Defeat Fighting," ibid.; "Robinson Wins Senate Election on first Joint Ballot," January 29, 1913, p. 1; "The Changes That Made Robinson Senator," ibid., January 30, 1913, p. 4; William K. Oldham and Earle W. Hodges [to clerk of the United States Senate], certification of Robinson as senator, 1913, RP; Niswonger, *Arkansas Democratic Politics, 1896–1920*, p. 202.

42. "Message of Joe T. Robinson, Governor, to the Thirty-ninth General Assembly," in the possession of Grady Miller Jr., Little Rock, Arkansas (hereafter cited as "Message of Governor"); "Governor Robinson Explains Handicap under Which His Administration Begins," *Arkansas Gazette*, January 17, 1913, p. 5; "Economy and Efficiency Are Keynotes of Governor Robinson's First Message," ibid., January 22, 1913, p. 5; "Governor Robinson Takes Oath of Office Today," *Arkansas Democrat*, January 16, 1913, p. 1; "Harmony Should Prevail in Working Out Problems Says the New Executive," ibid., January 21, 1913, p. 10; Neal, "Robinson Biography," pp. 118–22.

43. "Message of Governor"; "Economy and Efficiency Are Keynotes of Governor Robinson's First Message," *Arkansas Gazette*, January 22, 1913, p. 5; "Harmony Should Prevail in Working Out Problems Says the New Executive," *Arkansas Democrat*, January 21, 1913, p. 10; "The Governor's Voice," ibid., February 7, 1913, p. 6; Neal, "Robinson Biography," pp. 118–22.

44. "Message of Governor"; "Economy and Efficiency Are Keynotes of Governor Robinson's First Message," *Arkansas Gazette*, January 22, 1913, p. 5; "Governor Favors State Health Bill," ibid., February 6, 1913, p. 14; "Assembly Warned to Provide Funds," ibid., February 18, 1913, p. 1; "Robinson Asks End of Local Measures," ibid., March 1, 1913, p. 2; "Pass Health Bill at Once, Says Governor," *Arkansas Democrat*, February 6, 19113, p. 5; "Urges Passage of Bills for Financial Aid," ibid., February 17, 1913, p. 5; "Robinson Again Urges Action on Revenue Matter," ibid., February 24, 1913, p. 1; "Governor Urges Game Protection," ibid., March 3, 1913, p. 1.

45. "Governor Favors State Health Bill," *Arkansas Gazette*, February 6, 1913, p. 14; "House Votes for Pen Commission," ibid., p. 3; "Health Board Bill Favored by Senate," ibid., February 11, 1913, p. 5; "Senate Shelves Anti-liquor Bill," ibid., February 12, 1913, p. 5; "Cross-state Road Sought by Bill," ibid., February 13, 1913, p. 5; "House Turns Down Suffrage Measure," ibid., February 20, 1913, p. 1; "Bank Department Created in State," ibid., February 26, 1913, p. 5; "Good Roads Bill Passed by House," ibid., February 28, 1913, p. 5; "Senators Ignore Governor's Plea," ibid., March 1, 1913, p. 5; "Old Pen Board Is Abolished by House Measure," *Arkansas Democrat*, February 5, 1913, p. 1; "Health Bill Is Passed by House," ibid., February 18, 1913, p. 1; Jane Zimmerman, "The Convict Lease System in Arkansas and the Fight for Abolition," *Arkansas Historical Quarterly*, VII (autumn 1949): 186; Seagraves, "Arkansas Politics, 1878–1918," pp. 356–59; Neal, "Robinson Biography," pp. 121–22.

46. "House Passes Bill to Purify the Ballot," *Arkansas Gazette*, February 22, 1913, p. 5; "Senators Ignore Governor's Plea," ibid., March 1, 1913, p. 5; "Robinson Asks End of Local Measures," ibid., March 1, 1913, p. 2; "Robinson Urges Legislature to Hurry Up Work," *Arkansas Democrat*, February 28, 1913, p. 1; "Campaigns' Cost to Be Limited by Legislature," ibid., February 28, 1913, p. 1; Seagraves, "Arkansas Politics, 1878–1918," pp. 356–59; Neal, "Robinson Biography," pp. 121–22.

47. "Robinson to Resign Within Two Weeks," *Arkansas Gazette*, March 1, 1913, p. 1; "Robinson Resigns; Oldham Is Governor," ibid., March 9, 1913, p. 1; "State Again Faces Political Puzzle," ibid., March 10, 1913, p. 1; "Four More Days for Legislature," ibid., p. 3; "Governor Will Not Leave Until March 13, 1913," *Arkansas Democrat*, March 4, 1913, p. 5.

48. "Robinson Resigns; Oldham Is Governor," *Arkansas Gazette*, March 9, 1913, p. 1; "State Again Faces Political Puzzle," ibid., March 10, 1913, p. 1; "Four More Days for Legislature," ibid., p. 3; "Senator Futrell President Pro Tem," ibid., March 11, 1913, p. 1; "Clash Is Expected over Governorship," ibid., March 12, 1913, p. 1; "Crisis Expected in Governorship Row," ibid., March 13, 1913, p. 1; "Two Aspirants Now Claim the Executive Chair," ibid., March 14, 1913, p. 1; "Futrell Wins over Ashley in the Senate," *Arkansas Democrat*, March 10, 1913, p. 1; "Legislature Adjourned Today, Sine Day, After 60 Days," ibid., March 13, 1913, p. 1.

49. W. J. Robinson to Robinson, January 17, 1913, W. E. Edwards to Robinson, January 8, 1913, W. L. Thompson to Robinson, January 10, 1913, RP; Hinshaw, *Call the Roll*, p. 155.

50. "Robinson Offered Post in Brazil," *Arkansas Gazette*, March 18, 1913; Neal, "Robinson Biography," p. 124.

6 SENATOR

1. Arthur S. Link, *Woodrow Wilson and the Progressive Era, 1910–1917*, New American Nation Series (New York: Harper and Row, 1963), pp. 25–34; Neal, "Robinson Biography," pp. 125–26.

2. Grady Miller Jr. interview; Mrs. Grady Miller interview; Joe T. Robinson Jr. interview.

3. Grady Miller Jr. interview; Mrs. Grady Miller interview; Joe T. Robinson Jr. interview.

4. Grady Miller Jr. interview; Mrs. Grady Miller interview; Joe T. Robinson Jr. interview.

5. Link, *Woodrow Wilson*, pp. 36–43; Evans C. Johnson, *Oscar W. Underwood: A Political Biography* (Baton Rouge: Louisiana State University Press, 1980), pp. 197–210; Mowry, *Era of Roosevelt*, pp. 127–29, 239–49, 283–86; John A. Garraty, *The New Commonwealth, 1877–1890*, New American Nation Series (New York: Harper and Row, 1968), pp. 244–46, 278–80, 291–93; Harold U. Faulkner, *Politics, Reform, and Expansion, 1890–1900*, New American Nation Series (New York: Harper and Row, 1959), pp. 105–9, 158–61, 264–65.

6. *Congressional Record*, 63d Cong., 1st sess., pp. 3537, 3773, 3818, 3830, 3834, 3836, 3866, 3872, 3884, 3889, 4306, 4335, 4387, 4420, 4611–13, 4617, 5305, 5347; Niswonger, *Arkansas Democratic Politics, 1896–1920*, pp. 127–28; Ray S. Baker to Robinson, March 8, 1929, RP.

7. *Congressional Record*, 63d Cong., 2d sess., pp. 1120–21, 1126, 1128, 1144, 1149, 1194, 1196, 1200, 1202, 1204, 1214, 1216–17, 1225, 1230, 1488; Link, *Woodrow Wilson*, pp. 43–53; Neal, "Robinson Biography," p. 128.

8. *Congressional Record*, 63d Cong., 2d sess., pp. 11288–32, 12804, 12993, 13109, 13150, 13235, 13305, 13307, 13314, 13317, 14796–97, 14802; "Now Plan to Pass Only One Trust Bill," *New York Times*, April 12, 1914, III: 2; Neal, "Robinson Biography," pp. 128, 131–32; Link, *Woodrow Wilson*, pp. 68–74.

9. Neal, "Robinson Biography," pp. 131–32.

10. *Congressional Record*, 63d Cong., 2d sess., pp. 11228–32; "Seeks to Increase Trade Board Power," *New York Times*, June 28, 1914, p. 3.

11. *Congressional Record*, 63d Cong., 3d sess., pp. 3–4, 18–24; "Ovation to Clark as Congress Meets," *New York Times*, December 8, 1914, p. 6.

12. *Congressional Record*, 63d Cong., 2d sess., p. 5914.

13. Ibid., pp. 1263–76; Neal, "Robinson Biography," pp. 130–31.

14. *Congressional Record*, 63d Cong., 2d sess., pp. 1266–76, 10776–83, 10937–39, 10943, 11019–24, 11029–36; Neal, "Robinson Biography," pp. 130–31.

15. Link, *Woodrow Wilson*, pp. 59–60, 226–27; Arthur S. Link, *Wilson: Campaigns for Progressivism and Peace* (Princeton, New Jersey: Princeton University Press, 1965), pp. 56–59.

16. *Congressional Record*, 64th Cong., 1st sess., p. 12052; "Child Labor Bill Urged in Senate," *New York Times*, August 4, 1916, p. 9; "To Prevent Interstate Commerce in the Products of Child Labor," S. Rept. No. 358, 64th Cong., 1st sess. (hereafter cited as "Child Labor," S. Rept. No. 358).

17. *Congressional Record*, 64th Cong., 1st sess., pp. 12052–55; "Child Labor," S. Rept. No 358; "Child Labor Bill Urged in Senate," *New York Times*, August 4, 1916, p. 9.

18. *Congressional Record*, 64th Cong., 1st sess., pp. 12055–57, 12060–62; "Child Labor Bill Urged in Senate," *New York Times*, August 4, 1916, p. 9.

19. *Congressional Record*, 64th Cong., 1st sess., pp. 12306–13, 12917–18; P. Edward Haley, *Revolution and Intervention: The Diplomacy of Taft and Wilson with Mexico, 1910–1917* (Cambridge: Massachusetts Institute of Technology Press, 1970), pp. 129–40; Link, *Woodrow Wilson*, pp. 226–27; Link, *Campaigns*, pp. 58–60.

20. *Congressional Record*, 63d Cong., 3d sess., p. 1502; ibid., 64th Cong., 1st sess., pp. 1502–4, 6354, 6374–75, 11366–79, 11384; "Senate Debates Two War Issues," *New York Times*, January 6, 1916, p. 1; "Tammany Urges a Defense Inquiry," ibid., July 6, 1915, p. 18.

21. Link, *Woodrow Wilson*, pp. 254–73; *Congressional Record*, 68th Cong., 1st sess., p. 2651; Neal, "Robinson Biography," pp. 147–48; William G. McAdoo, *Crowded Years: The Reminiscences of William G. McAdoo* (Port Washington, New York: Kennikat Press, 1971), pp. 366–73; Foster Rhea Dulles, *America's Rise to World Power, 1898–1954*, New American Nation Series (New York: Harper and Row, 1963), pp. 101–5.

22. *Congressional Record*, 64th Cong., 2d sess., pp. 4988–89; "Bitter Wrangle as Senate Closes," *New York Times*, March 5, 1917, pp. 1–2; David M. Kennedy, *Over Here: The First World War and American Society* (New York: Oxford University Press, 1980), p. 74; Walter LaFeber, *The American Age: United States Foreign Policy at Home and Abroad* (New York: W. W. Norton and Company, 1989), pp. 278–79; Link, *Woodrow Wilson*, pp. 271–73; Neal, "Robinson Biography," pp. 148–51.

23. The text of the statement read: "The Undersigned United States Senators favor the passage of S. 8322, to authorize the President of the United States to arm American Merchant vessels and to protect American citizens in their peaceful pursuits upon the sea. A similar bill has already passed the House of Representatives by a vote of 403 to 13. Under the rules of the Senate allowing debate without limit it now appears to be impossible to obtain a vote prior to noon March 4, 1917, when the session of Congress expires. We desire this statement entered into the *Record* to establish the fact that the Senate favors the legislation and would pass it if a vote could be had." A facsimile of the original with all of the signatures may be found in the RP. *Congressional Record*, 64th Cong., 2d sess., pp. 4988–89; "Bitter Wrangle as Senate Closes," *New York Times*, March 5, 1917, pp. 1–2; Neal, "Robinson Biography," pp. 148–50.

24. *Congressional Record*, 64th Cong., 2d sess., pp. 4988–89; "Bitter Wrangle as Senate Closes," *New York Times*, March 5, 1917, pp. 1–2; Neal, "Robinson Biography," pp. 148–50.

25. "Bitter Wrangle as Senate Closes," *New York Times*, March 5, 1917, pp. 1–2; *Congressional Record*, 64th Cong., 2d sess., pp. 5012–13ff; Neal, "Robinson Biography," pp. 149–51.

26. "Bitter Wrangle as Senate Closes," *New York Times*, March 5, 1917, pp. 1–2; *Congressional Record*, 64th Cong., 2d sess., pp. 5012–13ff; Neal, "Robinson Biography," pp. 149–51.

27. "Bitter Wrangle as Senate Closes," *New York Times*, March 5, 1917, pp. 1–2; *Congressional Record*, 64th Cong., 2d sess., pp. 5012–13ff; Neal, "Robinson Biography," pp. 149–51; Link, *Woodrow Wilson*, pp. 274–75.

28. Link, *Woodrow Wilson*, pp. 274–75; "Thirty-three Senators Give Pledge to Mend Rules to Halt Filibuster," *New York Times*, p. 1; Neal, "Robinson Biography," pp. 151–52.

29. *Congressional Record*, 65th Cong., 1st sess., p. 261; Robert H. Ferrell, *Woodrow Wilson and World War I, 1917–1921* (New York: Harper and Row, 1985), p. 3; LaFeber, *American Age*, p. 279; Kennedy, *Over Here*, p. 10.

7 WAR AND PEACE

1. For a thorough look at America during the war, see David M. Kennedy, *Over Here: The First World War and American Society* (New York: Oxford University Press, 1980).

2. Grady Miller interview; Joe T. Robinson Jr. interview. Many letters throughout the RP also underscore the importance of loyalty to Robinson. See also Joseph

Alsop Jr. and Turner Catledge, "Joe Robinson, The New Deal's Old Reliable," *Saturday Evening Post*, September 26, 1936, pp. 5–7, 66–74.

3. *Congressional Record*, 65th Cong., 1st sess., pp. 1485, 1624–25, 2457, 5367, 7353, 7764; "Record Budget Is Voted for War," *New York Times*, May 20, 1917, p. 4.

4. *Congressional Record*, 65th Cong., 1st sess., pp. 7888–93; "La Follette Says He Will Continue to Oppose War," *New York Times*, October 7, 1917, pp. 1, 17; Neal, "Robinson Biography," p. 153.

5. *Congressional Record*, 65th Cong., 1st sess., pp. 7888–93; "La Follette Says He Will Continue to Oppose War"; Neal, "Robinson Biography," pp. 154–56.

6. *Congressional Record*, 65th Cong., 1st sess., pp. 742, 2701–3, 2706, 5846–47, 5935; "Enlargement of Interstate Commerce Commission," Senate Report no. 10, 65th Cong., 1st sess.

7. *Congressional Record*, 65th Cong., 2d sess., pp. 6305, 10095; Neal, "Robinson Biography," p. 152.

8. Robinson to Earl Hardin, January 5, 1918, RP; E. O. Mahoney to Robinson, February 2, 1918, RP; Robinson to Mahoney, February 13, 1918, RP; Grady Miller to Robinson, February 21, 1918, RP; Charles Jacobson to Robinson, February 26, 1918, RP; Neal, "Robinson Biography," p. 156.

9. Hardin to Robinson, January 1, 1918, RP; Robinson to Hardin, January 5, 1918, RP; Mahoney to Robinson, February 2, 1918, RP; Robinson to Mahoney, February 13, 1918, RP; Robinson to M. F. Dickinson, February 4, 1918, RP; Miller to Robinson, February 21, 1918, RP; Robinson to Thomas Trimble, February 25, 1918, RP; Jacobson to Robinson, February 26, 1918, RP; Robinson to A. J. Walls, February 28, 1918, RP; Robinson to Miller, March 4, 1918, RP.

10. Robinson to Miller, March 4, 1918, RP; Miller to Robinson, April 5, 1918, RP; Robinson to Stephen Brundige, April 27, 1918, RP; Neal, "Robinson Biography," pp. 157–58.

11. "Arkansas with Wilson," *New York Times*, March 6, 1917, p. 2; Robinson to Miller, March 4, 1918, RP; "A Real Statesman, A True Patriot, A Friend of Labor," February 25, 1918, RP; Woodrow Wilson to Robinson, February 6, 1918, Miller Collection (a copy exists in the RP); "A Letter from the President," RP; Neal, "Robinson Biography," pp. 156–58. Numerous untitled articles in Arkansas newspapers mention Wilson's letter and copies of the articles may be found in the Robinson Scrapbooks, RP.

12. *Congressional Record*, 65th Cong., 2d sess., pp. 2201–8, 2436–42, 2492–95, 2505–9, 3151, 3306–12, 3418–25, 3433–43, 4329, 4784, 4883, 10085; "Fight on Railroad Bill," *New York Times*, January 26, 1918, p. 13; "Senate Kills Amendments to Railroad Bill," ibid., February 22, 1918, p. 1.

13. *Congressional Record*, 65th Cong., 2d sess., pp. 6097, 8554, 10984, 11038–39.

14. "Filibuster on in Senate; Fate of Bond Bill in Doubt; Knox Attacks League Draft, Proposes Court of Nations; Wilson's Plans Unchanged by Congress Threat of Delay," *New York Times*, March 2, 1919, pp. 1–3; Thomas A. Bailey, *Woodrow Wilson and the Great Betrayal* (Chicago: Quadrangle Books, 1963), pp. 1–15, 49–50; Kennedy, *Over Here*, p. 358, 360; Walter LaFeber, *The American Age: United States Policy at Home and Abroad since 1750* (New York: W. W. Norton and Company,

1987), pp. 302–3; Alexander DeConde, *A History of American Foreign Policy*, II: *Global Power (1900 to the present)* (3d ed.; New York: Charles Scribner's Sons, 1978), pp. 72–75; Samuel Flagg Bemis, *A Diplomatic History of the United States* (5th ed.; New York: Holt, Rinehart and Winston, 1965), pp. 654–56; Thomas A. Bailey, *A Diplomatic History of the American People* (8th ed.; New York: Appleton-Century-Crofts, 1969), pp. 606–8. For a good overview of the peace conference, see Ferrell, *Wilson and World War I*, pp. 135–55.

15. *Congressional Record*, 66th Cong., 1st sess., pp. 328–42; "Challenges Reed: Resign on League," *New York Times*, May 29, 1919, p. 15; William C. Widenor, *Henry Cabot Lodge and the Search for American Foreign Policy* (Berkeley: University of California Press, 1980), pp. 171–73, 258–59, 268–69; Robert James Maddox, *William E. Borah and American Foreign Policy* (Baton Rouge: Louisiana State University Press, 1969), pp. 59–59.

16. "League Opponents Uniting," *New York Times*, June 29, 1919, pp. 1, 5; "Pittman Opposes Any Reservations," ibid., July 26, 1919, p. 2; LaFeber, *American Age*, pp. 307–10; Kennedy, *Over Here*, p. 360; Herbert F. Margulies, *The Mild Reservationists and the League of Nations Controversy in the Senate* (Columbia: University of Missouri Press, 1989), pp. ix–x; Maddox, *Borah*, pp. 58–59, 66; Bailey, *Great Betrayal*, pp. 42, 53–71; DeConde, *Global Power*, pp. 72–73.

17. E. David Cronon, ed., *The Cabinet Diaries of Josephus Daniels, 1913–1921* (Lincoln: University of Nebraska Press, 1963), pp. 462–73; Margulies, *Mild Reservationists*, pp. x, 8–9, 108–9; Widenor, *Lodge*, pp. 267–68, 307–9; LaFeber, *American Age*, pp. 307–10; Ferrell, *Wilson and World War I*, pp. 169–70; LaFeber, *American Age*, pp. 303, 308–10; Kennedy, *Over Here*, pp. 361–62; Bailey, *Great Betrayal*, pp. 72–113; Bemis, *Diplomatic History*, pp. 658–59; DeConde, *Global Power*, pp. 75–77; Bailey, *Diplomatic History*, pp. 616–20.

18. *Congressional Record*, 66th Cong., 1st sess., pp. 8068–74, 8137–39, 8434–35, 8555–71, 8634–40, 8738–59; "Lodge in Dilemma, Holds Up Vote on Article X," *New York Times*, November 12, 1919, p. 1; Cronon, ed., *Daniels Diary*, pp. 462–66; Ferrell, *Wilson and World War I*, p. 309; Margulies, *Mild Reservationists*, pp. 108–13, 140–64; Bailey, *Great Betrayal*, pp. 151–86; Ferrell, *Wilson and World War I*, pp. 173–75; Bemis, *Diplomatic History*, pp. 659–60; DeConde, *Global Power*, pp. 76–78; Bailey, *Diplomatic History*, pp. 621–22.

19. *Congressional Record*, 66th Cong., 1st sess., pp. 8801–3; Margulies, *Mild Reservationists*, pp. 165–84; Ferrell, *Wilson and World War I*, pp. 175–76; LaFeber, *American Age*, pp. 310–11; Kennedy, *Over Here*, pp. 362–63; Bailey, *Great Betrayal*, pp. 187–97; Bemis, *Diplomatic History*, pp. 621–22.

20. *Congressional Record*, 66th Cong., 2d sess., pp. 4600–4603; Margulies, *Mild Reservationists*, pp. 249–53; Ferrell, *Wilson and World War I*, pp. 176–77; LaFeber, *American Age*, p. 311; Bailey, *Great Betrayal*, pp. 254–70; Bemis, *Diplomatic History*, p. 661; DeConde, *Global Power*, pp. 77–78; Bailey, *Diplomatic History*, pp. 617–18, 620–22; Cronon, ed., *Daniels Diary*, p. 520.

21. *Congressional Record*, 66th Cong., 2d sess., pp. 4601–3; Margulies, *Mild Reservationists*, pp. 253–56; Bailey, *Great Betrayal*, pp. 268–70; DeConde, *Global Power*, p. 79; Bailey, *Diplomatic History*, pp. 622–23.

22. Joe T. Robinson Jr. interview; W. T. Robinson interview.

23. Bailey, *Great Betrayal*, pp. 314–16; "Murphy Drops Cox, May Go to M'Adoo; Ex-Secretary's Boom Gaining Fast and Backers Say He Will Accept," *New York Times*, June 28, 1920, pp. 1–2; "Glass Captures Resolutions Post," ibid., June 29, 1920, pp. 1–2; "Wilson Forces Will Dominate about Platform," *Atlanta Constitution*, June 29, 1920, pp. 1–2; "Glass Wins and Administration in Full Control," *Houston Post*, June 29, 1920, pp. 1–2; Edward G. Hoffman, comp., *Official Report of the Proceedings of the Democratic National Convention Held in San Francisco, California, June 28, 29, 30, July 1, 2, 3, 5, and 6, 1920* (Indianapolis: Bookwalter-Ball Printing Company, [1920]), pp. 72–74; James M Cox, *Journey through My Years* (New York: Simon and Schuster, 1946), p. 228.

24. "Issues Must Be Settled First at San Fran Meet," *Houston Post*, June 26, 1920, pp. 1–2; "McAdoo Strength Grows as Cox Trickery Is Nailed; Love Leads Fight," ibid., June 28, 1920, pp. 1–2; "Fight Is on Prohibition," *New York Times*, July 1, 1920, pp. 1–2; James Holloman, "Palmer or Darkhorse Will Win Nomination, Hollowman's Prediction," *Atlanta Constitution*, June 24, 1920; Bailey, *Great Betrayal*, pp. 314–19; Cox, *Journey through My Years*, pp. 225–26.

25. Hoffman, comp., *Democratic Proceedings*, 1920, pp. 74–77; "M'Adoo Foes Organize, Marshall and Davis Talk Grows," *New York Times*, June 30, 1920, pp. 1–2; "Permanent Chairman Assails Republican Record," ibid., p. 4; "Democrats Entitled to Win in November, Declares Robinson," *Atlanta Constitution*, June 30, 1920, p. 4; "G.O.P. Lambasting Gets Wild Cheers from Convention," *Houston Post*, June 30, 1920, p. 1; Cox, *Journey through My Years*, p. 228.

26. Hoffman, comp., *Democratic Proceedings*, 1920, pp. 77–83; "M'Adoo Foes Organize, Marshall and Davis Talk Grows," *New York Times*, June 30, 1920, pp. 1–2; "Permanent Chairman Assails Republican Record," ibid., p. 4; "Democrats Entitled to Win in November, Declares Robinson," *Atlanta Constitution*, June 30, 1920, p. 4; "G.O.P. Lambasting Gets Wild Cheers from Convention," *Houston Post*, June 30, 1920, p. 1; Cox, *Journey through My Years*, p. 228.

27. Hoffman, comp., *Democratic Proceedings*, 1920, pp. 415–20; "Palmer Given Big Demonstraton as Name Presented," *Houston Post*, July 1, 1920, pp. 1–2; "Administration Loses Fight for Unamended League Plank," ibid., July 2, 1920, pp. 1–2; "Commoner Loses His Fight after Turning Convention Upside Down with Oratory," ibid., July 3, 1920, pp. 1–2; "Governor Cox, with 454 Votes, Leads on Sixteenth Ballot; Dark Horse Talk," ibid., July 4, 1920, pp. 1–2; "Cox-Roosevelt Democratic Ticket," ibid., July 7, 1920, pp. 1–2; Cox, *Journey through My Years*, pp. 229–33; David Burner, "The Democratic Party, 1910–1932" in Arthur M. Schlesinger Jr., ed., *History of U.S. Political Parties, III: 1910–1945: From Square Deal to New Deal* (New York: Chelsea House Publishers, 1973), p. 1819.

8 MINORITY LEADER

1. John D. Hicks, *Republican Ascendancy, 1921–1933*, New American Nation Series (New York: Harper and Row, 1963), pp. 106–29, 170–73; William E.

Leuchtenburg, *The Perils of Prosperity, 1914–1932*, Chicago History of American Civilization (Chicago: University of Chicago Press, 1958), pp. 152–55, 170–93.

2. Hicks, *Republican Ascendancy*, pp. 17–19, 94–96, 168–83; Leuchtenburg, *Perils of Prosperity*, pp. 66–83, 204–24; Arthur Schlesinger Jr., *The Age of Roosevelt*, I: *The Crisis of the Old Order, 1910–1932* (Boston: Houghton Mifflin Company, 1957), pp. 95–99, 105–10, 128, 174–75.

3. Hicks, *Republican Ascendancy*, pp. 23–34, 53–65; Leuchtenburg, *Perils of Prosperity*, pp. 56–65, 96–97; Schlesinger Jr., *Crisis of the Old Order*, pp. 51–63.

4. Joan Hoff Wilson, *American Business and Foreign Policy, 1920–1933* (Lexington: University Press of Kentucky, 1971), pp. 31–44; Maddox, *Borah*, pp. 112–13; *Republican Ascendancy*, pp. 32–49; Francis Russell, *The Shadow of Blooming Grove: Warren G. Harding in His Times* (New York: McGraw-Hill Book Company, 1968), pp. 481–85; Bemis, *Diplomatic History*, pp. 697–703; Alexander DeConde, *Global Power*, pp. 80–90.

5. *Congressional Record*, 67th Cong., 2d sess., pp. 3101–4, 3564, 3606–11, 3666–67, 3722–23, 3845, 3857–58; "Bitter Enders Start Attack on Treaty," *New York Times*, February 28, 1922, p. 1; "Reservations Run Wild," ibid., March 1, 1922, p. 4; "More Treaty Facts Asked of Harding," ibid., March 7, 1922, p. 1; "Declares Japanese and British Framed 4-Power Treaty," ibid., March 10, 1922, p. 1; "First Senate Vote Forecasts Victory of 4-Power Treaty," ibid., March 15, 1922, p. 1; Evans C. Johnson, *Oscar W. Underwood: A Political Biography* (Baton Rouge: Louisiana State University Press, 1980), pp. 319–21; George F. Sparks, ed., *A Many Colored Toga: The Diary of Henry Fountain Ashurst* (Tucson: University of Arizona Press, 1962), p. 169; Norman Davis to Robinson, March 13, 1922, RP; Bernard Baruch to Robinson, March 25, 1922, RP.

6. *Congressional Record*, 67th Cong., 2d sess., pp. 3564, 3606–7, 3609; "Lodge Is Heckled in Plea to Senate," *New York Times*, March 9, 1922, p. 3; "Treaty Foes Busy, Claim Recruits," ibid., March 11, 1922, p. 3; Wilson, *Foreign Policy*, pp. 46–47; Hicks, *Republican Ascendancy*, pp. 48–49; Neal, "Robinson Biography," pp. 177–78.

7. *Congressional Record*, 67th Cong., 2d sess., pp. 3608, 3715, 3722–23, 3845, 3857; "More Treaty Facts Asked of Harding," *New York Times*, March 7, 1922, p. 1; "Treaty Foes Busy, Claim Recruits," ibid., March 11, 1922, p. 1; "Heavy Assault on Treaty," ibid., March 12, 1922, p. 1; "First Senate Vote Forecasts Victory of 4-Power Treaty," ibid., March 15, 1922, p. 1; Johnson, *Underwood*, pp. 319–21; Neal, "Robinson Biography," p. 181.

8. *Congressional Record*, 67th Cong., 2d sess., pp. 4486–88, 4497; "First Senate Vote Forecasts Victory of 4-Power Treaty," *New York Times*, March 15, 1922, p. 1; Wilson, *Foreign Policy*, pp. 47–48; Russell, *Harding*, pp. 484–85; Johnson, *Underwood*, p. 321; DeConde, *Global Power*, p. 89.

9. U.S. Senate, *Rural Credits: Hearings before the Committee on Banking and the Currency* (Washington, D.C.: Government Printing Office, 1923), pp. 1–67; Edwin R. A. Seligman, *The Economics of Farm Relief: A Survey of the Agricultural Problem* (New York: Columbia University Press, 1929), pp. 16–29; Theodore Saloutos and John D. Hicks, *Agricultural Discontent in the Middle West, 1900–1939* (Madison: University of Wisconsin Press, 1951), pp. 324–35; Hicks, *Republican Ascendancy*, p. 193; Theodore Saloutus, *The American Farmer and the New Deal* (Ames: Iowa

State University Press, 1982), pp. 14–17; Gilbert C. Fite, *Cotton Fields No More: Southern Agriculture, 1865–1980* (Lexington: University of Kentucky Press, 1984), pp. 103–7. For a good overview of the entire agricultural problem, see U.S. Senate, *Rural Credits: Hearings before the Committee on Banking and the Currency* (Washington, D.C.: Government Printing Office, 1923).

10. Seligman, *Economics of Farm Relief*, pp. 16–29; Fite, *Cotton Fields No More*, pp. 103–7; Saloutos and Hicks, *Agricultural Discontent*, pp. 324–35; Saloutus, *The American Farmer and the New Deal*, pp. 14–17; Hicks, *Republican Ascendancy*, p. 193.

11. Saloutus, *The American Farmer and the New Deal*, pp. 19–21; Philip A. Grant Jr., "Southern Congressmen and Agriculture, 1921–1932," *Agricultural History*, 53 (January 1979): 338–41; Fite, *Cotton Fields No More*, p. 105; Hicks, *Republican Ascendancy*, pp. 193–95; Grant McConnell, *The Decline of Agrarian Democracy* (Berkeley: University of California Press, 1953), pp. 56–58;

12. *Congressional Record*, 67th Cong., 2d sess., pp. 2256–82, 2453–55; Joe T. Robinson Jr. interview; W. T. Robinson interview; Grady Miller Jr. interview.

13. *Congressional Record*, 69th Cong., 2d sess., p. 3518; ibid., 70th Cong., 1st sess., p. 8647; ibid., 71st Cong., 1st sess., pp. 1269, 2886, 2894; Grant, "Southern Congressmen," pp. 341–48; McConnell, *Decline of Agrarian Democracy*, pp. 57–58; Saloutos, *The American Farmer and the New Deal*, pp. 20–29; Hicks, *Republican Ascendancy*, pp. 197–201, 217–18.

14. *Congressional Record*, 67th Cong., 1st sess., pp. 3598–99; ibid., 2d sess., pp. 6238, 6253–56, 7228–29, 7704–6, 7771, 8371, 9011, 11627, 11635, 11734, 11898–99, 12671–72; ibid., 4th sess., pp. 3492–95, 3538; "Fight for Housing Taken to Congress," *New York Times*, May 20, 1922, p. 1; "Bonus Bill Goes In; May Pass Saturday," ibid., August 24, 1922, p. 1; "Robinson Demands Bonus over Tax Cut," ibid., November 26, 1923, p. 1; "Newberry Letter Scored in Senate," ibid., August 25, 1922, p. 1.

15. *Congressional Record*, 67th Cong., 2d sess., pp. 11773, 12192–94; "Edge Offers Bill to Buy Coal Mines," *New York Times*, August 26, 1922, p. 1; "Move for Peace on 52 Roads Reported; Toning Down Strike Injunction Likely; Robinson Denounces It in the Senate," ibid., September 7, 1922, p. 1.

16. Sidney Anderson to Robinson, July 16, 1921, RP; *Congressional Record*, 67th Cong., 1st sess., pp. 744, 1056–57; ibid., 2d sess., pp. 11830–31.

17. *Congressional Record*, 67th Cong., 2d sess., pp. 6253–56, 6870, 12672.

18. "Minority Leader Sought," *New York Times*, November 9, 1922, p. 5; "Start Leadership Fight," ibid., December 6, 1922, p. 2.

19. Richard L. Watson, "Furnifold Simmons: Jehovah of the Tarheels," *North Carolina Historical Review*, XLIV (April 1967): 166–87; *Biographical Directory of the American Congress* (Washington, D.C.: Government Printing Office, 1928), p. 1525; Frank Hampton to Woodbridge Ferris, January 25, 1923, Furnifold M. Simmons Papers, William R. Perkins Library, Duke University (hereafter cited as SP).

20. Hampton to Ferris, January 25, 1922, SP; Claude Kitchen to Lee Overman, November 20, 1922, SP; Hampton to Kitchin, November 21, 1922, SP; Furnifold Simmons to Hampton (telegram), December 2, 1922, SP; Hampton to George Gordon Battle, December 2, 1922, SP; Simmons to E. D. Smith, December 2, 1922, SP; Hampton to Simmons (telegram), December 6, 1922, SP.

21. Grady Miller to Robinson, November 26, 1922, RP; "Close Fight in Senate for Minority Leader," *New York Times*, January 20, 1923, p. 8; Robinson to C. C. Dill, December 15, 1922, RP; Simmons to Smith, December 2, 1922, SP; Hampton to Ferris, January 25, 1922, SP; Neal, "Robinson Biography," pp. 181–83.

22. "Close Fight in Senate for Minority Leader," *New York Times*, January 20, 1923, p. 8; "Robinson Will Lead Senate Democrats," ibid., February 9, 1923; Hampton to Simmons, February 9, 1923, SP; Robinson to Bernard Baruch, December 13, 1922, RP; Neal, "Robinson Biography," p. 183.

23. "South Starts Filibuster in Congress," *New York Times*, March 4, 1923, p. 1; "Assails the Record of Dying Congress," ibid., March 4, 1923, p. 1; "Harding's Whole Program Failed, Says Minority Leader in Senate," ibid. March 4, 1923, p. 1; "Harding to Back Up World Court Stand in This City Today," ibid., April 24, 1923, p. 1.

24. L. Borggins [?] to Robinson August 30, 1923, RP; "Five Senators Sail for Geneva Parley," *New York Times*, August 7, 1923, p. 18; "Asks Europe to Speed Balancing of Budgets," ibid., August 18, 1923, p. 4; W. B. McKinley to Robinson, June 23, 1922, RP; Arthur D. Call to Robinson, June 23, 1922; McKinley to Robinson, June 23, 1922; Grady Miller Jr. interview; Mrs. Grady Miller interview.

25. *Congressional Record*, 68th Cong. 1st sess., pp. 1782, 2244–45; "Demand in Senate That Denby Quit; House Votes Oil Prosecution Fund; Coolidge in Conference on Scandal," *New York Times*, January 29, 1924, p. 1; Burl Noggle, *Teapot Dome: Oil and Politics in the 1920s* (New York: W. W. Norton and Company, 1965), pp. 46–50, 65–67, 75–76, 83–84, 97–98, 105–6, 117–18; Neal, "Robinson Biography," pp. 206–11.

26. *Congressional Record*, 68th Cong., 1st sess., pp. 1541–43, 1782, 1974–79, 1986–87, 2173–74, 2234–35, 2244–45, 2980–82, 3300–3305, 3399–3401, 3408–12; "Demand in Senate That Denby Quit; House Votes Prosecution Funds; Coolidge in Conference on Scandals," *New York Times*, January 29, 1924, p. 1; "Senate Broadens Scope of Inquiry," ibid., February 14, 1924, p. 3; "Daugherty Must Go, Borah Tells Senate; He Is Ready to Support Impeachment; Robinson Says Adams Injects Politics," ibid., February 24, 1924, p. 1; "Senators Wrangle over W. G. M'Adoo," ibid., February 27, 1924, p. 1; Noggle, *Teapot Dome*, pp. 49–50, 97–98, 105, 117–18; Neal, "Robinson Biography," pp. 207–11.

27. Robert K. Murray, *The 103rd Ballot: Democrats and the Disaster in Madison Square Garden* (New York: Harper and Row, 1976), pp. 41–50, 58–71; Hicks, *Republican Ascendancy*, pp. 94–97; Matthew and Hanna Josephson, *Al Smith: Hero of the Cities A Political Portrait Drawing on the Papers of Frances Perkins* (Boston: Houghton Mifflin Company, 1969), pp. 302–14; Burner, "The Democratic Party, 1910–1932," pp. 1821–22.

28. "Arkansas Brings Robinson Boom," *New York Times*, June 24, 1924, p. 6; "Sen. Robinson's Platform," ibid., June 25, 1924, p. 16.

29. Harvey Couch to Robinson, June 30, 1923, RP; W. Morton Carden to Robinson, July 3, 1923, RP; Robinson to Carden, July 9, 1923, RP.

30. Grady Miller to W. T. Sitlington, February 18, 1924, RP; Miller to Joe W. House Jr., March 2, 1924, RP; Sitlington to Robinson, March 7, 1924, RP; Clarence P. Newton to Robinson, March 7, 1924, RP; William Jennings Bryan to Robinson, March 5, 1924, RP; Bryan to [?], March 6, 1924, RP; Robinson to C. H. Brough,

March 15, 1924, C. H. Brough Papers, Arkansas Historical Commission, Little Rock (hereafter cited as BP).

31. Robinson to House, March 17, 1924, RP; Miller to Sitlington, February 18, 1924, RP.

32. Charles A. Greathouse, comp., *Official Report of the Proceedings of the Democratic Convention . . . 1924* (Indianapolis: Bookwalter-Ball-Greathouse Printing Company, 1924), pp. 103–5; "Robinson Offered by Ex-Gov. Brough," *New York Times*, June 26, 1924, p. 6; William H. Harbaugh, *Lawyer's Lawyer: The Life of John W. Davis* (New York: Oxford University Press, 1973), pp. 209–11.

33. "Peace Move Is Welcomed," *New York Times*, July 6, 1924, p. 1; "Smith Forces See Hope in Conference," ibid., p. 1; "Darkhorse Activity as Parley Begins," ibid., p. 3; "Proposals by Smith and Minority Candidates, and the Counter Proposals Offered by McAdoo," ibid., July 7, 1924, p. 1; "Conferees Split," ibid., p. 1; Greathouse, comp., *Official Report, 1924*, pp. 780–85; Murray, *103rd Ballot*, pp. 187–94. Murray's book is an excellent overview of the Democratic convention; he follows the events day by day and, at times, hour by hour.

34. "Drive Starts for Robinson," *New York Times*, July 7, 1924, p. 1; "Darkhorses Ready for New Contests," ibid., p. 3; "Peace Move Is Welcomed," ibid., July 6, 1924, p. 1; Murray, *103rd Ballot*, pp. 202–5; Harbaugh, *Lawyer's Lawyer*, pp. 214–17; Burner, "The Democratic Party, 1910–1932," p. 1823.

35. "J. F. Mitchell Felled by Senator Robinson," *New York Times*, June 20, 1924, p. 4; "Club Plans Inquiry into Senator's Blow," ibid., June 21, 1924, p. 13; "Senator Robinson Is Suspended by Golf Club for Felling a Player on Chevy Chase Links," ibid., June 26, 1924, p. 1.

36. *Congressional Record*, 68th Cong., 1st sess., pp. 1540–42, 1604–5, 3399–3401, 5553–59.

37. Ibid., pp. 5569–76, 6019–21, 6075–76, 8330, 9507–13; 2d sess., pp. 3493–94, 3607–14; "Asks Sugar Inquiry, Aiming at Coolidge," *New York Times*, January 3, 1925, p. 1; "Hits Pullman Surcharge," ibid., February 11, 1925, p. 22; "Hits Pullman Surcharge," ibid., February 12, 1925, p. 3.

38. *Congressional Record*, 68th Cong., 1st sess., pp. 9993, 10011, 10139–42.

39. *Congressional Record*, 68th Cong., 1st sess., pp. 6693–6703, 6774, 8788, 8869–71.

40. *Congressional Record*, 68th Cong., 2d sess., pp. 1204–6, 1363–64; "Dial Denounced, Withdraws Speech," *New York Times*, January 8, 1925, p. 1.

41. "Robinson Predicts Deep Cut in Taxes," *New York Times*, July 16, 1925, p. 3; "Fifteen Ships Dock, Causing Congestion," ibid., September 22, 1925, p. 9; Grady Miller Jr. interview; [MacLeish], "Senator from Arkansas," p. 90; Joe T. Robinson, "A New Ireland Rising out of Turmoil," *New York Times*, October 11, 1925, IX, 1; "Denies Ireland Prospers," ibid., October 17, 1925, p. 14; Robinson, "Ulster and Free State Still Deadlocked," ibid., October 18, 1925, X, 5; Robinson, "Leftover Issues Hamper Irish Free State," ibid., October 25, 1925, X, 5.

42. *Congressional Record*, 69th Cong., 1st sess., pp. 830–31, 918–22, 2022–24, 2182–86, 2572, 2590–92, 2673–76, 2824–25, 3423–27, 5140–41, 5266–67, 5377–79, 5388; ibid., 2d sess., pp. 1259–61, 1333, 3121–22; 5015–16, 5556–58; "Motion for

Closure on World Court Offered in Senate," *New York Times*, January 23, 1926, p. 1; "Closure Wins, 68–26, Assuring Victory for World Court," ibid., January 26, 1926, II, 1; "Favor Peace Treaty Briand Suggested," ibid., June 19, 1927, p. 1; "Robinson Assails Voters' Corruption," ibid., June 16, 1926, p. 2; "Robinson Assails Coolidge Silence," ibid., September 10, 1926, p. 22; "Vare Investigation Proposed," ibid., January 11, 1927, p. 4; "Coal Relief Demand Grows in Congress," ibid., January 17, 1926, p. 22; "Democrats Line Up behind Coal Bills," ibid., February 7, 1926, p. 26; "Coolidge Radio Plan Loses in Committee," ibid., April 29, 1926, p. 9; "Tariff Commission Assailed in Senate," ibid., March 7, 1926, p. 5; "Tariff Commission to Be Investigated," ibid., March 10, 1926, p. 11.

43. *Congressional Record*, 69th Cong., 1st sess., pp. 10485–86, 11357–60, 11674–77, 11856–58, 12212; ibid., 2d sess., pp. 3129, 3134–36, 3431, 3518; Hicks, *Republican Ascendancy*, pp. 198–200; Neal, "Robinson Biography," pp. 223–26.

44. Joe T. Robinson Jr. interview; Mrs. Grady Miller interview.

45. Walter G. Riddick to Robinson, June 28, 1922, RP; Robinson to Coleman, Robinson, and House, February 20, 1924, RP; Joe T. Robinson Jr. interview; Mrs. Grady Miller interview; Grady Miller interview; Neal, "Robinson Biography," pp. 40–41.

46. Robinson to House, March 13, 1926, RP; Robinson to Riddick, March 13, 1926, RP; Riddick to Robinson, March 11, 1926, RP; House to Robinson, March 17, 1926, RP; Robinson to House, March 20, 1926, RP; Robinson to Moses, October 21, 1926, RP; Robinson to Moses, March 11, 1935, RP; Grady Miller interview; Joe T. Robinson Jr. interview; Neal, "Robinson Biography," pp. 41–44.

47. Robinson to Robinson, House, & Moses, February 2, 1927, RP; Robinson to Moses, February 27, 1927, RP; Grady Miller interview; Joe T. Robinson Jr. interview.

48. Grady Miller interview; Mrs. Grady Miller interview; Joe T. Robinson Jr. interview; Neal, "Robinson Biography," p. 44.

9 VICE-PRESIDENTIAL CANDIDATE

1. Roy V. Peel and Thomas C. Donnelly, *The 1928 Campaign: An Analysis* (New York: Richard R. Smith, 1931), pp. 9–11.

2. "Robinson a Sturdy Partner for Smith," *New York Times*, July 15, 1928, RP; Calvin Ledbetter Jr., "Joe T. Robinson and the Presidential Campaign of 1928," *Arkansas Historical Quarterly*, XLV (summer 1986): 100; Neal, "Robinson Biography," pp. 242–43.

3. *Congressional Record*, 70th Cong., 1st sess., pp. 1649–59; "Heflin Attack on Smith Puts Democratic Senators into Caucus Test Today," *New York Times*, January 19, 1928, p. 1; Ledbetter, "Campaign," pp. 100–101; Neal, "Robinson Biography," pp. 242–43; "Heflin Vs. Robinson," *Atlanta Constitution*, January 19, 1928, p. 6.

4. *Congressional Record*, pp. 1659–63; "Heflin Attack on Smith Puts Democratic

Senators into Caucus Test Today," *New York Times*, January 19, 1928, p. 1; Ledbetter, "Campaign," pp. 101–2; Neal, "Robinson Biography," pp. 242–43.

5. *Congressional Record*, pp. 1660–63; "Heflin Attack on Smith Puts Democratic Senators into Caucus Test Today," *New York Times*, January 19, 1928, p. 1; Ledbetter, "Campaign," pp. 101–2; Neal, "Robinson Biography," pp. 242–43.

6. Robinson to Thomas Heflin, January 19, 1928, RP; "Democrats, 35 to 1, Uphold Robinson against Heflin," *New York Times*, January 20, 1928, p. 1; Ledbetter, "Campaign," pp. 101–2; Neal, "Robinson Biography," pp. 242–43.

7. "Press of Alabama Repudiates Heflin," *New York Times*, January 20, 1928, p. 2; "A Showdown for Tom-Tom," ibid., p. 20; "The Spirit of Jefferson Speaks," *New York Evening World*, January 20, 1928, RP; "Heflin Vs. Robinson," *Atlanta Constitution*, January 19, 1928, p. 6; "Hon. Joseph Robinson," *Alexandria Gazette*, January 27, 1928, RP; Resolution of the Geneva County, Alabama, Democratic Party, January 21, 1928, RP; W. A. Gunter Jr. to Robinson [telegram], January 19, 1928, RP; John Brunner to Robinson, January 19, 1928, RP; [Congressman] John Clarke to Robinson, January 19, 1928, RP; H. T. Rogers to Robinson, January 20, 1928, RP; Earl Hardin to Robinson, January 20, 1928, RP; Claude Fuller to Robinson, January 21, 1928, RP; O. Gardener to Robinson, January 18, 1928, RP; Bishop Jonathan Morris to Robinson, January 23, 1928, RP; [Governor] John Martineau to Robinson, January 21, 1928, RP; S. E. Tull to Robinson, January 24, 1928, RP; W. T. Robinson interview.

8. Joe T. Robinson Jr. interview; Grady Miller Jr. interview.

9. "Robinson Speech Widely Heralded," *Chicago Daily News*, February 11, 1928, RP; "Massachusetts Is for Joe Robinson," *Arkansas Gazette*, March 5, 1928, RP; "Rogers on Robinson," RP; "Robinson Rises in Party Esteem," *New York Times*, January 29, 1928, RP; "Robinson Viewed as Still in the Race," ibid., March 26, 1928, RP; "Robinson May Be Democrats' Compromise," *Arkansas Democrat*, March 4, 1928, p. 1; "Walsh-Smith Row Seen at Houston Meet," ibid., March 5, 1928, RP; Robinson to J. S. Utley, March 16, 1928, RP; Peel and Donnelly, *The 1928 Campaign*, p. 31.

10. "J. W. Davis Favored to Nominate Smith," *New York Times*, February 19, 1928, p. 3; "Robinson Favored to Lead at Houston," ibid., March 24, 1928, p. 2; "Walker Is Slated to Nominate Smith," ibid., April 23, 1928, p. 12; "Senator Robinson Likely to Handle Gavel at Houston," *St. Louis Star*, March 24, 1928, RP; "Robinson Favored to Lead at Houston," n.p., n.d, RP; "Robinson Sure to Be Power in Convention," *Arkansas Democrat*, January 24, 1928, RP; Fred L. Israel, *Nevada's Key Pittman* (Lincoln: University of Nebraska Press, 1963), p. 62; Neal, "Robinson Biography," pp. 243–44; Ledbetter, "Campaign," p. 105.

11. "Vice Presidency Race Open in Both Parties," *New York Times*, May 27, 1928, pp. ix, 9; "Robinson Forecast for Second Place," ibid., June 19, 1928, p. 12; "Robinson Leading for Vice President," ibid., June 25, 1928, p. 4; "Robinson Boom Gains Momentum," *Arkansas Democrat*, June 26, 1928, p. 1; "Senator Robinson Gains in Strength for Second Place," *Washington Post*, June 26, 1928, p. 1; John Robert Moore, *Senator Josiah William Bailey of North Carolina: A Political Biography* (Durham, North Carolina: Duke University Press, 1968), p. 52; Rexey Smith and Norman Beasley, *Carter Glass: A Biography* (New York: Longmans, Green, and

Company, 1939), p. 258; Ledbetter, "Campaign," pp. 103–5; Neal, "Robinson Biography," pp. 243–46.

12. Key Pittman to Mrs. Henry [Belle] Moskowitz, June 18, 1928, Key Pittman Papers, Library of Congress, Washington, D.C. (hereafter cited as PP); Pittman to Robinson, June 18, 1928, PP. Copies of these letters may also be found in the RP.

13. "Hague Pushing Robinson," *New York Times*, June 26, 1928, p. 2; "Robinson Stronger for Second Place," ibid., p. 3; "Robinson Gets Second Place Boom," *Austin Statesman*, June 25, 1928, Democratic Party National Convention 1928 Collection, Houston Metropolitan Research Center, Houston Public Library, Houston, Texas (hereafter cited as DPNC). Many of the newspaper articles in DPNC are pasted into scrapbooks and do not include the page numbers of the articles. "Travelers to Give Banquet Honoring Senator Robinson of Arkansas Next Monday," *Houston Post*, June 21, 1928, DPNC; "Edge to Robinson," *Kansas City Star*, June 26, 1928, DPNC; "Robinson Boom Gains Momentum," *Arkansas Democrat*, June 26, 1928, p. 1; "Senator Robinson Gains in Strength for Second Place," *Washington Post*, June 26, 1928, p. 1; Neal, "Robinson Biography," pp. 246–47; Ledbetter, "Campaign," pp. 106–7.

14. Peel and Donnelly, *The 1928 Campaign*, p. 30; "Official Souvenir Program of the National Democratic Convention," 1928, DPNC; "'Happy Warrior' Al Smith Nominated in 'Miracle' House That Jesse Built," *Houston Chronicle*, n.d., DPNC; "How 25,000 Will Be Seated at the Coliseum," *Houston Post-Dispatch*, May 19, 1928, DPNC; "Democrats Chose Houston as Site of '28 Convention," *Houston Post*, January 13, 1985, DPNC; "Like a Carnival, Usher Recalls," *Houston Post*, n.d., DPNC; numerous pictures of the exterior, DPNC.

15. "How 25,000 Will Be Seated at the Coliseum," *Houston Post-Dispatch*, May 19, 1928, DPNC; "Democrats Chose Houston as Site of '28 Convention," *Houston Post*, January 13, 1985, DPNC; "Like a Carnival, Usher Recalls," *Houston Post*, n.d., DPNC; numerous pictures of the interior, DPNC.

16. Charles Greathouse, comp., *Official Report of the Proceedings of the Democratic National Convention* (Indianapolis: Bookwalter-Ball-Greathouse Printing Company, 1928), pp. 71–76; "Shaver Gets New Gavel to Start Things," *Dallas News*, June 27, 1928, p. 1; "Combat among Delegates," *New York Times*, June 27, 1928, p. 1; "Text of Senator Robinson's Plea for Tolerance Which Set Off Explosion on Convention Floor," ibid., p. 1; "Robinson Warns Party against Wet Plank and Assails Corruption of G.O.P.," *Washington Star*, June 27, 1928, p. 1; "Tumult over Al," *Washington Star*, June 28, 1928, p. 1; "Fists, Police Clubs Fly at Houston," *Fort Worth Star-Telegram*, June 28, 1928, p. 1; Peel and Donnelly, *The 1928 Campaign*, p. 31; Moore, *Bailey*, p. 52; Ledbetter, "Campaign," p. 107; Neal, "Robinson Biography," p. 247.

17. "Senator Slated Days Ago," *New York Times*, June 27, 1928, p. 1; "Drive Is Started against Robinson," *New York Times*, June 29, 1928, p. 1; "Delegates Cheer Message," ibid., June 30, 1928, p. 1; "Delegates Hasten End of Convention," ibid., p. 2; Greathouse, comp., *Official Proceedings*, 1928, pp. 244–52; Burner, "The Democratic Party, 1910–1932," p. 1827.

18. Sam Rorex to H. D. Knickerbocker, September 1, 1928, RP; "Pastor Rebuked for Robinson Attacks," n.d., clipping in RP; S. E. Tull to Robinson, January 24, 1928, RP; Ledbetter, "Campaign," pp. 111–15; Nevin Neal, "The Smith-Robinson

Arkansas Campaign of 1928," *Arkansas Historical Quarterly*, XIX (spring 1960): 3–4; Neal, "Robinson Biography," pp. 276–81. Arkansas was similar to the rest of the nation in the anti-Catholic rhetoric of the Protestant clergy. See Burner, "The Democratic Party, 1910–1932," pp. 1827–29, and Peel and Donnelly, *The 1928 Campaign*, pp. 62–64. While the author believes, as do many others, that Smith's Catholicism and his anti-prohibitionists hurt him in many areas, for a differing view, see Joan Hoff Wilson, *Herbert Hoover: Forgotten Progressive* (Boston: Little, Brown and Company, 1975), pp. 129–33.

19. James Comer to J. Carroll Cone, July 16, 1928, RP; Harry Lee Williams to Robinson, July 24, 1928, RP. For a view of the Klan on the national level, see Peel and Donnelly, *The 1928 Campaign*, pp. 62–63.

20. "Address of Senator Joe T. Robinson, State Teachers College, July 17, 1928," RP; "Address of Senator Joe T. Robinson, Hope, Arkansas, August 9, 1928," RP; T. H. Caraway to Robinson, August 14, 1928, RP; Cone to Comer, RP; Neal, "The Smith-Robinson Arkansas Campaign of 1928," pp. 4–5; untitled two-page manuscript on the campaign, n.d., RP; Ledbetter, "Campaign," pp. 111–13; Neal, "Robinson Biography," pp. 274–76.

21. Utley to Robinson, July 21, 1928, RP; Ledbetter, "Campaign," pp. 111–12; Neal, "The Smith-Robinson Arkansas Campaign of 1928," pp. 5–7; Neal, "Robinson Biography," pp. 275–78.

22. Robinson to John J. Raskob, August 10, 1928, RP; "Great Throng Hears Senator as He Accepts," *Arkansas Gazette*, August 31, 1928, p. 1; "Robinson Accepts in Vigorous Talk," ibid.; "Robinson Officially Accepts Nomination," *Sentinel-Record*, Hot Springs National Park, Arkansas, August 30, 1928, p. 1; Claude Bowers Oral History, p. 80, Columbia Oral History Colection, Columbia University, New York, New York (hereafter cited as COHC); Ledbetter, "Campaign," pp. 115–16; Neal, "Robinson Biography," pp. 265–72, 282–83; Neal, "The Smith-Robinson Arkansas Campaign of 1928," p. 7.

23. "Great Throng Hears Senator as He Accepts," *Arkansas Gazette*, August 31, 1928, p. 1; "Robinson Accepts in Vigorous Talk," ibid., p. 1; "Robinson Officially Accepts Nomination," *Sentinel-Record*, Hot Springs National Park, Arkansas, August 30, 1928, p. 1; Ledbetter, "Campaign," pp. 115–16; Neal, "Robinson Biography," pp. 265–72, 282–83; Neal, "The Smith-Robinson Arkansas Campaign of 1928," p. 7.

24. Robinson to Raskob, November 3, 1928, RP; Millard Tydings to Robinson, September 1, 1928, RP; Grady Miller to Edwin Halsey, October 1, 1928, RP; Pittman to Robinson, October 3, 1928, RP; Pat Harrison to Robinson, August 15, 1928, RP; [Miller?] to Vint Miles, September 11, 1928, RP; "Second Tour Senator Joe T. Robinson" [itinerary], n.d., RP; "Senator Joe T. Robinson's Midwestern Tour" [itinerary], n.d., RP; Ledbetter, "Campaign," pp. 117–18; Neal, "Robinson Biography," pp. 284–85.

25. Robinson to Mrs. Henry Moskowitz, October 4, 1928, RP; Robinson to Raskob, September 11, 1928, RP; Robinson to Harrison, September 11, 1928, RP; Robinson to B. M. Baruch, September 18, 1928, RP; [Miller?] to Miles, September 11, 1928, RP; Ledbetter, "Campaign," p. 121; Neal, "Robinson Biography," pp. 287–89.

26. "15,000 Applaud Robinson's Message to Organized Labor," *Dallas Morning News*, September 4, 1928, RP; "Keep Crooks Out, Says Robinson," *Nashville*

Tennessean, September 7, 1928, p. 1; "Senator Robinson, in Masterly Address, Outlines Leading Issues of the Campaign to Great Crowd at Memorial Auditorium," *Chattanooga Daily Times*, September 8, 1928, p. 1; "Address of Senator Joe T. Robinson, Raleigh, North Carolina, September 11, 1928," RP; "Address of Senator Joseph T. Robinson, Charlotte, North Carolina, September 12, 1928," RP; Robinson to Baruch, September 18, 1928, RP; Ledbetter, "Campaign," pp. 117–20; Neal, "Robinson Biography," pp. 285–89; Peel and Donnelly, *The 1928 Campaign*, pp. 76–77.

27. Robinson to Tydings, September 19, 1928, RP; itinerary of Robinson's entire tour, n.d., RP; Neal, "Robinson Biography," p. 285.

28. Robinson to Raskob, September 11, 1928, RP; Robinson to Harrison, September 12, 1928, RP; Robinson to Baruch, September 18, 1928, RP; Neal, "Robinson Biography," pp. 285–88.

29. Pittman to Robinson, October 3, 1928, RP; Robinson to John Raskob, August 10, 1928, RP; "Robinson Raps G.O.P. Boulder Dam Politics," *San Francisco Chronicle*, October 12, 1928, p. 1; "Address of Senator Joe T. Robinson, Muskogee, Oklahoma, October 3, 1928," RP; "Address of Senator Joe T. Robinson, Des Moines, Iowa, October 27, 1928," RP; David Burner, *The Politics of Provincialism: The Democratic Party in Transition, 1918–1932* (Cambridge: Harvard University Press, 1986), p. 215; Ledbetter, "Campaign," pp. 118–19; Neal, "Robinson Biography," pp. 289–91, 293–99; Peel and Donnelly, *The 1928 Campaign*, pp. 67–69.

30. Pittman to Robinson, October 3, 1928, RP; Robinson to Harry Hawes, October 4, 1928, RP; Robinson to Moskowitz, October 4, 1928, RP; "Address of Senator Joseph T. Robinson, Kansas City, Missouri, September 26, 1928," RP; "Joe Robinson in Wichita," *Wichita Sunday Beacon*, September 30, 1928, p. 1, RP; "Robinson Flays Owen and Hoover in Tulsa Speech," *Tulsa Daily World*, October 3, 1928, p. 1, RP; Richard Lowitt, *Bronson M. Cutting* (Albuquerque: Univeristy of New Mexico Press, 1992), p. 149; "Senator Robinson Here Today," *Arizona Republican*, October 8, 1928, p. 1, RP; "Scores G.O.P. for Neglect of Veterans," *Los Angeles Examiner*, October 10, 1928, p. 1, RP; "Senator Robinson Guest Here Today," *Sioux City Tribune*, October 23, 1928, p. 1, RP; "Senator Robinson Arrives Today; Gives Address Tonight at Armory," *Duluth News-Tribune*, October 26, 1928, p. 1, RP; Ledbetter, "Campaign," pp. 120–21; Neal, "Robinson Biography," pp. 289–91, 294–98; Burner, "The Democratic Party, 1910–1932," p. 1829.

31. Burner, *Politics*, p. 238; Robinson to Miller, October 21, 1928, RP; "Address of Senator Joe T. Robinson, East St. Louis, Illinois, October 30, 1928," p. 1.

32. "Address of Senator Joe T. Robinson, Clarksburg, West Virginia, November 3, 1928," RP; Ledbetter, "Campaign," pp. 118, 121; Neal, "Robinson Biography," p. 291.

33. "Robinson Welcome Committees Named," *Arkansas Gazette*, November 1, 1928, p. 1; "Homecoming Will Be Made State Event," *Arkansas Democrat*, October 30, 1928, p. 1; "'Homefolks' Will Welcome Robinson," ibid., p. 1; Ledbetter, "Campaign," p. 121; Neal, "Robinson Biography," pp. 291–92.

34. Robinson to Pittman, November 21, 1928, RP; "Address of Senator Joe T. Robinson, Clarksburg, West Virginia, November 3, 1928," RP; Ledbetter, "Campaign," pp. 122–23; Neal, "Robinson Biography," p. 323; Harbaugh, *Lawyer's*

Lawyer, pp. 275–76; Wilson, *Herbert Hoover*, pp. 128–29. Allan J. Lichtman, in *Prejudice and the Old Politics: The Presidential Election of 1928* (Chapel Hill: University of North Carolina Press, 1979), sees religious bigotry as the most important factor in the election, pp. 231–46; Joan Hoff Wilson, in *Herbert Hoover: Forgotten Progressive*, pp. 128–33, disagrees, seeing religious bigotry as unimportant in Hoover's victory, arguing that Hoover was too popular and the economy in too good a shape for anyone else to win. For other views of the issues and their impact, see Peel and Donnelly, *The 1928 Campaign*, pp. 53–71. They placed continued prosperity as the most important issue while ranking the "religion" issue as fourth in importance, albeit a loud and acrimonious fourth.

10 DIPLOMAT AND OPPOSITION LEADER

1. Herbert Hoover, *The Memoirs of Herbert Hoover: The Cabinet and the Presidency, 1920–1933* (New York: Macmillan, 1952), pp. 253–55, 291–93; Wilson, *Herbert Hoover*, pp. 134–45; Hicks, *Republican Ascendancy*, pp. 217–18; Martin L. Fausold, *The Presidency of Herbert Hoover* (Lawrence: University Press of Kansas, 1985), pp. 49–53.

2. "Congress Leaders Clash as to Scope of Extra Session," *New York Times*, April 14, 1929, p. 1; "Congress Leaders Sum Up Prospects," ibid., April 15, 1929, p. 2; "Leaders in Congress Comment on Message," ibid., April 17, 1929, p. 2.

3. "House Passes Farm Bill Without Debenture Plan; Hailed as Hoover Victory," ibid., April 26, 1929, p. 1; "Hoover's Farm Stand Upheld by Watson," ibid., May 2, 1929, p. 4; "Congressmen Score New Tariff Valuing," ibid., May 9, 1929, p. 20; Wilson, *Herbert Hoover*, p. 134; Hicks, *Republican Ascendancy*, pp. 217–18; Fausold, *The Presidency of Herbert Hoover*, pp. 50–52.

4. *Congressional Record*, 71st Cong., 1st sess., pp. 598–600, 714, 1239–41; "Hoover Men Press Plans in Senate to Kill Debentures," *New York Times*, April 27, 1929, p. 1; "Fess Assails Borah on Farm Debenture," ibid., May 10, 1929, p. 3; "Senate Group Takes Threatening Stand," ibid., May 15, 1929, p. 1; "Senate Passes Debentures Farm Bill and Lively Battle with House Impends; Hoover Raises Duty on 3 Farm Products," ibid., May 15, 1929, p. 1; Fausold, *The Presidency of Herbert Hoover*, pp. 50–51.

5. *Congressional Record*, 71st Cong., 1st sess., pp. 1249–50; "Senate Passes Debentures Farm Bill and Lively Battle with House Impends; Hoover Raises Duty on 3 Farm Products," *New York Times*, May 15, 1929, p. 1; "Senate Group Takes Threatening Stand," ibid., May 15, 1929, p. 1; "Debenture Test Due Today with Senate Vote in Doubt; Borah Hits Hoover Stand," ibid., June 11, 1929, p. 1; "Senate Accepts Hoover Farm Bill," ibid., June 15, 1929, p. 1; "Laud Achievements of Senate Minority," ibid., June 22, 1929, p. 18; Hicks, *Republican Ascendancy*, pp. 218; Fausold, *The Presidency of Herbert Hoover*, pp. 51–52.

6. *Congressional Record*, 71st Cong., 1st sess., pp. 2731, 2871–72; ibid., 2d sess., pp. 10622–23; "Laud Achievements of Senate Minority," *New York Times*, June 22,

1929, p. 18; "Tariff Foes Agree on Their Strategy," ibid., September 6, 1929, p. 8; Hoover, *Memoirs*, pp. 219–97; Wilson, *Herbert Hoover*, pp. 134–35; Hicks, *Republican Ascendancy*, pp. 219–22; Fausold, *The Presidency of Herbert Hoover*, pp. 53–54, 94–97.

7. John Kenneth Galbraith, *The Great Crash, 1929* (Boston: Houghton Mifflin Company, 1961), pp. 93–148; Hicks, *Republican Ascendancy*, pp. 223–34; Schlesinger, *The Crisis of the Old Order*, pp. 156–60.

8. Radio address by Henry Stimson, London, February 6, 1930, in U.S. State Department, *London Naval Conference: Speeches and Press Statements by Members of the American Delegation, January 20–April 29, 1930* (Washington, D.C.: Government Printing Office, 1930), pp. 18–19; "Washington Ready for Wide Navy Cuts in Agreement with MacDonald's Plans; Our Delegates Sail with High Hopes," *New York Times*, January 10, 1930, p. 1; Robert Goron Kaufman, *Arms Control during the Pre-Nuclear Era: The United States and Naval Limitation between the Two World Wars* (New York: Columbia University Press, 1990), pp. 1–3, 122–24; L. Ethan Ellis, *Republican Foreign Policy, 1921–1933* (New Brunswick, New Jersey: Rutgers University Press, 1968), pp. 155–65; Wilson, *Foreign Policy*, pp. 51–53; Raymond O'Connor, *Perilous Equilibrium: The United States and the London Naval Conference of 1930* (Lawrence: University of Kansas Press, 1962), p. 59. For a good overview of efforts to limit naval forces, see Kaufman, *Arms Control during the Pre-Nuclear Era*. For a more in-depth look at the London Naval Conference, see Raymond O'Connor, *Perilous Equilibrium: The United States and the London Naval Conference of 1930* (Lawrence: University of Kansas Press, 1962).

9. Henry Stimson to Herbert Hoover, January 19, 1930, [telegram, paraphrased], Presidential Papers, Herbert C. Hoover Library, West Branch, Iowa (hereafter cited as HCH Library); Benjamin H. Williams, *A Series of Twelve Radio Talks on the London Naval Conference: Its Background and Results* (Pittsburgh, Pennsylvania: University of Pittsburgh, 1930), pp. 37–83; Kaufman, *Arms Control during the Pre-Nuclear Era*, pp. 125–27; O'Connor, *Perilous Equilibrium*, pp. 62–62; Ellis, *Republican Foreign Policy*, pp. 163–65; Hugh Lattimer, *Naval Disarmament: A Brief Record from the Washington Conference to Date* (London: Royal Institute of International Affairs, Chatham House, 1930), pp. 3–77.

10. "Washington Ready for Wide Navy Cuts in Agreement with MacDonald's Plans; Our Delegates Sail with High Hopes," *New York Times*, January 10, 1930, p. 1; "U.S. Delegates Sail," *The Times* (London), January 10, 1930, p. 12; Robert H. Ferrell, *American Diplomacy in the Great Depression: Hoover Stimson Foreign Policy, 1929–1933* (New York: W. W. Norton and Company, 1957), p. 87; O'Connor, *Perilous Equilibrium*, p. 58; Kaufman, *Arms Control during the Pre-Nuclear Era*, pp. 123–24; Elllis, *Republican Foreign Policy*, p. 165; Williams, *Radio Talks*, pp. 61–92; Henry L. Stimson and McGeorge Bundy, *On Active Service in Peace and War* (New York: Harper and Brothers, 1948), pp. 166–67.

11. Robinson to Charles Brough, January 27, 1930, Charles Brough Papers, David Mullins Library, University of Arkansas, Fayetteville, Arkansas (hereafter cited as BP); Stimson to Hoover, January 20, 1930, [telegram, paraphrased], Presidential Papers, HCH Library; "Washington Ready for Wide Navy Cuts in Agreement with MacDonald's Plans; Our Delegates Sail with High Hopes," *New York Times*, January 10, 1930, p. 1; "What Demos Think," ibid., February 23, 1930, p. 4E; Stimson and Bundy, *Active Service*, pp. 166–67.

12. Radio address by Joseph T. Robinson, February 2, 1930, in State Department, *Speeches and Press Releases*, pp. 15–17; Foreign Office, *Documents of the London Naval Conference* (London: His Majesty's Stationery Office, 1930), pp. 39–53; Ferrell, *American Diplomacy*, pp. 88–90; "Conference Plans," *The Times* (London), January 13, 1930, p. 11; "Five Power Conference," ibid., January 18, 1930, p. 10; "London Naval Conference," ibid., January 21, 1930, p. 14; "Conference Opened," ibid., January 22, 1930, p. 14; O'Connor, *Perilous Equilibrium*, p. 64; Ellis, *Republican Foreign Policy*, pp. 167–68.

13. Charles G. Dawes, *Journal as Ambassador to Great Britain* (New York: Macmillan, 1939), pp. 139, 172; Robinson to Brough, January 27, 1930, BP; Foreign Office, *Documents*, pp. 100–101; O'Connor, *Perilous Equilibrium*, pp. 64–66, 72; Ferrell, *American Diplomacy*, pp. 90–94; "Conference Agenda," *The Times* (London), January 25, 1930, p. 12; "Senate and the Conference," ibid., January 27, 1930, p. 12; "Conference in Committee," ibid., February 1, 1930, p. 12; "Limitation of Tonnage," ibid., February 5, 1930, p. 14; "Next Task of Conference," ibid., February 6, 1930, p. 14; "Adams and Gibson in Steering Group," *New York Times*, January 31, 1930, p. 1; "Robinson on Radio Appeals to Senate," ibid., February 3, 1930, p. 2.

14. "Radio Address by Joseph T. Robinson, London, February 19, 1930," in State Department, *Speeches and Press Releases*, pp. 28–30; Cotton to Stimson, March 3, 1930, [telegram, paraphrased], Presidential Papers, HCH Library; Stimson to Cotton, March 10, 14, 1930, [telegram], ibid.; "Remarks of the Honorable Senator Joseph T. Robinson, at Luncheon of the American Association of Correspondents, London, February 19, 1930," press copy of speech in RP; "Conference Agenda," *The Times* (London), January 25, 1930, p. 12; "American Policy at the Conference," ibid., February 20, 1930, p. 13; "London Naval Conference," ibid., February 24, 1930, p. 12; "Navy Parley Halts for a Week at Call of American Leader," *New York Times*, February 20, 1930, p. 1; "Senator Robinson's Speech," ibid., February 20, 1930, p. 19; O'Connor, *Perilous Equilibrium*, p. 72; Gilbert Richard Grant, "Joseph Taylor Robinson in Foreign Affairs," *Arkansas Historical Quarterly*, IX (autumn 1950): 160–61.

15. Dawes, *Journal*, p. 174; Grant, "Foreign Affairs," pp. 161–62; State Department, *London Naval Treaty of 1930* (Washington, D.C.: Government Printing Office, 1930), p. 15; Foreign Office, *Documents*, pp. 2–36; *Congressional Record*, 71st Cong., special sess., pp. 118–19; O'Connor, *Perilous Equilibrium*, p. 142.

16. Radio Address by Joseph T. Robinson, London, February 2, 1930, in State Department, *Speeches and Press Statements*, pp. 15–17; Dawes, *Journal*, p. 128; Ferrell, *American Diplomacy*, p. 98; "London Naval Conference," *The Times* (London), January 20, 1930, p. 12; "London Naval Conference," ibid., January 21, 1930, p. 12; "The Third Week," ibid., February 3, 1930, p. 12; "Robinson Wants a Letter," *New York Times*, January 31, 1930, p. 4; "Lady Astor Shows Sights," ibid., February 26, 1930, p. 8; "Trade Stories at Parley," ibid., March 12, 1930, p. 2; Mrs. Joe T. Robinson to Mrs. Grady Miller, February 27, 1930, RP; Joe T. Robinson Jr. interview; Grant, "Foreign Affairs," p. 160; Neal, "Robinson Biography," pp. 346–47.

17. "Radio Address by Joseph T. Robinson, London, April 20, 1930," in State Department, *Speeches and Press Releases*, pp. 48–53; "Radio Address by Joseph T. Robinson, City of New York, April 29, 1930," ibid., pp. 66–67; State Department, *London Treaty*, pp. 1–18; Foreign Office, *Documents*, pp. 2–36; "Robinson Hails Navy

Pact as Marking Achievements of Magnitude and Value," *New York Times*, April 21, 1930, p. 1; "City Greets Arms Envoys; Treaty Taken to Capital with Plea to Ban Politics," ibid., April 30, 1930, p. 1; "The Tonnage Inquiry," *The Times* (London), March 31, 1930, p. 14; "The Security Formula," ibid., April 5, 1930, p. 14; "U.S. Delegate on Naval Treaty," ibid., April 21, 1930, p. 9; "Naval Treaty," ibid., April 22, 1930, p. 14; "Naval Treaty Signed," ibid., April 23, 1930, p. 12; [William T. Stone], "The London Naval Conference, January 21–April 22, 1930," *Foreign Policy Association Information Service*, VI (May 28, 1930): 115–30, in the Thomas Walsh Papers, Library of Congress, Washington, D.C.; O'Connor, *Perilous Equilibrium*, pp. 104–9; Kaufman, *Arms Control during the Pre-Nuclear Era*, pp. 134–39; Stimson and Bundy, *Active Service*, pp. 167, 171–72; LaFeber, *American Age*, pp. 333–34.

18. "Stimson under Barrage of Questions on Parity as Senators Study Pact," *New York Times*, May 14, 1930, p. 1; "Bristol Attacks Treaty as Navy Board Chairman; Denies It Gives Us Parity," ibid., May 17, 1930, p. 1; "Stimson Overruled Jones at London, Admiral Testifies," ibid., May 20, 1930, p. 1; "Borah Confident of Action on Treaty at This Session Despite Threats of Delay," ibid., May 23, 1930, p. 1; "Treaty Majority Solid in Committee," ibid., June 22, 1930, p. 11; O'Connor, *Perilous Equilibrium*, pp.109–11; Kaufman, *Arms Control during the Pre-Nuclear Era*, pp. 139–40; Grant, "Foreign Affairs," p. 162. For a text of the treaty, see O'Connor, *Perilous Equilibrium*, pp. 129–44.

19. *Congressional Record*, 71st Cong., special sess., pp. 44–47, 86, 118–22, 327–31, 377–78; "Naval Gun Dispute Trivial, Says Robinson," *New York Times*, June 6, 1930, p. 17; "Fight over Treaty Papers Occupies Senate Session; Swanson Pleads for Pact," ibid., July 9, 1930, p. 1; "Senate Wrangles 5 Hours on Secret Treaty Papers; No Vote on Them in Sight," ibid., July 10, 1930, p. 1; "Senate, 53–4, Asks Hoover for Secret Treaty Data, But on His Own Terms," ibid., July 11, 1930, p. 1; "Hoover Gets Compromise for a Quick Treaty Vote; Norris Reservation Eased," ibid., July 15, 1930, p. 1; "President Signs Treaty; Calls Our Action a Move to Renew 'World Faith,'" ibid., July 23, 1930, p. 1; Stimson and Bundy, *Active Service*, pp. 167, 172–73; O'Connor, *Perilous Equilibrium*, pp. 114–17, 122–28; Kaufman, *Arms Control during the Pre-Nuclear Era*, pp. 4, 139–45; Ferrell, *American Diplomacy*, pp. 104–5; Grant, "Foreign Affairs," pp. 163–65; Wilson, *Foreign Policy*, pp. 60–61; Ellis, *Republican Foreign Policy*, pp. 153, 180. For a good overview on the effects of the London Naval Conference, see Kaufman, *Arms Control during the Pre-Nuclear Era*, pp. 141–145. For a different view, in particular on the role of the conference in Japan, see Ferrell, *American Diplomacy*, pp. 100–105.

20. Miller to Robinson, April 6, 8, 26, May 5, 1930, and C. H. Moses and J. W. House to Robinson, April 30, 1930, RP; Neal, "Robinson Biography," pp. 360–61.

21. Miller to Robinson, April 6, 8, 26, May 5, 1930, and C. H. Moses and J. W. House to Robinson, April 30, 1930, RP; Neal, "Robinson Biography," pp. 360–61.

22. Miller to Robinson, April 6, 8, 26, May 5, 1930, and C. H. Moses and J. W. House to Robinson, April 30, 1930, RP; Neal, "Robinson Biography," pp. 360–61; "Analysis of the Vote for United States Senator in the Arkansas Primary Election Held August 12, 1930," manuscript in RP.

23. *Congressional Record*, 71st Cong., 3d sess., pp. 1101–4, 1367–69, 1533–39, 2141–42, 3576, 4315, 4560–61; "Hoover Asks Democrats to Aid Congress Program,

Averting Special Session," *New York Times*, November 13, 1930, p. 1; "Hoover and Robinson Agree on Eve of Congress Session to Expedite Relief Bills," ibid., December 1, 1930, p. 1; "Robinson Has Bill for Use of Wheat," ibid., December 2, 1930, p. 2; "Employment Bills Pour in on Congress," ibid., December 3, 1930, p. 20; "Sheppard Denies Democratic Rift," ibid., December 5, 1930, p. 19; "Footnotes on a Week's Headliners," ibid., December 7, 1930, sec. X, p. 6; "Robinson Asks Cooperation on Relief, but He Condemns President's Criticism; Hoover Submits World Court Protocol," ibid., December 11, 1930, p. 1; "Robinson Condemns Relief Measure as Short of Needs," ibid., December 26, 1930, p. 1; "Drought Relief Bill Accepted by Senate; New Battle Looms," ibid., January 15, 1931, p. 1; "Senators Assail Hoover on Relief," ibid., February 4, 1931, p. 1; "Hoover Ends Doubts on Relief Measure," ibid., February 10, 1931, p. 1; "Food Is Not Barred, Hyde Tells Senate," ibid., February 13, 1931, p. 1; Fred Greenbaum, *Fighting Progressive: A Biography of Edward P. Costigan* (Washington, D.C.: Public Affairs Press, 1971), p. 121; Burner, *Politics*, pp. 175–76; Neal, "Robinson Biography," p. 375.

24. *Congressional Record*, 71st Cong., 3d sess., pp. 3837–38, 5716; *ibid.*, 72d Cong., 1st sess., pp. 1180–81; "Suggests Congress Omit Next Session," *New York Times*, May 25, 1931, p. 2; "Robinson Says Hoover Forced Hebert Choice," ibid., March 21, 1931, p. 33; "Robinson Ridicules Humanizing Hoover," ibid., May 23, 1931, p. 5; "Resuming Hostilities," ibid., July 9, 1931, p. 22; "Democrats Warn Rivals on Boasting," ibid., December 18, 1931, p. 2; "Robinson Assails Hoover on Economy," ibid., June 14, 1932, p. 2; "Robinson Retorts Quickly to Mills," ibid., July 13, 1932, p. 4; "$2,300,000,000 Relief Proposed to Senate in Democratic Plan," *New York Times*, May 12, 1932, p. 1; "Young and Smith for Robinson Plan," ibid., May 12, 1932, p. 6; "Hoover Urges 3-point Relief Plan of $1,500,000,000 to Use as Loans," ibid., May 13, 1932, p. 1; "Rail Labor Urges Smith Debt Plan," ibid., May 14, 1932, p. 8; "Senate Body Weighs Relief Compromise," ibid., May 17, 1932, p. 12; "Democrats at Odds on Garner Aid Bill," ibid., June 12, 1932, p. 1; Eugene Meyer Oral History, p. A-42, COHC; Wilson, *Herbert Hoover*, pp. 141–42.

25. *Congressional Record*, 72d Cong., 1st sess., pp. 1481–85, 1701–5; Meyer Oral History, pp. 627–28, 693; Stephen Wilson, *Harvey Couch: An Entrepreneur Brings Electricity to Arkansas* (Little Rock, Arkansas: August House Publishers, 1986), pp. 100–101; Wilson, *Herbert Hoover*, pp. 155–56; Neal, "Robinson Biography," pp. 371–73.

26. *Congressional Record*, 72d Cong., 1st sess., pp. 9212–16; "Huey Long Revolts; Quits Senate Posts," *New York Times*, April 30, 1932, p. 1; Alan Brinkley, *Voices of Protest: Huey Long, Father Coughlin, and the Great Depression* (New York: Random House, 1983), pp. 42–43; T. Harry Williams, *Huey Long* (New York: Alfred A. Knopf, 1969), pp. 560–62; Diane D. Kinkaid, ed., *Silent Hattie Speaks: The Journal of Senator Hattie Caraway* (Westport, Connecticut: Greenwood Press, 1979), pp. 125–26.

27. *Congressional Record*, 72d Cong., 1st sess., pp. 9216–20; "Huey Long Revolts; Quits Senate Posts," *New York Times*, April 30, 1932, p. 1; Williams, *Huey Long*, pp. 561–62.

28. *Congressional Record*, 72d Cong., 1st sess., pp. 10062–68; "Huey Long Loses Committee Posts," *New York Times*, May 4, 1932, p. 1; Brinkley, *Voices of Protest*, p. 43; Williams, *Huey Long*, pp. 562–64; Joe T. Robinson Jr. interview.

29. Numerous materials from Long's campaign swing through Arkansas are located in the Robinson Papers such as "Wall Street vs. the People," "A Letter from Uncle Trusty," and an itinerary of the Long-Caraway campaign swing. Numerous petitions from Arkansas "Share the Wealth" clubs, urging Robinson to support Long, can also be found in the RP. These clubs would have been a natural avenue for Long to oppose Robinson in his 1936 reelection bid, although most Arkansas political pundits did not believe the clubs would succeed. Hugh Williamson to Robinson, May 1, 1935, RP; D. L. Slaughter to Robinson, March 22, 1934, ibid.; W. B. Eason to Robinson, March 24, 1934, ibid.; Isaac Flint to Robinson, April 6, 1934, ibid.; Robinson to Homer Adkins, May 27, 1935, ibid.; George H. Page to Robinson, May 10, 1935, ibid.; Bill Shepherd to Robinson, February 14, 1935, ibid.; Harry Williams to Robinson, April 8, 1935, ibid.; Robinson to Williams, April 12, 1935, ibid.; Brinkley, *Voices of Protest*, pp. 47–53; Joe T. Robinson Jr. interview; Hermann Deutsch, "Hattie and Huey," *Saturday Evening Post*, October 15, 1932, pp. 88–90; Harper, ed., *Arkansas Historical Report*, p. 230; Williams, *Huey Long*, pp. 583–93; "Arkansas Awaits Huey Long's Visit," *New York Times*, July 31, 1932, p. 6; David Malone, *Hattie and Huey: An Arkansas Tour* (Fayetteville: University of Arkansas Press, 1989), pp. 46–96. For an in-depth look at the entire campaign, including background on each of the candidates, *Hattie and Huey* is a good source.

30. Joe T. Robinson Jr. interview; Mrs. Grady Miller interview; W. T. Robinson interview; Mrs. Tom Trimble interview; "Senate Curbs Long in Midst of Attack," *New York Times*, May 13, 1932, p. 13; Malone, *Hattie and Huey*, pp. 5–17, 110–11; Williams, *Huey Long*, pp. 628, 680, 711, 804–10, 842.

31. "Campaign Oratory Loosed in Senate," *New York Times*, July 16, 1932, p. 1; "Robinson Attacks Four Hoover Points," ibid., August 13, 1932, p. 1; "Robinson Denounces Treasury 'Mistakes,'" ibid., September 9, 1932, p. 5; "Hoover 'Desperate' Robinson Declares," ibid., October 11, 1932, p. 11; "The Distinguished Nominee for President Has a Distinguished Visitor," ibid., October 17, 1932, p. 3; Neal, "Robinson Biography," pp. 379–82.

11 MAJORITY LEADER

1. Raymond Moley, *The First New Deal* (New York: Harcourt, Brace, and World, 1966), pp. 350–51; Raymond Moley, *After Seven Years* (New York: Harper and Brothers, 1939), p. 111; Betty Glad, *Key Pittman: The Tragedy of a Senate Insider* (New York: Columbia University Press, 1986), p. 177; Neal, "Robinson Biography," p. 385.

2. Mrs. Tom Trimble interview; Frank Freidel, *Franklin D. Roosevelt: Launching the New Deal* (Boston: Little, Brown and Company, 1973), pp. 47–48; James F. Byrnes, *All in One Lifetime* (New York: Harper and Brothers, 1958), p. 68; Robinson to Lee Miles, January 17, 1933, RP.

3. Freidel, *Launching the New Deal*, pp. 47–48; Byrnes, *All in One Lifetime*, p. 68; Robinson to Miles, January 17, 1933, RP; Robinson to William Shepherd,

February 27, 1933, ibid.; Robinson to Milton Fies, March 10, 1933, ibid.; "Couzens Attacks Woodin in Senate," *New York Times*, March 5, 1933, p. 10.

4. "Democrats Assign Senate Positions," *New York Times*, March 9, 1933, p. 9; "Congress Leaders to Speed Bank Aid," ibid., March 7, 1933, p. 1; E. Pendleton Herring, "First Session of the Seventy-third Congress, March 9, 1933, to June 16, 1933," *American Political Science Review*, XXVII (1934): 65–69; Williams, *Long*, p. 560.

5. "Roosevelt Inaugurated, Ready to Call Congress," *New York Times*, March 5, 1933, p. 1; "Congress Leaders to Speed Bank Aid," ibid., March 7, 1933, p. 1; "President Tells Plans," ibid., March 9, 1933, p. 1; Arthur Schlesinger Jr., *The Age of Roosevelt*, II: *The Coming of the New Deal* (Boston: Houghton Mifflin Company, 1958), pp. 4–7; William E. Leuchtenburg, *Franklin D. Roosevelt and the New Deal, 1932–1940*, New American Nation Series (New York: Harper and Row, 1963), pp. 41–43. Perhaps the best one-volume overview of the New Deal is William Leuchtenburg, *Franklin D. Roosevelt and the New Deal, 1932–1940* (1963), which argues that FDR was a pragmatic politician who tried to ameliorate the suffering of the times. Other positive views of Roosevelt and his policies may be seen in Arthur M. Schlesinger Jr., *The Age of Roosevelt* (3 vols., 1957–1960), James MacGregor Burns, *Roosevelt: The Lion and the Fox, 1882–1940* (1956), and Frank Freidel, *Franklin D. Roosevelt: A Rendezvous with Destiny* (1990). For a negative view of the New Deal, see John T. Flynn, *The Roosevelt Myth* (1956), which argues that FDR had abandoned free enterprise and had concentrated too much power in the presidency; Richard Hofstadter, *The Age of Reform* (1955), which says that the New Deal dealt with specific issues, but neglected to look at the larger problems of the era which would have led to rational planning; Rexford Tugwell, *The Democratic Roosevelt* (1957), which, while praising Roosevelt, also paints him as someone who missed the opportunity of making far-reaching reforms; and Paul Conkin, *The New Deal* (1967), which argued that FDR was too shallow and too concerned with immediate issues to enact real reforms. Other good works include Ellis Hawley, *The New Deal and the Problem of Monopoly* (1966); Albert U. Romasco, *The Politics of Recovery: Roosevelt's New Deal* (1983); Anthony Badger, *The New Deal: the Depression Years, 1933–1940* (1989); and Roger Biles, *A New Deal for the American People* (1991).

6. *Congressional Record*, 73d Cong., 1st sess., pp. 45–47; "Bank Bill Is Enacted," *New York Times*, March 10, 1933, pp. 1–3; Schlesinger Jr., *The Coming of the New Deal*, pp. 7–8; Leuchtenburg, *FDR and the New Deal*, pp. 43–44; Richard Lowitt, *George W. Norris: The Triumph of a Progressive, 1933–1944* (Urbana: University of Illinois Press, 1978), pp. 16–17. Because of Robinson's friendship with Harvey Couch, the leading utility operator in the mid-south, some historians have contended that Robinson was opposed to TVA and thus personally scuttled a similar proposal for the Arkansas River and its tributaries. No evidence exists in the records at the Franklin D. Roosevelt Library, Hyde Park, New York (hereafter cited as FDRL), the Manuscript Division of the Library of Congress, Washington, D.C. (hereafter cited as LC), or in the RP, showing that Robinson opposed this idea. Instead, he apparently favored federal development similar to TVA. In a letter to Roosevelt on December 5, 1934, he suggested that the White River in Arkansas should be considered for future power developments. Roosevelt, however, nixed the idea in a reply on December 21, 1934, Official Files (hereafter cited as OF), FDRL.

7. *Congressional Record,* 73d Cong., 1st sess., pp. 117, 194, 470–71; "Maintenance of the Credit of the United States," S. Rept. No. 1, 73d Cong., 1st sess.; "Congress Set to Back Roosevelt on Veteran and Federal Pay Cut," *New York Times,* March 11, 1933, p. 1; "Economy Victory Looms," ibid., March 13, 1933, p. 1; "President Speaks on Economy Bill," ibid., March 14, 1933, p. 1; Martha H. Swain, *Pat Harrison: The New Deal Years* (Jackson: University of Mississippi Press, 1978), pp. 38–39; Schlesinger, *The Coming of the New Deal,* pp. 10–11; Leuchtenburg, *FDR and the New Deal,* p. 45; Freidel, *Launching the New Deal,* pp. 244–47.

8. *Congressional Record,* 73d Cong., 1st sess., pp. 249, 331–35, 651, 707–9, 711–21, 723, 789, 813–14, 850, 897; "Direct Loans to State Banks and Trust Companies," S. Rept. No. 4, 73d Cong., 1st sess.; "Senate Acts to Aid Non-member Banks," *New York Times,* March 15, 1933, p. 4; "New Move to Help Non-member Banks," ibid., March 17, 1933, p. 5; "Senators Revise State Banks' Aid," ibid., March 22, 1933, p. 7.

9. *Congressional Record,* 73d Cong., 1st sess., pp. 249, 331–35, 651, 707–9, 711–21, 723, 789, 813–14, 850, 897; "Direct Loans to State Banks and Trust Companies," S. Rept. No. 4, 73d Cong., 1st sess.; "Senate Acts to Aid Non-member Banks," *New York Times,* March 15, 1933, p. 4; "New Move to Help Non-member Banks," ibid., March 17, 1933, p. 5; "Senators Revise State Banks' Aid," ibid., March 22, 1933, p. 7.

10. *Congressional Record,* 73d Cong., 1st sess., pp. 650–51, 861–62; "Roosevelt Asks Congress to Make Work for 250,000," *New York Times,* March 24, 1933, p. 1; J. Joseph Huthmacher, *Senator Robert F. Wagner and the Rise of Urban Liberalism* (New York: Atheneum, 1971), pp. 139–40.

11. *Congressional Record,* 73d Cong., 1st sess., pp. 863–70, 914–16, 937, 953, 995, 1012–13, 1102.

12. Ibid., p. 786; "To Relieve the Existing National Economic Emergency by Increasing Agricultural Purchasing Power," S. Rept. No. 16, 73d Cong., 1st sess.

13. *Congressional Record,* 73d Cong., 1st sess., p. 1103; "To Relieve the Existing National Economic Emergency by Increasing Agricultural Purchasing Power," S. Rept. 16, 73d Cong., 1st sess.; "Emergency Farm Mortgage Act of 1933," S. Rept. No. 17, 73d Cong., 1st sess.

14. *Congressional Record,* 73d Cong., 1st sess., pp. 786, 1103, 1281, 1389–98, 1737; "To Relieve the Existing National Economic Emergency by Increasing Agricultural Purchasing Power," S. Rept. 16, 73d Cong., 1st sess.; "Emergency Farm Mortgage Act of 1933," S. Rept. No. 17, 73d Cong., 1st sess.; "Robinson Opens Farm Bill Fight," *New York Times,* April 8, 1933, p. 4; Freidel, *Launching the New Deal,* pp. 315–18.

15. *Congressional Record,* 73d Cong., 1st sess., pp. 1551–63, 1630–37, 1645, 1737–41; "Roosevelt Loses a Farm Bill Vote," *New York Times,* April 14, 1933, p. 3; Lowitt, *Norris,* pp. 7–8.

16. *Congressional Record,* 73d Cong., 1st sess., pp. 1888–95, 1932–44; "Senate Chiefs Win Farm Bill Limit," *New York Times,* April 20, 1933, p. 3.

17. *Congressional Record,* 73d Cong., 1st sess., pp. 1994–2005, 2007–9, 2091.

18. Ibid., pp. 1835–1842, 2004, 2170; Moley, *After Seven Years,* pp. 156–61; Burton K. Wheeler with Paul Healey, *Yankee from the West: The Turbulent Life Story*

of the Yankee-born U.S. Senator from Montana (Garden City, New York: Doubleday and Company, 1962), p. 302; Israel, *Pittman*, p. 101; Leuchtenburg, *FDR and the New Deal*, p. 50; Schlesinger Jr., *The Coming of the New Deal*, pp. 41–42; "Inflation Moves Delay Farm Bill," *New York Times*, April 15, 1933, p. 2; "Senate Rejects 16-1 Silver as Clause in Farm Bill; Inflationists Get 33 Votes," ibid., April 18, 1933, pp. 1–2.

19. *Congressional Record*, 73d Cong., 1st sess., pp. 2216–17; Moley, *After Seven Years*, pp. 158–61; "Currency Amendment to Farm Relief Bill," S. Rept No. 40, 73d Cong., 1st sess.

20. *Congressional Record*, 73d Cong., 1st sess., pp. 1782–84, 2246, 2307–13, 2407–9, 2411, 2468; "Party Chiefs Fight to Unsnarl Senate for Farm Aid Vote," *New York Times*, April 22, 1933, p. 1; Henry Wallace to Franklin Roosevelt, April 22, 1933, OF, FDRL; "Robinson Threatens Any Inflation Filibuster with Closure [sic]," *New York Times*, April 22, 1933, p. 1; "Silver Plan Added to Inflation Bill," ibid., April 27, 1933, p. 1.

21. *Congressional Record*, 73d Cong., 1st sess., pp. 2468, 2522–23; "Silver Plan Added to Inflation Bill," *New York Times*, April 27, 1933, p. 1.

22. *Congressional Record*, 73d Cong., 1st sess., pp. 2531, 2551–52, 2563; "Senate Passes Inflation-Farm Bill by 64-20; Industry Control Bill Permits Price Fixing; Three Nations to Act to Stabilize Exchange," *New York Times*, April 29, 1933, p. 1; "Points in the Farm Inflation Bill," ibid., April 29, 1933, p. 1.

23. "Rise to 36 Hours Asked in Work Bill," *New York Times*, April 6, 1933, p. 5; "Senate Votes 30 Hour Work Week, 53-30," ibid., April 7, 1933, p. 1; "30-Hour Week Is Asked by Teagle," ibid., May 3, 1933, p. 5; Virginia Van der Veer Hamilton, *Hugo Black: The Alabama Years* (Tuscaloosa: University of Alabama Press, 1982), pp. 217–19; Monroe Lee Billington, *The Political South in the Twentieth Century* (New York: Charles Scribner's Sons, 1975), pp. 65–66; Michael E. Parrish, *Securities Regulation and the New Deal* (New Haven, Connecticut: Yale University Press, 1970), pp. 68–70; Moley, *The First New Deal*, p. 313.

24. "Highlight of Senator Joseph T. Robinson's Record Since March 4, 1933," RP; Joe T. Robinson Jr. interview; *Congressional Record*, 73d Cong., 1st sess., pp. 6133–39; WLM [initials only listed] to Stephen Early, April 5, 1933, OF, FDRL.

25. Bronson Cutting to his mother [Olivia Cutting], September 11, 1933, Bronson Cutting Papers, LC; Lowitt, *Cutting*, p. 246; Joe T. Robinson Jr. interview; Grady Miller interview; Mrs. Grady Miller interview; Mrs. Tom Trimble interview; Robinson to Roosevelt, August 14, 1933, RP.

12 LEGISLATIVE LEADER

1. *Congressional Record*, 74th Cong., 1st sess., pp. 432–33; Allan Nevins, *The New Deal and World Affairs: A Chronicle of International Affairs, 1933–1945*, Chronicles of America Series (New Haven, Connecticut: Yale University Press, 1950), pp. 45–46;

Wilson, *Foreign Policy*, pp. 48, 55–56; A. Beatrice Busse, et al. to Robinson (telegram), January 9, 1935, RP; F. J. Clark to the Members of the United States Senate, January 5, 1935, ibid.; Frederick Smith to Robinson, January 9, 1935, ibid.; Arthur J. Barton to Robinson, January 28, 1935, ibid.; Marguerite Wells to Robinson, January 20, 1935, ibid.; Henry I. Harriman to Robinson, January 16, 1935, ibid.

2. *Congressional Record*, 74th Cong., 1st sess., pp. 432–33; Thomas J. Walsh to Franklin D. Roosevelt, January 24, 1933, Thomas J. Walsh Papers, LC (hereafter cited as TJW Papers); D. Y. Thomas to Esther Everett Lape, May 7, 1933, OF, FDRL; Roosevelt to Robinson, January 8, 1935, ibid.; Roosevelt to Cordell Hull, January 3, 1935, ibid.; Key Pittman to Roosevelt, January 4, 1935, ibid.; Jonas Manfred, "The United States and the Failure of Collective Security in the 1930s," in *Twentieth-Century American Foreign Policy*, ed. John Braeman, Robert H. Bremner, and David Brody (Columbus: Ohio State University Press, 1971), p. 271; Cordell Hull, *The Memoirs of Cordell Hull* (New York: Macmillan, 1940), I, 387–89; Israel, *Pittman*, pp. 135–36; Robert Dallek, *Franklin D. Roosevelt and American Foreign Policy, 1932–1945* (New York: Oxford University Press, 1979), pp. 17, 70–71; Wayne S. Cole, *Roosevelt and the Isolationists, 1932–1945* (Lincoln: University of Nebraska Press, 1983), pp. 120–21; Nevins, *New Deal and World Affairs*, pp. 45–46.

3. Nevins, *New Deal and World Affairs*, p. 47; Leuchtenburg, *FDR and the New Deal*, pp. 215–16; Arthur M. Schlesinger Jr., *The Age of Roosevelt*, III: *The Politics of Upheaval* (Boston: Houghton Mifflin Company, 1966), pp. 4–5; Cole, *Isolationists*, pp. 121, 123; "Roosevelt Pushes World Court Issue," *New York Times*, January 6, 1935, p. 1; "World Court Foes in Senate Dwindle to 12 and Ratification in Next Week Expected," ibid., January 12, 1935, p. 2; Walsh to Roosevelt, January 24, 1933, TJW Papers; *Congressional Record*, 74th Cong., 1st sess., p. 249; Roosevelt to Elihu Root, February 9, 1935, President's Personal File (hereafter cited as PPF), FDRL; Pittman to Roosevelt, January 9, 1935, OF, ibid.; Roosevelt to Manley Hudson, January 11, 1935, ibid.

4. *Congressional Record*, 74th Cong., 1st sess., pp. 432–36; "President to Urge World Court Vote," *New York Times*, January 16, 1935, p. 4; Monroe Lee Billington, *Thomas P. Gore: The Blind Senator from Oklahoma* (Lawrence: University of Kansas Press, 1967), pp. 172–73; Maddox, *Borah*, pp. 222–23; Cole, *Isolationists*, p. 121.

5. *Congressional Record*, 74th Cong., 1st sess., pp. 434–37.

6. Ibid., pp. 479–84, 573–79, 643–48, 799; "Johnson Assails World Court Plan," *New York Times*, January 13, 1935, p. 3; Jonas, "Collective Security," pp. 271–76; Cole, *Isolationists*, pp. 121-22; Dallek, *American Foreign Policy*, p. 95; Billington, *Thomas P. Gore*, pp. 172–73.

7. *Congressional Record*, 74th Cong., 1st sess., pp. 479–84, 573–79, 643–48, 799, 801–2, 873, 892; "World Court Talks Limited by Senate," *New York Times*, January 25, 1935, p. 11; Cole, *Isolationists*, pp. 122–23.

8. *Congressional Record*, 74th Cong., 1st sess., pp. 636–43, 893; "World Court Foes Try New Strategy," *New York Times*, January 23, 1935, p. 6; [John S. Dickey], "Re: Senator Vandenberg's 'Traditional Policy' Understanding," January 19, 1935, memorandum, RP; Cole, *Isolationists*, p. 122; Jonas, "Collective Security," pp. 272–73.

9. *Congressional Record*, 74th Cong., 1st sess., pp. 964–66, 977, 1039–44, 1055; "Roosevelt Fights World Court Curb," *New York Times*, January 24, 1935, p. 14;

"World Court Vote Backs Roosevelt," ibid., January 26, 1935, p. 14; Cole, *Isolationists*, p. 122; Jonas, "Collective Security," p. 273.

10. Elizabeth Eastman to Roosevelt, January 11, 1935, OF, FDRL; Hull, *Memoirs*, I, 389; Brinkley, *Voices of Protest*, pp. 135–36; Cole, *Isolationists*, p. 123; Dallek, *American Foreign Policy*, pp. 95–96; Israel, *Pittman*, p. 136; Billington, *Thomas P. Gore*, p. 173; Nevins, *New Deal and World Affairs*, pp. 47–48; Leuchtenburg, *FDR and the New Deal*, pp. 215–16; Schlesinger Jr., *The Politics of Upheaval*, pp. 4–5.

11. *Congressional Record*, 74th Cong., 1st sess., pp. 1055–56, 1117–40; "Senate Beats World Court 52–36, 7 Less Than 2/3 Vote; Defeat for President," *New York Times*, January 30, 1935, p. 1; Cole, *Isolationists*, 123–24; Billington, *Thomas P. Gore*, p. 173; Maddox, *Borah*, p. 223; Jonas, "Collective Security," p. 273.

12. Roosevelt to Root, February 9, 1935, PPF, FDRL; "The Congress: Up Senate, Down Court," *Time*, February 11, 1935, pp. 13–15; Robert Dalleck, *Democrat and Diplomat: The Life of William E. Dodd* (New York: Oxford University Press, 1968), p. 251; Leuchtenburg, *FDR and the New Deal*, pp. 215–16; Schlesinger Jr., *The Politics of Upheaval*, pp. 4–5; Nevins, *New Deal and World Affairs*, pp. 47–49; Brinkley, *Voices of Protest*, pp. 136–37; Manley O. Hudson, "Memorandum Submitted to the Trustees of the World Peace Foundation on the Senate and the World Court," February 16, 1935, RP. Hudson was a professor of law at Harvard University and a major supporter of the tribunal. After having traveled with Woodrow Wilson to Europe as part of the American delegation after World War I, he eventually gained renown in international law. According to Cordell Hull, the "ambition of his [Hudson's] life" was to serve on the World Court. Hull to Roosevelt, n.d., OF, FDRL.

13. Cordell Hull to Robinson, February 5, 1935, RP; John S. Dickey to Robinson, February 5, 1935, ibid.; Roosevelt to Robinson, January 30, 1935, Joseph Taylor Robinson Papers in the personal collection of Grady Miller Jr., Little Rock, Arkansas, as well as in PPF, FDRL; Cole, *Isolationists*, pp. 124–25; Dallek, *American Foreign Policy*, p. 96.

14. Leuchtenburg, *FDR and the New Deal*, pp. 146–62; Schlesinger Jr., *The Politics of Upheaval*, pp. 291–338, 400–406.

15. Joe T. Robinson Jr. interview; W. T. Robinson interview; numerous speeches and letters in the RP.

16. Burton A. Zorn and George Feldman, *Business under the New Price Laws: A Study of the Economic and Legal Problems Arising out of the Robinson-Patman Act and the Various Fair Trade and Unfair Practices Laws* (New York: Prentice-Hall, 1937), pp. ix–xii, 28–39, 85, 91–94; Federal Trade Commission, "Final Report on the Chain Store Investigation," S. Doc. No. 4, 74th Cong., 1st sess., pp. 24–25, 46–50 (hereafter cited as FTC, "Final Report"); Wright Patman, "Curbing the Chain Store," *Nation*, November 28, 1936, pp. 625–26; Institute of Distribution, "A Robinson-Patman Bill Picture Book," RP; *Congressional Record*, 74th Cong., 1st sess., p. 10129; Schlesinger Jr., *The Politics of Upheaval*, pp. 279–85; Leuchtenburg, *FDR and the New Deal*, pp. 145-46. For a more in-depth look at Robinson's role in the passage of the Robinson-Patman Act, see Cecil E. Weller Jr., "Joseph Taylor Robinson and the Robinson-Patman Act," *Arkansas Historical Quarterly*, XLVII (spring 1988): 29–36.

17. Wright Patman, *Complete Guide to the Robinson-Patman Act* (Englewood Cliffs, New Jersey: Prentice-Hall, 1963), pp. 11, 89, 102, 109, 125, 129, 148, 151, 167–69; Zorn and Feldman, *New Price Laws*, pp. 54–57; FTC, "Final Report," pp. 23–28.

18. S. Rept. No. 1502, 74th Cong., 2d sess., p. 2; W. H. Holmes and C. H. Moses to Robinson (telegram), February 10, 1936, RP; Robinson to Moses and Holmes (telegram), February 18, 1936, ibid.

19. Zorn and Feldman, *New Price Laws*, pp. 52–53; "Hard Fight Looms on Trade Measure," *New York Times*, February 23, 1936, p. 18; "Fight to be Pushed on Price Measure," ibid., March 22, 1936, sec. 3, p. 1; Institute of Distribution, "The 28 Questions . . . And Their Answers," RP.

20. *Congressional Record*, 74th Cong., 2d sess., pp. 6425–36; "Chain Store Bill Passed by Senate," *New York Times*, May 1, 1936, p. 8.

21. *Congressional Record*, 74th Cong., 2d sess., pp. 8418–19, 9413–22, 9902–4, 10219, 10700; "Chain Store Curb Is Voted by the House," *New York Times*, May 29, 1936, p. 37; "Congress Passes Chain Store," ibid., June 19, 1936, p. 5; H. B. Teegarden to Robinson May 4, 1936, RP.

22. Joe T. Robinson, "Pertaining to the Robinson-Patman Act," copy of a speech delivered August 5, 1936, Jonesboro, Arkansas, RP; "They Led the Fight for the Robinson-Patman Anti-Price Discrimination Act," *National Association of Retail Druggists Journal*, June 18, 1936, p. 790, Wright Patman Papers, Lyndon Baines Johnson Library, Austin, Texas; Schlesinger Jr., *The Politics of Upheaval*, p. 510.

23. Copies of the speech may be found in RP; Matthew Josephson and Hanna Josephson, *Al Smith: Hero of the Cities, A Political Biography Drawing on the Papers of Frances Perkins* (Boston: Houghton Mifflin Company, 1969), pp. 457–61; George Wolfskill, *The Revolt of the Conservatives: A History of the Liberty League, 1934–1940* (Boston: Houghton Mifflin Company, 1962), pp. 20–21, 133, 147, 151–60; Frank Freidel, "The Conservative South," in *The South and the Sectional Image: The Sectional Theme since Reconstruction*, ed. Dewey W. Grantham Jr. (New York: Harper and Row, 1967), pp. 104–5; Billington, *Political South*, p. 75; Neal, "Robinson Biography," pp. 425–28.

24. Copies of the speeches may be found in RP; Farley Diary, February 7, April 20, 1936, James Farley Papers, LC (hereafter cited as Farley Papers); Josephson and Josephson, *Al Smith*, pp. 457–61; Wolfskill, *Revolt of the Conservatives*, pp. 133, 147, 151–60; Neal, "Robinson Biography," pp. 425–28.

25. Norman Thomas to Franklin Roosevelt, April 22, 1936, OF, FDRL; Roosevelt to [Arkansas Governor] J. Marion Futrell, n.d. [1936], ibid.; Frances Perkins to Roosevelt, June 8, 1936, ibid.; Homer Cummings to Roosevelt, August 4, 1936, ibid.; Sam Whitaker to Brian McMahan, June 16, 1936, ibid.; Futrell to Cummings, July 14, 1936, ibid.; H. L. Mitchell, *Mean Things Happening in This Land: The Life and Times of H. L. Mitchell, Co-Founder of the Southern Tenant Farmers Union* (Montclair, New Jersey: Allanheld, Osmun and Company, 1979), pp. 86–103; James R. Green, *Grass-Roots Socialism: Radical Movements in the Southwest, 1895–1943* (Baton Rouge: Louisiana State University Press, 1978), pp. 424–25; M. S. Venkataramani, "Norman Thomas, Arkansas Sharecroppers and the Roosevelt Agricultural Policies, 1933–1937," *Mississippi Valley Historical Review*, 47 (September 1960): 226–35; Donald H. Grubbs, *Cry from the Cotton: The Southern Tenant Farmers Union and the New Deal* (Chapel Hill: University of North Carolina Press, 1971), pp. 89–125; Jerold S. Auerbach, "Southern Tenant Farmers: Socialist Critics of the New Deal," *Labor History*, v. 7 (winter, 1966), pp. 3–18; David Conrad, *The Forgotten Farmers* (Urbana:

University of Illinois Press, 1965), pp. 154–76. For a complete, and favorable, look at the Southern Tenant Farmers Union, see Mitchell, *Southern Tenant Farmers Union*. Mitchell was an organizer and tactician for the union. For a complete, yet less biased, view of the STFU, see Grubbs, *Cry from the Cotton*. For shorter versions, see Green, *Grass-Roots Socialism*, pp. 419–31.

26. Norman Thomas to Franklin Roosevelt, April 22, 1936, OF, FDRL; Roosevelt to Futrell, n.d. [1936], ibid.; Perkins to Roosevelt, June 8, 1936, ibid.; Cummings to Roosevelt, August 4, 1936, ibid.; Whitaker to McMahan, June 16, 1936, ibid.; Futrell to Cummings, July 14, 1936, ibid.; Norman Thomas Oral History, COHC, pp. 97–98; Mitchell, *Southern Tenant Farmers Union*, pp. 89–104; Grubbs, *Cry from the Cotton*, p. 99; Venkataramani, "Thomas and Arkansas," pp. 228–29, 235–37; Green, *Grass-Roots Socialism*, p. 425.

27. Robinson to Mrs. Franklin D. Roosevelt April 20, 1936, OF, FDRL; H. L. Mitchell Oral History, COHC, pp. 72–73; Venkataramin, "Thomas and Arkansas," pp. 234–35.

28. Robinson to Mrs. Roosevelt, April 20, 1936, OF, FDRL; Mitchell Oral History, pp. 72–73; Mitchell, *Southern Tenant Farmers Union*, pp. 98–100; Venkataramin, "Thomas and Arkansas," pp. 239–40; Green, *Grass-Roots Socialism*, p. 426; Robinson to Archibald MacLeish (telegram), November 19, 1936, RP; MacLeish to Robinson, November 23, 1936, ibid.

29. Leuchtenburg, *FDR and the New Deal*, pp. 140–41.

30. Mrs. Grady Miller interview; Joe T. Robinson Jr. interview; Mrs. Tom Trimble interview.

31. Mrs. Grady Miller interview; Joe T. Robinson Jr. interview; Mrs. Tom Trimble interview; Stephen Wilson, *Harvey Couch: An Entrepreneur Brings Electricity to Arkansas* (Little Rock, Arkansas: August House Publishers, 1986), pp. 116, 120.

32. Bill Shepherd to Robinson, February 14, 1935, RP; Robinson to Shepherd, February 18, 1935, ibid.; B. J. Parrish to Robinson, February 13, 1935, ibid.; Robinson to Parrish, February 18, 1935, ibid.; Robinson to Harry Williams, April 8, 12, 1935, ibid.; Robinson to Homer Adkins, May 27, 1935, ibid.; Jonathan Page to Robinson, May 10, 1936, ibid.; Joe T. Robinson Jr. interview.

33. Farley Diary, February 7, April 20, June 1, 1936, Farley Papers; Proceedings, Committee on Arrangements for the Democratic National Convention, April 25, 1936, ibid.; Neal, "Robinson Biography," pp. 429–31; Oliver A. Quayle Jr., comp., *Official Report of the Proceedings of the Democratic National Convention, 1936* (n.p.: n.p., 1936), pp. 87–94.

13 THE FINAL ACT

1. Program for the Inaugural Ceremonies, January 20, 1937, RP; Joe T. Robinson Jr. interview; W. T. Robinson interview.

2. Samuel I. Rosenman, ed., *The Public Papers and Addresses of Franklin D. Roosevelt* (New York: Macmillan, 1941), pp. vi, 51–66; James Roosevelt to Marvin

McIntyre, February 5, 1937, OF, FDRL; James T. Patterson, *Congressional Conservatism and the New Deal: The Growth of the Conservative Coalition in Congress, 1933–1939* (Lexington: University of Kentucky Press, 1967), pp. 90–91; Moore, *Bailey*, pp. 129–30.

3. "Cummings Scores 'Hysteria' on Roosevelt's Court Plan; Senate Revolt Is Spreading," *New York Times*, February 15, 1937, pp. 1–2; "Senators Advance Compromise Plan for Court Reform," ibid., February 17, 1937; Charles Michelson, *The Ghost Talks* (New York: G. P. Putnam's Sons, 1944), p. 179; Ron C. Law, "Congressman Hatton W. Sumners of Dallas, Texas: His Life and Congressional Career, 1876–1937," Ph.D. dissertation, Texas Christian University, Fort Worth, Texas, 1990, pp. 116–20; Lionel V. Patenude, "Garner, Sumners, and Connally: The Defeat of the Roosevelt Court Bill in 1937," *Southwestern Historical Quarterly*, 74 (July 1970): 36–40; Patterson, *Congressional Conservatism*, pp. 91–92; Michael L. Collins, "The Influence of Texans upon Roosevelt's Court-Packing Plan," M.A. thesis, Texas Christian University, Fort Worth, Texas, 1975, pp. 13–18; Joseph Alsop and Turner Catledge, *The 168 Days* (Garden City, New York: Doubleday, Doran and Company, 1938; reprint ed., New York: Da Capo Press, 1973), pp. 88–89.

4. *Congressional Record*, 75th Cong., 1st sess., p. 956; Gerald Nye Oral History, p. 6, Gerald Nye Papers, Herbert Hoover Library, West Branch, Iowa; Thomas G. Corcoran to Mr. Rowe, Mr. Katz, Mr. Weiner, May 6, 1937, Thomas G. Corcoran Papers (hereafter cited as Corcoran Papers), LC; Moore, *Bailey*, pp. 130–31; Homer E. Socolofsky, *Arthur Capper: Publisher, Politician, and Philanthropist* (Lawrence: University of Kansas Press, 1962), p. 178; Jesse Palmer Jr., *Carter Glass—Unreconstructed Rebel: A Biography* (Roanoke, Virginia: Institute of American Biography, 1938), p. 300; Bascom N. Timmons, *Garner of Texas: A Personal History* (New York: Harper and Brothers, 1948), p. 219; Frank Freidel, *F.D.R. and the South* (Baton Rouge: Louisiana State University Press, 1965), pp. 93–94; Patterson, *Congressional Conservatism*, pp. 93–94, 107–12; Alsop and Catledge, *The 168 Days*, pp. 65–67.

5. Frank E. Gannett to William E. Borah, July 23, 1937, Borah Papers, LC; R. Emmet Digney to Robinson, March 2, 1937, RP. In the RP there are many completed Gannett petitions in Robinson's files on the Supreme Court proposal; Corcoran to Rowe, Katz, Weiner, May 6, 1937, Corcoran Papers.

6. *Congressional Record*, 75th Cong., 1st sess., pp. 677–80; Neal, "Robinson Biography," pp. 447–48.

7. "Supreme Court Upholds Wagner Labor Law; Hailed by Friends and Foes of Bench Change; Unions See Sweeping Progress within a Year," *New York Times*, April 13, 1937, p. 1; Moore, *Bailey*, p. 134; Patterson, *Congressional Conservatism*, pp. 119–20; Neal, "Robinson Biography," pp. 449–50; Alsop and Catledge, *The 168 Days*, pp. 145–47.

8. Harold L. Ickes, *The Secret Diary of Harold L. Ickes*, II: *The Inside Struggle, 1936–39* (New York: Simon and Schuster, 1954), pp. 108, 126; Marvin Jones Oral History, COHC, pp. 981–82; Michael Weatherson and Hal Bochin, *Hiram Johnson: A Bio-Bibliography* (New York: Greenwood Press, 1988), p. 57; Patterson, *Congressional Conservatism*, p. 122; Moore, *Bailey*, p. 135; Alsop and Catledge, *The 168 Days*, p. 153.

9. "Van Devanter, 78, Retires; Adverse Court Bill Report Voted by Committee, 10 to 8," *New York Times*, May 19, 1937, p. 1; Patrick J. Maney, *"Young Bob" La Follette: A Biography of Robert M. La Follette, Jr., 1895–1953* (Columbia: University of Missouri Press, 1978), p. 194; Moore, *Bailey*, pp. 134–35; Patterson, *Congressional Conservatism*, p. 122; Neal, "Robinson Biography," pp. 450–51.

10. Ickes, *Diary, 1936–1939*, p. 144; Michelson, *The Ghost Talks*, p. 179; James MacGregor Burns, *Roosevelt: The Lion and the Fox* (New York: Harcourt, Brace and Company, 1956), p. 304.

11. "Robinson Will Not Do!" *Nation*, May 29, 1937, pp. 607–8; Ickes, *Diary, 1936–1939*, pp. 144–45; Henry Morgantheau Diaries, May 24, 1937, FDRL; M. William Zucker to Franklin Roosevelt, May 19, 1937, OF, FDRL; Irving Brant to Corcoran [copy], June 12, 1937, Irving Brant Papers, LC; Brant to Corcoran, August 13, 1937, Corcoran Papers; Beatrice Bishop Berle and Travis Beal Jacobs, eds., *Navigating the Rapids: From the Papers of Adolphe A. Berle* (New York: Harcourt, Brace, Jovanovich, 1973), p. 127; Neal, "Robinson Biography," p. 451.

12. Borah to Roosevelt, May 19, 1937, RP; "Five More to Quit Court, Capitol Hears; Robinson Boomed for Appointment," *Washington Herald*, May 20, 1937, p. 1; Berle and Jacobs, *Berle Papers*, p. 127; "Court Plan Dead but Not Buried," *The Literary Digest*, May 29, 1937, p. 3; William G. McAdoo, to Roosevelt, May 21, 1937, OF, FDRL; McIntyre to Kenneth McKellar, May 28, 1937, RP; Moore, *Bailey*, p. 135; Neal, "Robinson Biography," p. 451.

13. Farley Diary, May 20, 1937, Farley Papers; Michelson, *The Ghost Talks*, p. 181; Patterson, *Congressional Conservatism*, pp. 122–23; Alsop and Catledge, *The 168 Days*, pp. 213–14.

14. Farley Diary, July 18, 1937, Farley Papers; James Farley Oral History, COHC, p. 173; James A. Farley, *Jim Farley's Story: The Roosevelt Years* (New York: Whittlesey House, McGraw-Hill Book Company, 1948), pp. 86, 91; Neal, "Robinson Biography," pp. 454–55; Alsop and Catledge, *The 168 Days*, pp. 214–16.

15. Farley, *Farley's Story*, p. 86; Ickes, *Diary, 1936–1939*, p. 153; Moore, *Bailey*, p. 135; Neal, "Robinson Biography," p. 453.

16. Roosevelt to Robinson, June 11, 1937, RP.

17. *Congressional Record*, 75th Cong., 1st sess., pp. 6788–89; "Memorandum on Features of Proposed Plan," n.d., Ben Cohen Papers, LC; "Draft No. 1," n.d., ibid.; Brant to Corcoran, July 2, 1937, Corcoran Papers; Alsop and Catledge, *The 168 Days*, pp. 223–24.

18. "Parley Called by Democrats to Heal Breach," *Washington Post*, June 17, 1937, p. 1; Ickes, *Diary*, p. 156; Henry A. Wallace Oral History, COHC, pp. 454–55; Robinson to B. M. Baruch, July 12, 1937, RP; Joe T. Robinson Jr. interview; Moore, *Bailey*, p. 135.

19. *Congressional Record*, 75th Cong., 1st sess., pp. 6788–98; Moore, *Bailey*, p. 136.

20. *Congressional Record*, pp. 6895–97; Ickes, *Diary, 1936–1939*, p. 159; Burns, *Lion and Fox*, p. 308; Glad, *Pittman*, pp. 183–84; Moore, *Bailey*, p. 136; "Control of Court Is Roosevelt Aim, Bailey Declares," *New York Times*, July 13, 1937, pp. 1, 8; Joe T. Robinson Jr. interview.

21. *Congressional Record*, 75th Cong., 1st sess., pp. 7033–39; "The Congress: End of Strife," *Time*, July 26, 1937, p. 10; "Senator Robinson Dies Suddenly; Senate Faces Fight on Leadership and Fate of Court Bill Is Doubtful," *New York Times*, July 15, 1937, pp. 1, 13; Joe T. Robinson Jr. interview; Baker, *Senate*, p. 84; Glad, *Pittman*, p. 184; Neal, "Robinson Biography," pp. 459–61; Alsop and Catledge, *The 168 Days*, pp. 262–67.

22. Neal, "Robinson Biography," p. 465; "The Congress: End of Strife," *Time*, pp. 10–13; Burns, *Lion and Fox*, p. 308; "Senator Robinson Dies Suddenly; Senate Faces Fight on Leadership and Fate of Court Bill Is Doubtful," *New York Times*, July 15, 1937, pp. 1, 13; Brant to Corcoran, July 21, 1937, Corcoran Papers; Farley Oral History, pp. 173–74; Marvin Jones Oral History, pp. 981–82; William Leuchtenburg Oral History, COHC, p. 57; Palmer, *Glass*, p. 304; Moore, *Bailey*, p. 137.

23. "The Congress: End of Strife," *Time*, pp. 10–13; "Senator Robinson Dies Suddenly; Senate Faces Fight on Leadership and Fate of Court Bill Is Doubtful," *New York Times*, July 15, 1937, pp. 1, 13; Farley Oral History, p. 21; Collins, "Influence of Texans," pp. 70–73; Timmons, *Garner*, pp. 221–23; Moore, *Bailey*, pp. 137–38; Patenude, "Roosevelt Court Bill," pp. 48–49; Alsop and Catledge, *The 168 Days*, pp. 279–80.

24. Timmons, *Garner*, p. 220; John Nance Garner to Robinson, June 28, 1937, RP; Patenude, "Roosevelt Court Bill," pp. 47–48.

25. Robinson to Garner, July 2, 1937, cited in Neal, "Robinson Biography," p. 465; Hiram Johnson to Garret W. McEnerney, July 7, 1937, cited in William E. Leuchtenburg, "Franklin D. Roosevelt's Supreme Court Packing Plan," in *Essays on the New Deal*, ed. Harold Hollingsworth and William F. Holmes (Austin: University of Texas Press, 1969), p. 103; Collins, "Influence of Texans," p. 68; Alsop and Catledge, *The 168 Days*, p. 187.

26. Frances Perkins Oral History, COHC, pp. 55–56.

BIBLIOGRAPHY

PRIMARY SOURCES

Government Documents

Arkansas. General Assembly. *Journal of the House of Representatives of Arkansas, Thirtieth Session.* [1895.]

———. *Journal of the Senate of Arkansas, Thirty-ninth Regular Session.* [1913.]

Crockett, John W. *Arkansas: Biennial Report of the Secretary of State.* Little Rock, Arkansas: Tunnah and Pittard, 1903.

Harper, C. Armitage, ed. *Historical Report of the Secretary of State (Arkansas).* Little Rock, Arkansas: State of Arkansas, 1968.

Parliament of the Commonwealth of Australia. *Limitation of Naval Armament Conference Held at London January–April, 1930: Report of the Australian Delegate (The Hon. J. E. Fenton).* Canberra: Commonwealth of Australia, 1930.

United Kingdom Foreign Office. *Documents of the London Naval Conference, 1930.* London: His Majesty's Stationery Office, 1930.

U.S. Congress. *Congressional Record.* 1903–1937.

U.S. Congress. House of Representatives. *Boundary Reservation at Hot Springs, Arkansas.* H.R. Rept. No. 1683, 59th Cong., 1st sess., 1906.

U.S. Congress. Senate. *Currency Amendment to Farm Relief Bill.* S. Rept. 40, 73d Cong., 1st sess., 1933.

———. *Direct Loans to State Banks and Trust Companies.* S. Rept. 4, 73d Cong., 1st sess., 1933.

———. *Emergency Farm Mortgage Act of 1933.* S. Rept. 17, 73d Cong., 1st sess., 1933.

———. *Enlargement of Interstate Commerce Commission.* S. Rept. 10, 65th Cong., 1st sess., 1918.

———. *Maintenance of Credit of the United States.* S. Rept. 1, 73d Cong., 1st sess., 1933.

———. *National Industrial Recovery Bill.* S. Rept. 114, 73d Cong., 1st sess., 1933.

———. *Relieve the Existing National Economic Emergency by Increasing Agricultural Purchasing Power.* S. Rept. 16, 73d Cong., 1st sess., 1933.

———. *Rural Credits: Hearings before the Committee on Banking and Currency United States Senate.* 67th Cong., 4th sess., 1923. Washington, D.C.: Government Printing Office, 1923.

———. *To Amend Antitrust Act.* S. Rept. 1502 to Accompany S. 3154, 74th Cong., 2d sess., 1936.

———. *To Prevent Interstate Commerce in the Products of Child Labor.* S. Rept. No. 358, 64th Cong., 1st sess., 1916.

U.S. Department of State. *London Naval Conference: Speeches and Press Statements by Members of the American Delegation, January 20–April 29, 1930.* Washington, D.C.: Government Printing Office, 1930.

———. *London Naval Treaty of 1930.* Washington, D.C.: Government Printing Office, 1930.

U.S. Federal Trade Commission. *Chain Stores: Final Report on the Chain-Store Investigation.* S. Doc. 4, 74th Cong., 2d sess., 1936.

Manuscript Collections

Homer Adkins Papers. Arkansas Historical Commission. Little Rock, Arkansas.

George Akerson Papers. Herbert Hoover Library. West Branch, Iowa.

Alsop Family Papers. Manuscript Division, Library of Congress. Washington, D.C.

Arkansas State Council of Defense Papers. Arkansas Historical Commission. Little Rock, Arkansas.

Edward Anthony Papers. Herbert Hoover Library. West Branch, Iowa.

Arthur Ballantine Papers. Herbert Hoover Library. West Branch, Iowa.

Hugo Black Papers. Manuscript Division, Library of Congress. Washington, D.C.

S. Bledsoe Oral History. Columbia Oral History Collection. Columbia University. New York, New York.

William Borah Papers. Manuscript Division, Library of Congress. Washington, D.C.

Claude Bowers Oral History. Columbia Oral History Collection. Columbia University. New York, New York.

Irving Brandt Papers. Manuscript Division, Library of Congress. Washington, D.C.

Charles Brough Papers. Arkansas Historical Commission. Little Rock, Arkansas.

———. Special Collections, David Mullins Library, University of Arkansas. Fayetteville, Arkansas.

William R. Castle Papers. Herbert Hoover Library. West Branch, Iowa.

Benjamin Cohen Papers. Manuscript Division, Library of Congress. Washington, D.C.

Tom Connally Papers. Manuscript Division, Library of Congress. Washington, D.C.

Thomas Corcoran Papers. Manuscript Division, Library of Congress. Washington, D.C.

Harvey Couch Papers. Arkansas Power and Light. Little Rock, Arkansas.

Bronson Cutting Papers. Manuscript Division, Library of Congress. Washington, D.C.

Josephus Daniels Papers. Manuscript Division, Library of Congress. Washington, D.C.

James J. Davies Papers. Manuscript Division, Library of Congress. Washington, D.C.

Democratic National Committee Papers. Franklin D. Roosevelt Library. Hyde Park, New York.

Martha W. Donaghey Papers. Arkansas Historical Commission. Little Rock, Arkansas.

Lavinia Engle Oral History Collection. Columbia Oral History Collection. Columbia University. New York, New York.

James Farley Oral History. Columbia Oral History Collection. Columbia University. New York, New York.

James Farley Papers. Manuscript Division, Library of Congress. Washington, D.C.

Felix Frankfurter Papers. Manuscript Division, Library of Congress. Washington, D.C.

J. M. Futrell Papers. Arkansas Historical Commission. Little Rock, Arkansas.

Edwin Halsey Papers. Manuscript Division, Library of Congress. Washington, D.C.

Brooks Hays Papers. Special Collections, David Mullins Library, University of Arkansas. Fayetteville, Arkansas.

Herbert Hoover Campaign and Transition Papers. Herbert Hoover Library. West Branch, Iowa.

Herbert Hoover Commerce Department Papers. Herbert Hoover Library. West Branch, Iowa.

Herbert Hoover Post-Presidential (Individual) Papers. Herbert Hoover Library. West Branch, Iowa.

Herbert Hoover Post-Presidential (Subject) Papers. Herbert Hoover Library. West Branch, Iowa.

Herbert Hoover Presidential Papers. Herbert Hoover Library. West Branch, Iowa.

Cordell Hull Papers. Manuscript Division, Library of Congress. Washington, D.C.

Harry Hopkins Papers. Franklin D. Roosevelt Library. Hyde Park, New York.

Robert Jackson Papers. Manuscript Division, Library of Congress. Washington, D.C.

Marvin Jones Oral History. Columbia Oral History Collection. Columbia University. New York, New York.

Theodore Joslin Papers. Herbert Hoover Library. West Branch, Iowa.

William Leuchtenburg Oral History. Columbia Oral History Collection. Columbia University. New York, New York.

James H. MacLafferty Papers. Herbert Hoover Library. West Branch, Iowa.

Archibald MacLeish Papers. Manuscript Division, Library of Congress. Washington, D.C.

John Martineau Papers. Arkansas Historical Commission. Little Rock, Arkansas.

Felix Marley Papers. Herbert Hoover Library. West Branch, Iowa.

Charles McNary Papers. Manuscript Division, Library of Congress. Washington, D.C.

Eugene Meyer Oral History. Columbia Oral History Collection. Columbia University. New York, New York.

H. L. Mitchell Oral History. Columbia Oral History Collection. Columbia University. New York, New York.

Henry Morgenthau Diaries. Franklin D. Roosevelt Library. Hyde Park, New York.

George Norris Papers. Manuscript Division, Library of Congress. Washington, D.C.

Gerald Nye Papers. Herbert Hoover Library. West Branch, Iowa.

R. L. O'Brien Oral History. Columbia Oral History Collection. Columbia University. New York, New York.

Wright Patman Papers. Lyndon Baines Johnson Library. Austin, Texas.

Frances Perkins Oral History. Columbia Oral History Collection. Columbia University. New York, New York.

Key Pittman Papers. Manuscript Division, Library of Congress. Washington, D.C.

Donald Richberg Papers. Manuscript Division, Library of Congress. Washington, D.C.

E. R. Robinson Papers. In the possession of Mrs. Lloyd Willmon, Lonoke, Arkansas.

———. In the possession of W. T. Robinson, England, Arkansas.

Joseph Taylor Robinson Papers. Special Collections, David Mullins Library, University of Arkansas. Fayetteville, Arkansas.

———. Arkansas Historical Commission. Little Rock, Arkansas.

———. In the possession of Grady Miller Jr. Little Rock, Arkansas.

Eleanor Roosevelt Papers. Franklin D. Roosevelt Library. Hyde Park, New York.

Franklin D. Roosevelt, Official Files. Franklin D. Roosevelt Library. Hyde Park, New York.

Franklin D. Roosevelt, President's Personal Files. Franklin D. Roosevelt Library. Hyde Park, New York.

Elihu Root Papers. Manuscript Division, Library of Congress. Washington, D.C.

Lewis Schwellenbach Papers. Manuscript Division, Library of Congress. Washington, D.C.

Furnifold M. Simmons Papers. William R. Perkins Library. Duke University. Durham, North Carolina.

Robert Simmons Papers. Herbert Hoover Library. West Branch, Iowa.

E. F. Strothers Papers. Herbert Hoover Library. West Branch, Iowa.

Swaim Family Genealogy. In the possession of Mrs. Lloyd Willmon. Lonoke, Arkansas.

Norman Thomas Oral History. Columbia Oral History Collection. Columbia University. New York, New York.

Henry A. Wallace Oral History. Columbia Oral History Collection. Columbia University. New York, New York.

Thomas J. Walsh Papers. Manuscript Division, Library of Congress. Washington, D.C.

Thomas J. Walsh and John Erickson Papers. Manuscript Division, Library of Congress. Washington, D.C.

Wallace White Papers. Manuscript Division, Library of Congress. Washington, D.C.

Burton K. Wheeler Oral History. Columbia Oral History Collection. Columbia University. New York, New York.

Interviews

Interview of Maysell Walls Currie, Pine Bluff, Arkansas, with author, February 12, 1988.

Interview of Grady Miller Jr., Little Rock, Arkansas, with author, August 20, 1986.

Interview of Mrs. Grady Miller, Little Rock, Arkansas, with author, August 20, 1986.

Interview of Claude Pepper, Washington, D.C., with author, November 20, 1987.

Interview of Joe T. Robinson Jr., England, Arkansas, with author, August 20, 1986.

Interview of W. T. Robinson, England, Arkansas, with author, February 12, 1988.

Interview of Mrs. Tom Trimble Jr., Lonoke, Arkansas, with Mrs. Lloyd Willmon, November 2, 1988.

Interview of Mrs. Lloyd Willmon, Lonoke, Arkansas, February 11, 1988.

Published Works

Barkley, Alben. *That Reminds Me*. Garden City, New York: Doubleday and Company, 1954.

Baruch, Bernard M. *Baruch: The Public Years*. New York: Holt, Rinehart and Winston, 1960.

Bellairs, Carlyon. *The Naval Conference and After*. London: Faber and Faber Limited, [1930].

Berle, Beatrice Bishop, and Travis Beal Jacobs, eds. *Navigating the Rapids, 1918–1971: From the Papers of Adolphe A. Berle*. New York: Harcourt, Brace, Jovanovich, 1973.

Bundy, McGeorge. *On Active Duty in Peace and War*. New York: Harper and Brothers, 1948.

Byrnes, James F. *All in One Lifetime*. New York: Harper and Brothers, 1958.

Catledge, Turner. *My Life and the Times*. New York: Harper and Row, 1963.

Connally, Tom, and Alfred Steinberg. *My Name Is Tom Connally*. New York: Thomas Y. Crowell Company, 1954.

Cox, James M. *Journey through My Years*. New York: Simon and Schuster, 1946.

Cronon, E. David, ed. *The Cabinet Diaries of Josephus Daniels, 1913–1921*. Lincoln: University of Nebraska Press, 1963.

Dawes, Charles G. *Journal as Ambassador to Great Britain*. New York: Macmillan, 1939.

Dodd, William E. *Ambassador Dodd's Diary, 1933–1938*. Edited by William E. Dodd Jr. and Martha Dodd. New York: Harcourt, Brace and Company, 1941.

Donaghey, George W. *Autobiography of George W. Donaghey, Governor of Arkansas, 1909–1913*. Benton, Arkansas: L. B. White Printing Company, 1939.

———. *Building a State Capitol*. Little Rock, Arkansas: Parke-Harper Company, 1937.

Farley, James A. *Behind the Ballots: The Personal History of a Politician*. New York: Harcourt, Brace, and Company, 1938.

———. *Jim Farley's Story: The Roosevelt Years*. New York: Whittlesey House, McGraw-Hill Book Company, 1948.

Greathouse, Charles A., comp. *Official Report of the Democratic Convention . . . 1924*. Indianapolis: Bookwalter-Ball-Greathouse Printing Company, 1924.

Hays, Brooks. *Politics Is My Parish*. Baton Rouge: Louisiana State University Press, 1981.

Hoffman, Edward G., comp. *Official Report of the Proceedings of the Democratic National Convention Held in San Francisco, California . . . 1920*. Indianapolis: Bookwalter-Ball Printing Company, [1920].

Hoover, Herbert Clark. *The Memoirs of Herbert Hoover: The Cabinet and the Presidency, 1920–1933*. New York: Macmillan, 1952.

Hull, Cordell. *The Memoirs of Cordell Hull*. New York: Macmillan, 1948.

Ickes, Harold L. *The Secret Diary of Harold L. Ickes*. I: *The First Thousand Days, 1933–1936*. New York: Simon and Schuster, 1953.

———. *The Secret Diary of Harold L. Ickes*. II: *The Inside Struggle, 1936–1939*. New York: Simon and Schuster, 1954.

Kincaid, Diane, ed. *Silent Hattie Speaks: The Personal Journal of Senator Hattie Caraway*. Westport, Connecticut: Greenwood Press, 1979.

Lodge, Henry Cabot. *The Senate and the League of Nations*. New York: Charles Scribner's Sons, 1925.

McAdoo, William G. *Crowded Years: The Reminiscences of William G. McAdoo*. Port Washington, New York: Kennikat Press, 1971.

Michelson, Charles. *The Ghost Talks*. New York: G. P. Putnam's Sons, 1944.

Mitchell, H. L. *Mean Things Happening in This Land: The Life and Times of H. L. Mitchell Co-Founder of the Southern Tenant Farmers Union*. Montclair, New Jersey: Allanheld, Osmun and Company, 1979.

Moley, Raymond. *After Seven Years*. New York: Harper and Brothers, 1939.

———. *The First New Deal*. New York: Harcourt, Brace, and World, 1966.

Norris, George W. *Fighting Liberal: The Autobiography of George W. Norris*. New York: Macmillan, 1945.

Pepper, Claude Denson, and Hays Gorey. *Pepper: Eyewitness to a Century*. San Diego, California: Harcourt Brace Jovanovich, 1987.

Pepper, George Wharton. *In the Senate*. Philadelphia: University of Pennsylvania Press, 1930.

——. *Philadelphia Lawyer: An Autobiography*. Philadelphia: J. B. Lippincott and Company, 1944.

Reidel, Richard Langham. *Halls of the Mighty: My Forty-seven Years at the Senate*. Washington, D.C.: Robert B. Luce, 1969.

Rosenman, Samuel I. ed. *The Public Papers and Addresses of Franklin D. Roosevelt*. New York: Macmillan, 1941.

Stimson, Henry L., and McGeorge Bundy. *On Active Service in Peace and War*. New York: Harper and Brothers, 1948.

Tully, Grace. *F.D.R.: My Boss*. Chicago: Peoples Book Club, 1949.

Tumulty, Joseph P. *Woodrow Wilson As I Know Him*. Garden City, New York: Doubleday, Page and Company, 1921.

Wheeler, Burton K., and Paul Healey. *Yankee from the West: The Candid, Turbulent Life Story of the Yankee-Born U.S. Senator from Montana*. Garden City, New York: Doubleday and Company, 1962.

White, William Allen. *The Autobiography of William Allen White*. New York: Macmillan, 1946.

Williams, Harry Lee. *Forty Years Behind the Scenes in Arkansas Politics*. Little Rock, Arkansas: Parkin Printing and Stationery Company, 1949.

SECONDARY SOURCES

Newspapers

Arkansas County Democrat (De Witt, Arkansas), 1895, 1911.

Arkansas Democrat, 1894–1937.

Arkansas Gazette, 1894–1937.

Atlanta Constitution, 1924, 1928.

Chattanooga Daily Times, September, 1928.

Fayetteville (Arkansas) Sentinel, 1895.

Fort Smith (Arkansas) Elevator, 1895.

Fort Smith (Arkansas) Times-Record, 1911–13.

Harrison (Arkansas) Times, 1911–12.

Hot Springs Sentinel-Record, 1928.

Houston Chronicle, 1920, 1924, 1928.

Houston Post, 1920, 1924, 1928.

Lonoke Democrat, 1870–1937.

Lonoke Citizen, 1896.

Memphis Commercial Appeal, 1895, 1911–13, 1928.

Nashville Tennessean, September, 1928.

New York Times, 1903–37.

Pine Bluff (Arkansas) Daily Commercial, 1895, 1911–13.

Pope County Record (Russellville, Arkansas), 1911–13.

San Francisco Chronicle, October, 1928.

Springdale (Arkansas) News, 1895.

The Times (London), 1929–30.

Washington Herald, 1928.

Washington Post, 1923, 1928, 1933–37.

Washington Star, 1903–37.

Articles

Alsop, Joseph, Jr., and Turner Catledge. "Joe Robinson, The New Deal's Old Reliable." *Saturday Evening Post*, September 26, 1936, pp. 5–7, 66–74.

Auerbach, Jerold S. "Southern Tenant Farmers: Socialist Critics of the New Deal." *Arkansas Historical Quarterly*, XXVII (summer 1968): 113–31.

Ball, Larry D., and William M. Clements. "The Very Last Timber: Harvesting Chemical Wood in Northeastern Arkansas." *Forest and Conservation History*, 36 (April 1992): 73–81.

"Bigness and the Chain Store." *Nation*, December 5, 1936, pp. 648–49.

"Business and Finance: Act in Action." *Time*, October 12, 1936. pp. 73–74.

"Congress: End of Strife." *Time*, July 26, 1937, p. 10.

"Court Plan Dead but Not Buried." *The Literary Digest*, May 29, 1937, p. 3.

Dew, Lee A. "The J.L.C. and E.R.R. and the Opening of the 'Sunk Lands' in Northeast Arkansas." *Arkansas Historical Quarterly*, XXVII (spring 1968): 22–39.

Farmer, Rod. "Direct Democracy in Arkansas, 1910–1918." *Arkansas Historical Quarterly*, XL (summer 1981): 99–118.

Freidel, Frank. "The Conservative South." In *The South and the Sectional Image: The Sectional Theme Since Reconstruction*, ed. Dewey W. Grantham Jr. New York: Harper and Row, 1967.

Grant, Gilbert Richard. "Joseph Taylor Robinson in Foreign Affairs." *Arkansas Historical Quarterly*, IX (autumn 1950): 133–71.

Grant, Philip A., Jr. "Southern Congressmen and Agriculture, 1921–1932," *Agricultural History*, LIII (January 1979): pp. 338–51.

Grantham, Dewey, Jr. "The Southern Senators and the League of Nations, 1918–1920." *North Carolina Historical Review*, XXVI (April 1949): 187–205.

Guthrie, Mildred Bush. "Anti-war Minority in Congress, 1916–1917." *Historian*, II (spring 1940): 85–104.

Herring, E. Pendleton. "First Session of the Seventy-third Congress, March 9, 1933 to June 16, 1933." *American Political Science Review*, XXVIII (1934): 65–83.

Hicks, Floyd W., and C. Roger Lambert. "Food for the Hungry: Federal Food Programs in Arkansas, 1933–1942." *Arkansas Historical Quarterly*, XXXVII (spring 1978): 23–43.

Holt, Wythe, Jr. "The Senator from Virginia and the Democratic Floor Leadership: Thomas S. Martin and Conservatism in the Progressive Era." *Virginia Magazine of History and Biography*, LXXXIII (January 1975): 3–21.

Kiser, G. Gregory. "The Socialist Party in Arkansas, 1900–1912." *Arkansas Historical Quarterly*, XL (summer 1981): 119–53.

Lambert, Roger. "Hoover and the Red Cross in the Arkansas Drought of 1930." *Arkansas Historical Quarterly*, XXIX (spring 1970): 3–19.

Ledbetter, Calvin R., Jr. "Joe T. Robinson and the Presidential Campaign of 1928." *Arkansas Historical Quarterly*, XLV (summer 1986): 95–125.

———. "The Long Struggle to End Convict Leasing in Arkansas." *Arkansas Historical Quarterly*, LII, (spring 1993): 1–27.

———. "The Office of Governor in Arkansas History." *Arkansas Historical Quarterly*, XXXVII (spring 1978): 44–73.

Leuchtenburg, William E. "Franklin D. Roosevelt's Supreme Court Packing Plan." In *Essays on the New Deal*. Edited by Harold Hollingsworth and William F. Holmes. Austin: University of Texas Press, 1969.

[MacLeish, Archibald.] "The Senator from Arkansas: The life and opinions of Joseph Taylor Robinson, upon whose ability to control the U.S. Senate now hangs the political destiny of President Franklin Delano Roosevelt." *Fortune*, January 1937, pp. 88–108.

Jonas, Manfred. "The United States and the Failure of Collective Security in the 1930s." In *Twentieth Century American Foreign Policy*, ed. John Braeman, Robert H. Brenner, and David Brody (Columbus: University of Ohio Press, 1972), pp. 241–93.

Mann, George R. "Appendix: George R. Mann's Comments on George W. Donaghey's *Building a State Capitol*." *Arkansas Historical Quarterly*, XXXI (summer 1972): 134–49.

Munk, Margaret. "Origin and Development of the Party Floor Leadership in the United States Senate." *Capitol Studies*, II (winter 1974): 23–41.

Murray, Gail S. "Forty Years Ago: The Depression Comes to Arkansas." *Arkansas Historical Quarterly*, XXIX (winter 1970): 291–312.

Neal, Nevin. "The Smith-Robinson Arkansas Campaign of 1928." *Arkansas Historical Quarterly*, XIX (spring 1960): 3–11.

Newby, Idus A. "States Rights and Southern Congressmen During World War I." *Phylon*, XXIV (spring 1963): 34–50.

Niswonger, Richard L. "A Study in Southern Demagoguery: Jeff Davis of Arkansas." *Arkansas Historical Quarterly*, XXXIX (summer 1980): 114–24.

———. "William F. Kirby, Arkansas's Maverick Senator." *Arkansas Historical Quarterly*, XXXVII (autumn 1978): 252–63.

O'Brien, Patrick G. "A Reexamination of the Senate Farm Bloc, 1921–1933." *Agricultural History*, XLVII (July 1973): 248–63.

Patman, Wright. "Curbing the Chain Stores." *Nation*, November 28, 1936. pp. 624–25.

Patenude, Lionel V. "Garner, Sumners, and Connally: The Defeat of the Roosevelt Court Bill in 1937." *Southwestern Historical Quarterly*, LXXIV (July 1970): 36–51.

Perkins, Frances. "Eight Years as Madame Secretary." *Fortune*, September, 1941, pp. 77–79+.

Petersen, Svend. "Arkansas' Favorite Son." *Arkansas Historical Quarterly*, III (1944): 137–46.

Robertson, Reynolds. "The Robinson-Patman Act: *Fortune* Presents a Legal Opinion upon the Constitutionality and the Effects of the Legislation, Whose Interpretation Is Today One of the Most Complex Problems of U.S. Business." *Fortune*, November, 1936, pp. 96–97+.

"Robinson Will Not Do!" *Nation*, May 29, 1937, pp. 607–8.

Ross, Margaret. "The New Madrid Earthquake." *Arkansas Historical Quarterly*, XXVII (summer 1968): 83–104.

Scott, Robert Carl. "William McCombs and the 1912 Democratic Presidential Nomination of Woodrow Wilson." *Arkansas Historical Quarterly*, XLIV (autumn 1985): 246–59.

"Shakeup in Selling Practices." *Business Week*, June 20, 1936, pp. 13–14.

Towns, Stuart. "Joseph T. Robinson and Arkansas Politics, 1912–1913." *Arkansas Historical Quarterly*, XXIV (winter 1965): 291–307.

Treon, John A. "Politics and Concrete: The Building of the State Capitol, 1899–1917." *Arkansas Historical Quarterly*, XXXI (summer 1972): 99–133.

Venkataramani, M. S. "Norman Thomas, Arkansas Share-croppers, and the Roosevelt Agricultural Policies, 1933–1937," *Mississippi Valley Historical Review*, XLVII (September 1960): 225–46.

Watson, Richard L. "Furnifold M. Simmons: Jehovah of the Tarheels." *North Carolina Historical Review*, XLIV (April 1967): 166–87.

Zimmerman, Jane. "The Convict Lease System in Arkansas and the Fight for Abolition." *Arkansas Historical Quarterly*, VIII (autumn 1949): 171–88.

Books

Allen, Frederick Lewis. *Only Yesterday: An Informal History of the Nineteen-Twenties*. New York: Harper and Brothers, 1931.

Arsenault, Raymond. *The Wild Ass of the Ozarks: Jeff Davis and the Social Bases of Southern Politics*. Philadelphia: Temple University Press, 1984.

Bailey, Thomas. *A Diplomatic History of the American People*. Eighth Edition, New York: Appleton-Century-Crofts, 1969.

——. *Woodrow Wilson and the Great Betrayal*. Chicago: Quadrangle Books, 1963.

Baker, Leonard. *Back to Back: The Duel between FDR and the Supreme Court*. New York: Macmillan, 1967.

Baker, Richard Allan. *The Senate of the United States: A Bicentennial History*. Malabar, Florida: Robert E. Kreiger Publishing Company, 1988.

Barnard, Harry. *Independent Man: The Life of Senator James Couzens*. New York: Charles Scribner's Sons, 1958.

Bemis, Samuel Flagg. *A Diplomatic History of the United States*. Fifth Edition, New York: Holt, Rinehart and Winston, 1965.

Biles, Roger. *A New Deal for the American People*. De Kalb: Northern Illinois University Press, 1991.

Billington, Monroe Lee. *The Political South in the Twentieth Century*. New York: Charles Scribner's Son, 1975.

———. *Thomas P. Gore: The Blind Senator from Oklahoma*. Lawrence, Kansas: University of Kansas Press, 1967.

Billington, Ray Allen. *The Far Western Frontier, 1830–1860*. New York: Harper and Row, 1962.

Brinkley, Alan. *Voices of Protest: Huey Long, Father Coughlin, and the Great Depression*. New York: Vintage Books, 1983.

Burner, David. *Herbert Hoover: A Public Life*. New York: Atheneum, 1984.

———. *The Politics of Provinicialism: The Democratic Party in Transition, 1918–1932*. Cambridge: Harvard University, 1986.

Burns, James MacGregor. *Roosevelt: The Lion and the Fox*. New York: Harcourt, Brace, and Company, 1956.

Cebula, James E. *James E. Cox: Journalist and Politician*. New York: Garland Publishing, 1985.

Coit, Margaret L. Mr. *Baruch: The Man, the Myth, the Eighty Years*. Boston: Houghton Mifflin Company, 1957.

Cole, Wayne S. *Roosevelt and the Isolationists, 1932–1945*. Lincoln: University of Nebraska Press, 1983.

Conrad, David. *The Forgotten Farmers*. Urbana: University of Illinois Press, 1965.

Currie, James T. *The United States House of Representatives*. Malabar, Florida: Robert E. Kreiger Publishing Company, 1988.

Dallek, Robert. *Democrat and Diplomat: The Life of William E. Dodd*. New York: Oxford University Press, 1968.

———. *Franklin D. Roosevelt and American Foreign Policy, 1932–1945*. New York: Oxford University Press, 1979.

Daniels, Josephus. *The Wilson Era. I: Years of Peace, 1910–1917*. Chapel Hill: University of North Carolina Press, 1944.

Davis, Polly Ann. *Alben W. Barkley: Senate Majority Leader and Vice-President*. New York: Garland Publishing, 1979.

DeConde, Alexander. *A History of American Foreign Policy*. II: *Global Power (1900 to the present)*. Third edition, New York: Charles Scribner's Sons, 1978.

Dethloff, Henry C. *A History of the American Rice Industry, 1685–1985*. College Station: Texas A & M University Press, 1988.

Dulles, Foster Rhea. *America's Rise to World Power, 1898–1954*. New American Nation Series. New York: Harper and Row, 1963.

Eldot, Paula. *Governor Alfred E. Smith: The Politician as Reformer*. New York: Garland Publishing, 1983.

Ellis, L. Ethan. *Republican Foreign Policy, 1921–1933*. New Brunswick, New Jersy: Rutgers University Press, 1968.

Fausold, Martin L. *The Presidency of Herbert Hoover*. Lawrence, Kansas: University Press of Kansas, 1985.

Ferrell, Robert H. *American Diplomacy in the Great Depression: Hoover Stimson Foreign Policy, 1929–1933*. New York: W. W. Norton and Company, 1957.

——. *Woodrow Wilson and World War I, 1917–1921*. New York: Harper and Row, 1985.

Fite, Gil. *Cotton Fields No More: Southern Agriculture, 1865–1980*. Lexington: University of Kentucky Press, 1984.

——. *George N. Peek and the Fight for Farm Parity*. Norman: Oklahoma University Press, 1954.

Fletcher, John Gould. *Arkansas*. Chapel Hill: University of North Carolina Press, 1947.

Fleming, Denna Frank. *The United States and the League of Nations*. New York: G. P. Putnam's Sons, 1932.

——. *The United States and the World Court*. Garden City, New Jersey: Doubleday, Doran, and Company, 1945.

Freidel, Frank. *F.D.R. and the South*. Baton Rouge: Louisiana State University Press, 1965.

——. *Franklin D. Roosevelt: Launching the New Deal*. Boston: Little, Brown and Company, 1973.

Galbraith, John Kenneth. *The Great Crash, 1929*. Boston: Houghton Mifflin Company, 1961.

Garraty, John A. *Henry Cabot Lodge: A Biography*. New York: Alfred A. Knopf, 1953.

Garraty, John A. *The Great Depression*. San Diego: Harcourt, Brace, Jovanovich, 1986.

——. *The New Commonwealth, 1877–1890*. New American Nation Series. New York: Harper and Row, 1968.

Glad, Betty. *Key Pittman: The Tragedy of a Senate Insider*. New York: Columbia University Press, 1986.

Goldman, Eric F. *Rendezvous with Destiny*. New York: Alfred A. Knopf, 1970.

Grantham, Dewey W. *Southern Progressivism: The Reconciliation of Progress and Tradition*. Knoxville: University of Tennessee Press, 1983.

——, ed. *The South and the Sectional Image: The Sectional Theme Since Reconstruction*. New York: Harper and Row, 1965.

——. *The South in Modern America: A Region at Odds*. New York: HarperCollins, 1994.

Green, Constance McLaughlin. *Washington: Capitol City, 1879–1950*. Princeton, New Jersey: Princeton University Press, 1963.

Green, James R. *Grass-Roots Socialism: Radical Movements in the Southwest, 1895–1943*. Baton Rouge: Louisiana State University Press, 1978.

Greenbaum, Fred. *Fighting Progressive: A Biography of Edward P. Costigan*. Washington, D.C.: Public Affairs Press, 1971.

Grubbs, Donald H. *Cry from the Cotton: The Southern Tenant Farmers Union and the New Deal*. Chapel Hill: University of North Carolina Press, 1971.

Haley, P. Edward. *Revolution and Intervention: The Diplomacy of Taft and Wilson with Mexico, 1910–1917*. Cambridge: Massachusetts Institute of Technology Press, 1970.

Hamilton, Virginia Van Der Veer. *Hugo Black: The Alabama Years*. Tuscaloosa: University of Alabama Press, 1972.

Hanson, Gerald T., and Carl H. Moneyhon. *Historical Atlas of Arkansas*. Norman: University of Oklahoma Press, 1989.

Harbaugh, William H. *Lawyer's Lawyer: The Life of John W. Davis*. New York: Oxford University Press, 1973.

Hicks, John D. *Republican Ascendancy, 1921–1933*. New American Nation Series. New York: Harper and Row, 1960.

Hinshaw, Jerry E. *Call the Roll: The First One Hundred and Fifty Years of the Arkansas Legislature*. Little Rock, Arkansas: Rose Publishing Company, 1986.

Hofstadter, Richard. *The Age of Reform: From Bryan to F.D.R.* New York: Random House, 1955.

Hogan, William Ransom. *The Texas Republic: A Social and Economic History*. Austin: University of Texas Press, 1969.

Huthmacher, J. Joseph. *Senator Robert F. Wagner and the Rise of Urban Liberalism*. New York: Atheneum, 1971.

Israel, Fred L. *Nevada's Key Pittman*. Lincoln: University of Nebraska Press, 1963.

Jackson, Robert H. *The New Deal: The Historical Debate*. New York: John Wiley and Sons, 1973.

Jessup, Phillip C. *Elihu Root*. New York: Dodd, Mead and Company, 2 vol., 1938.

Johnson, Claudius O. *Borah of Idaho*. Longman, Green, and Company, 1932.

Johnson, Evans C. *Oscar W. Underwood: A Political Biography*. Baton Rouge: Louisiana State University Press, 1980.

Kaufman, Robert Gordon. *Arms Control during the Pre-Nuclear Era: The United States and Naval Limitation between the Two World Wars*. New York: Columbia University Press, 1990.

Kennedy, David M. *Over Here: The First World War and American Society*. New York: Oxford University Press, 1980.

Key, V. O. *Southern Politics in State and Nation*. New York: Alfred A. Knopf, 1949.

Kirkendall, Richard S. *The New Deal: The Historical Debate*. New York: John Wiley and Sons, 1973.

La Follette, Belle Case and Fola La Follette. *Robert M. La Follette*. New York: Macmillan, 1953.

LaFeber, Walter. *The American Age: United States Foreign Policy at Home and Abroad since 1750*. New York: W. W. Norton and Company, 1989.

Lash, Joseph P. *Dealers and Dreamers: A New Look at the New Deal*. New York: Doubleday, 1988.

Latimer, Hugh. *Naval Disarmament: A Brief Record from the Washington Conference to date*. London: The Royal Institute of International Affairs, 1930.

Ledbetter, Calvin R., Jr. *Carpenter from Conway: George Washington Donaghey as Governor of Arkansas, 1909–1913*. Fayetteville: University of Arkansas Press, 1993.

Leuchtenburg, William E. *Franklin D. Roosevelt and the New Deal, 1932–1940*. New American Nation Series. New York: Harper and Row, 1963.

——. *The Perils of Prosperity*. Chicago History of American Civilization. Chicago: University of Chicago Press, 1958.

Lichtman Allan J. *Prejudice and the Old Politics: The Presidential Election of 1928*. Chappel Hill: University of North Carolina Press, 1979.

Link, Arthur S. *Woodrow Wilson and the Progressive Era, 1910–1917*. New American Nation Series. New York: Harper and Row, 1954.

——. *Wilson*. II: *The New Freedom*. Princeton, New Jersey: Princeton University Press, 1956.

——. *Wilson*. III: *The Struggle for Neutrality*. Princeton, New Jersey: Princeton University Press, 1960.

——. *Wilson*. IV: *Confusions and Crises, 1915–1916*. Princeton, New Jersey: Princeton University Press, 1964.

——. *Wilson*. V: *Campaigns for Progressivism and Peace*. Princeton, New Jersey: Princeton University Press, 1965.

Livermore, Seward W. *Woodrow Wilson and the War Congress, 1916–1918*. Seattle: University of Washington Press, 1966.

Louchheim, Katie, ed. *The Making of the New Deal: The Insiders Speak*. Cambridge, Massachusetts: Harvard University Press, 1983.

Lowitt, Richard. *Bronson M. Cutting: Progressive Politician*. Albuquerque: University of New Mexico Press, 1992.

——. *George W. Norris: The Triumph of a Progressive, 1933–1944*. Urbana: University of Illinois Press, 1978.

Ludwig Emil. *Roosevelt: A Study in Fortune and Power*. Translated from German by Maurice Samuel. New York: Viking Press, 1938.

Maddox, Robert James. *William E. Borah and American Foreign Policy*. Baton Rouge: Louisiana State University Press, 1969.

Malone, David. *Hattie and Huey: An Arkansas Tour*. Fayetteville: University of Arkansas Press, 1989.

Maney, Patrick J. *"Young Bob" La Follette: A Biography of Robert M. La Follette Jr., 1895–1953*. Columbia: Univeristy of Missouri Press, 1978.

Margulies, Herbert. *The Mild Reservationists and the League of Nations Controversy in the Senate*. Columbia: University of Missouri Press, 1989.

McConnell, Grant. *The Decline of Agrarian Democracy*. Berkeley: University of California Press, 1953.

McKenna, Marian C. *Borah*. Ann Arbor: University of Michigan Press, 1961.

Moore, John Robert. *Senator Josiah Weldon Bailey of North Carolina: A Political Biography*. Durham, North Carolina: Duke University Press, 1968.

Mowry, George. *Another Look at the Twentieth Century South*. Baton Rouge: Louisiana State University Press, 1973.

———. *The Era of Theodore Roosevelt and the Birth of Modern America, 1900–1912*. New American Nation Series. New York: Harper and Row, 1958.

Murray, Robert K. *The 103rd Ballot: Democrats and the Disaster in Madison Square Garden*. New York: Harper and Row, 1976.

Newsom, Gene, and Karl Kastner. *"Our Joe": An Illustrated, Biographical Sketch of Arkansas' Super-Senator, Joseph Taylor Robinson*. North Little Rock, Arkansas: Times Printing Company, n.d.

Niswonger, Richard L. *Arkansas Democratic Politics, 1896–1920*. Fayetteville: University of Arkansas Press, 1990.

Noggle, Burl. *Teapot Dome: Oil and Politics in the 1920s*. New York: W. W. Norton and Company, 1965.

O'Connor, Raymond. *Perilous Equilibrium: The United States and the London Naval Conference of 1930*. Lawrence: University of Kansas Press, 1962.

O'Keane, Josephine. *Thomas J. Walsh: A Senator from Montana*. Francistown, New Hampshire: Marshall Jones, 1955.

Palamountain, J. C., Jr. *The Politics of Distribution*. Cambridge: Harvard University Press, 1955.

Palmer, Jesse, Jr. *Carter Glass—Unreconstructed Rebel: A Biography*. Roanoke, Virginia: Institute of American Biography, 1938.

Parrish, Michael E. *Securities Regulation and the New Deal*. New Haven, Connecticut: Yale University Press, 1970.

Patman, Wright. *The Complete Guide to the Robinson-Patman Act*. Englewood Cliffs, New Jersey: Prentice-Hall, 1963.

Patterson, James T. *Congressional Conservatives and the New Deal: The Growth of the Conservative Coalition in Congress, 1933–1939*. Lexington, Kentucky: University of Kentucky Press, 1967.

Peel, Roy V., and Thomas C. Donnelly. *The 1928 Campaign: An Analysis*. New York: Richard R. Smith, 1931.

Perkins, Frances. *The Roosevelt I Knew*. New York: Viking Press, 1946.

Rauch, Basil. *The History of the New Deal, 1933–38*. New York: Creative Age Press, 1944.

Richberg, Donald R. *My Hero: The Indiscreet Memoirs of an Eventful but Unheroic Life*. New York: G. P. Putnam's Sons, 1954.

Roosevelt, Elliot, and James Brough. *An Untold Story: The Roosevelts of Hyde Park*. New York: G. P. Putnam's Sons, 1973.

Russell, Francis. *The Shadow of Blooming Grove: Warren G. Harding in His Times*. New York: McGraw-Hill Book Company, 1968.

Saloutos, Theodore, and J. D. Hicks. *A Discontent in the Middle West, 1900–1939*. Madison: University of Wisconsin Press, 1951.

Schlesinger, Arthur M., Jr. *The Age of Roosevelt*. I: *The Crisis of the Old Order*. Boston: Houghton Mifflin Company, 1957.

———. *The Age of Roosevelt*. II: *The Coming of the New Deal*. Boston: Houghton Mifflin Company, 1958.

———. *The Age of Roosevelt*. III: *The Politics of Upheaval*. Boston: Houghton Mifflin Company, 1960.

Schlesinger, Arthur M., Jr., ed. *History of U.S. Political Parties*. III: *1910–1945: From Square Deal to New Deal*. New York: Chelsea House Publishers, 1973.

Schlesinger, Arthur M., Jr., and Fred L. Israel. *History of American Presidential Elections*. VI: *1920–1928*. New York: Confucian Press, 1981.

Seligman, Edwin R. A. *The Economics of Farm Relief: A Survey of the Agricultural Problem*. New York: Columbia University Press, 1929.

Sitkoff, Harvard. *A New Deal for Blacks: The Emergence of Civil Rights as a National Issue*. I: *The Depression Decade*. Oxford: Oxford University Press, 1978.

Smith, Rexey, and Norman Beasley. *Carter Glass: A Biography*. New York: Longman's Green and Company, 1939.

Socolofsky, Homer E. *Arthur Capper: Publisher, Politician, and Philanthropist*. Lawrence: University of Kansas Press, 1962.

Sparks, George F., ed. *A Many Colored Toga: The Diary of Henry F. Ashurst*. Tuscon: University of Arizona Press, 1962.

Swaim, Martha H. *Pat Harrison: The New Deal Years*. Jackson: University Press of Mississippi, 1978.

Timmons, Bascom N. *Garner of Texas: A Personal Biography*. New York: Harper and Brothers, 1948.

Tindall, George B. *The Emergence of the New South, 1913–1945*. A History of the South. Baton Rouge: Louisiana State University Press, 1967.

———. *The Persistent Tradition in New South Politics*. Baton Rouge: Louisiana State University Press, 1975.

Tompkins, C. David. *Senator Arthur H. Vandenberg: The Evolution of a Modern Republican, 1884–1945*. [East Lansing, Michigan]: Michigan State University Press, 1970.

Watkins, T. H. *Righteous Pilgrim: The Life and Times of Harold L. Ickes, 1874–1952*. Henry Holt and Company, 1990.

White, William S. *Citadel: The Story of the U.S. Senate*. New York: Harper and Brothers, 1956.

Widenor, William C. *Henry Cabot Lodge and the Search for an American Foreign Policy*. Berkeley: University of California Press, 1980.

Williams, Benjamin H. *A Series of Twelve Radio Talks on the London Naval Conference: Its Background and Results*. Pittsburgh: University of Pittsburgh, 1930.

Williams, T. Harry. *Huey Long*. New York: Alfred A. Knopf, 1970.

Wilson, Joan Hoff. *American Business and Foreign Policy, 1920–1933*. Louisville: University Press of Kentucky, 1971.

———. *Herbert Hoover: Forgotten Progressive*. Boston: Little, Brown and Company, 1975.

Wolfskill, George. *The Revolt of the Conservatives: A History of the American Liberty League, 1934–1940*. Boston: Houghton Mifflin Company, 1962.

Woodward, C. Vann. *Origins of the New South, 1877–1913*. Baton Rouge: Louisiana State University Press, 1974.

Zorn, B. A., and G. F. Feldman. *Business under the Price Laws: A Study of the Economic and Legal Problems Arising out of the Robinson-Patman Act and the Various Fair Trade and Unfair Practices Laws*. New York: Prentice-Hall, 1937.

Theses and Dissertations

Chiles, John E. "The Early Public Career of Joseph Taylor Robinson." M.A. thesis, Vanderbilt University, Nashville, Tennessee, 1949.

Collins, Michael L. "The Influence of Texans Upon Roosevelt's Court Packing Plan." M.A. thesis, Texas Christian University, Fort Worth, Texas, 1975.

Drummond, Boyce Alexander, Jr. "Arkansas Politics: A Study of a One Party System." Ph.D. dissertation, University of Chicago, Chicago, Illinois, 1957.

Law, Ron C. "Congressman Hatton W. Sumners of Dallas, Texas: His Life and Congressional Career, 1876–1937." Ph.D. dissertation, Texas Christian University, Fort Worth, Texas, 1990.

Neal, Nevin Emil. "A Biography of Joseph Taylor Robinson." Ph.D. dissertation, University of Oklahoma, Norman, Oklahoma, 1958.

Niswonger, Richard L. "Arkansas Democratic Politics, 1896–1920." Ph.D. dissertation, University of Texas, Austin, Texas, 1974.

Pettus, Beryl Erwin. "The Senate Career of Joseph Taylor Robinson." M.A. thesis, University of Illinois, Urbana, Illinois. 1950.

Schmelzer, Janet L. "The Early Life and Early Congressional Career of Wright Patman: 1894–1941." Ph.D. dissertation, Texas Christian University, Fort Worth, Texas, 1978.

Seagraves, Joe Tolbert. "Arkansas Politics, 1874–1918." Ph.D. dissertation, University of Kentucky, Lexington, Kentucky, 1973.

INDEX